THE THEOLOGY OF KARL BARTH

THE THEOLOGY OF KARL BARTH

by Hans Urs von Balthasar

Translated by JOHN DRURY

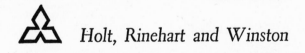 Holt, Rinehart and Winston

NEW YORK   CHICAGO   SAN FRANCISCO

Library of Congress Catalog Card Number: 69-10237

The Theology of Karl Barth was translated from the German
text, Karl Barth: Darstellung und Deutung seiner Theologie,
©Verlag Jakob Hegner, 1962.

First Edition

SBN: 03-068450-1

Design: Winston Potter

Printed in the United States of America

CONTENTS

PART THREE. A Closer Look at the Framework

PART FOUR. *Catholic Perspectives*

EPILOGUE

TRANSLATOR'S NOTE

Von Balthasar's study of the work of Karl Barth is already a classic in its field. First published in German in the early 1950's, it was a major attempt by a Catholic theologian to dialogue with the leading Protestant theologian of our age, at a time when this was not common practice. But *The Theology of Karl Barth* did more than lay the groundwork for fraternal debate; it remains a living part of an ongoing dialogue. Von Balthasar's considerations, like the ideas of Barth himself, constitute a necessary element in the present theological scene.

Because this translation was an attempt to do justice to a book for today, the most important consideration was to communicate its essential ideas, von Balthasar's respectful presentation of Barth's views, and his attempt to enter into dialogue with them. At the same time, since dialogue in history moves on, some ideas that had to be hammered home in their original German presentation could advantageously be set forth more briefly now. This translation was begun only after the whole book had been carefully reviewed, but any effort at abridgement entails risks. To the best of my knowledge, however, no substantive point has been omitted, distorted, or obscured. The German original remains for those who wish to relive a given historical moment in its entirety, but the translator did his work in the hope that this edition might bring out even more sharply the originality and permanent value of von Balthasar's contribution. The translation was, of course, sent to the author for his approval, but I do not wish to avoid responsibility for any failures that may have resulted.

The Foreword to the second German edition, which otherwise reproduced the first edition without alterration, has been here put back in the Epilogue as "A Few Years Later." Thus the reader can follow the original line of treatment as it was first published and then examine the author's comments written at a later date. The thrust of historical moment is thereby preserved.

The passionate ideas of Karl Barth and his Catholic interlocutor will stand on their own merits; my work will have been a success if it conveys these ideas to a new public.

John Drury

THE THEOLOGY OF KARL BARTH

PART ONE

Overture to a Dialogue

I · THE TORN GARMENT

"The enigmatic split which had divided the Church for four hundred years"[1] is a constant source of scandal to anyone who is aware of the nature of this Church. The very essence of the Church is agape—unity in love; and every move away from unity casts doubt on the ultimate roots of this Church. We cannot help but wonder about this scandal every day; we cannot help but ask how it happened, what it means, and whether it was necessary. The questions will remain for as long as we are divided, both for those of us who have stayed within the ancient precincts and for those who felt they had to leave.

If the Church's visible faults provided the occasion for this split, then we must atone for past mistakes with ever renewed penitence; and we must constantly check the present situation to weed out the scandalous elements that once made others sacrifice the Church's unity for the sake of a pure faith in Christ. Do we Catholics still ponder the question of Church unity as if our very salvation depended on it? Have we done everything we can to restore it? Are we to be reproached with the fact that others are more deeply concerned about this question than we are?

We are faced with "the paradoxical fact of heresy."[2] It is indeed a paradox and a *contradictio in adjecto*,[3] because the essential inner unity of Christ's body must necessarily manifest itself in external unity as well. "We have to seek the divine mystery of the Church in its human form, or else we shall not find it at all."[4] But, in fact, the Church's human form contradicts her essence. Her essence is in the charge which Christ gave her: united in him, she will lead all things to unity.

It is primarily this charge which compels us to set out in quest of Church unity, because it does not allow for a multiplicity of Churches. The New Testament, to be sure, recognizes a multiplicity of communities, a multiplicity of gifts, and a multiplicity of persons—*within* the one Church. But the multiplicity, of itself, has no meaning. Its origin, its justification, and its limits are to be found in the unity of Jesus Christ; or rather, in the one Jesus Christ, who is the one and only son of God, the dispenser of the one Holy Spirit. . . . Thus the New Testament does not recognize a polarity or a reciprocity between oneness and multiplicity. It sees only a one-sided relationship between these two realities. The many are dependent on the one, subservient to it, and incorporated into it. And that is why the many cannot found churches. To be able to do this, they would have to possess an independence that could only be procured at the expense of unity. The first Epistle to the Corinthians shows us how vigorously Paul opposed the first stirrings of such a process; and there it was only a question of party factionalism, not of separate Churches.[5]

It is for this reason that Karl Barth rejected theological deductions based on the existence of schism.

We should not try to explain Church plurality as a necessary characteristic of the visible, empirical Church, in contrast to

the invisible Church. We should not do this because . . . as
the New Testament sees it, the Church of Jesus Christ is one
in this respect also. It is invisible where the grace of the Word
of God and the Holy Spirit is concerned, but it is also clearly
visible . . . as a community with a communal ministry, in the
service of Word and sacrament. . . . Only these visible signs
of *being* and *action* enable us to believe in the existence of a
Church. We cannot escape from the visible Church to the
invisible one.

Nor should one try to explain the multiplicity of Churches
as the normal development willed by God for the kingdom of
grace brought to men by Jesus Christ,[6] [as] dissonant strains
that are to be woven into a larger harmony.[7]

In so doing, a person is evidently constructing a social philosophy or a philosophy of history, not theology. To solve the
problem of Church unity, he is fashioning his own ideas instead of listening to Christ's question and Christ's answer. If
we listen to Christ, we do not live above the differences that
divide the Churches, we are caught up in them.

Only one attitude is possible. "We should not try to explain the multiplicity of Churches at all. We should treat
it as we treat our own offenses and those of others, regarding it as a sin."[8] We should be "*shocked* by these divisions
and *pray* for their elimination."[9]

To be sure, there are signs that Christ's unity is not
totally absent from the divided Churches. But instead of
comforting us, these signs of accord, which indeed "cannot
make manifest the unity of the Church,"[10] should goad us
on to solve the problems that remain. For "if Jesus Christ
is the unity in his Church, while we suffer plurality, we
cannot escape the fact that the restoration of unity is a
duty, a commandment given to the Church by the Lord
himself."[11]

For the Protestant Church the first task is the reunifica-
tion of its own sister Churches. This goal preoccupied

Barth for a long time. The important point for us is not
the detailed working out of the project, but the basic considerations involved; they crop up again, almost unchanged,
when the question of Protestant–Catholic unity is raised.
The fundamental point of Barth's position was that church
reunion can never be achieved on a political or socio-
logical basis; it must be on an ecclesial (i.e., theological)
basis. That is why he rejected the union proposed by
Friedrich Wilhelm III in the nineteenth century and continued to regard the contemporary ecumenical movement
with distrust.[12] As he saw it, church reunion must be a
union in faith, an agreement on clearly formulated articles
of faith. The Churches will accomplish this through a
more authentic, more vital belief, not a leveling off or a
scaling down of dogmatic differences. An understanding
between Lutherans and Calvinists, for example, could arise
through laying stress once again on those points that
formerly caused their division. Perhaps the need to take a
common stand against some anti-Christian threat would
again awaken the original awareness of a true, living father.
Nevertheless, it should not involve hasty compromises
or irenicism[13] but rather a deeply earnest theological examination of each other's beliefs. "The move from division
to unity must take place without any compromise and,
most important of all, without resorting to forms and
formulas that cover up rather than overcome disunity."[14]

For a long time Barth remained skeptical about most
contemporary Protestant attempts to further interdenominational unity.[15] Yet, at the same time, he was quick to
advocate and undertake serious theological dialogue with
the Catholic Church. In a 1927 lecture on "The Concept
of the Church," he called for mutual discussions, and in
a 1928 lecture, "Roman Catholicism as a Question for the

Protestant Churches" he readily brought up the challenges posed by the Catholic Church.[16]

Barth called for a serious type of dialogue that had once taken place between Catholics and Protestants but was no longer in evidence. As he saw it, the present atmosphere of quiet tolerance was symptomatic of an unhealthy state. The bitter controversies of the past were, to some extent, healthier signs.

In the sixteenth and seventeenth century, Catholics and Protestants looked each other in the eye. It was a savage look, but they did look straight at each other. They talked sharply and angrily to each other, but it was a dialogue.

Today we have grown tired of the long continuing quarrel, but we may also have lost our Christian concern for the whole question. We now talk around the issues, showing no interest in basic discussions and saying nothing that is really worthwhile.[17]

But why shouldn't real dialogue be possible?

The quest for Christ's truth is always an inquiry of hope and love. It always contributes to Church reunion—even when neither side softens its position and the split seems at first to become wider.[18]

It is only when we have a clear picture of the reasons why we are divided that we shall be able to find ways to reunite.

I maintain that it should be possible to reach some clarification with a Catholic theologian, even about the sacrament of the altar, without trying to change a man's views. When all is said and done, the promise and the challenge of Christian teaching, of divine judgment and divine justification, also stands behind the Tridentine Church. There is enough Catholicism in us Protestants for us to realize that the thrust of reform is not dead there either.[19]

A real confrontation of views will force us to spell out our differences clearly and to carry them out to their logical conclusion. In such an encounter any well-meaning attempt to overlook differences, any hasty attempt to become buddies, and any shallow empathy will only compound the existing rift. In other words, "we must listen to Christ and engage in real, clear-headed theology."[20]

The truth is that it is not those who are seriously interested in theology that do not understand each other; it is the amateur, the dilettante, and the historian on both sides. Those who have spelled out their stand fully find a real encounter and a real community spirit developing between them, despite their differences. This could be the basis for Church unity.

Why is this? Because unity will not be found in some open no-man's-land *between* the denominations; it can only be found *within* the bounds of the Church. Theology is ecclesial, or it is nothing at all. And if each Church remains faithful to Revelation, "thinking its doctrines through to the end,"[21] both sides might come to agreement at some specific spot. Says Barth: "Let the Roman Catholic Church think through its doctrine on nature and grace, and the teaching on justification that was developed by Trent." And to him we say: "Let reformation theology think through its teaching on the visible Church, on obedience and law, and also its dialectic about *homo simul peccator et justus*. Then life will begin to flow through the Church's limbs. Questions will be posed, and the possibility of an answer will be real once again.

Unity is a gift of the Church's founder, not a man-made thing. We are "unprofitable servants" whose sins brought on disunity. Knowing these two things, we cannot rest until we have done everything we can. Only faith, which can move mountains, will face the task courageously. For faith knows that even mountains heed the Word of God, and that God chose to involve us in his own proper work. Awareness of this secret is shared by both sides in this split; and this unity in *belief* offers the promise of true *unity*.

Let us not become disturbed because Barth does not call Catholicism a "sister Church" as he calls the various Protestant Churches, or by the fact that he calls our Church "heretical,"[22] that he finds it to be a Church "in whose teaching we cannot recognize our own faith or the one true Church of Jesus Christ, a Church which we must *reject*, with heavy heart, as a false Church."[23] How can we hold this anathema against him when we feel forced to reiterate the anathema of Trent against his Church?

Yet Barth also sees another side to Catholicism: "Here is ecclesial *substance!* It may be distorted and tainted, but it is something substantial nevertheless."[24] He knows that despite the hard and fast differences, the things which divide us are "only relative."[25]

And how about us? We see Protestants as our brothers in Christ by baptism, as members of His visible body who should by rights belong to the One, Holy, Catholic Church. We share the same hope as they do. Trusting in that hope and not in our own power, we shall try to initiate a dialogue.[26]

II · PROTESTANT-CATHOLIC DIALOGUE

Such a dialogue presupposes that it is *possible* to understand one another. Here we are talking about a concrete possibility, really open to me as a speaker or listener. Moreover, we are not talking about a purely psychological pos-

sibility on the human level, but about a Christian possibility—one that can be realized within the context of faith
and its analogical process.

Having probed the reasoning through to the end, I can
accept the infallibility of the Pope and belief in the Im-
maculate Conception; yet, at the same time, I can understand why someone else rejects these things for reasons
that are not entirely conclusive. I can understand how a
Christian might not wish to consider the meritoriousness
of his deeds before God, and yet, at the same time, I can
believe that my worthless acts do merit a reward. I may
reject something, but that does not mean it is totally alien
to me. It is a possibility that I am aware of, but one which
I have moved beyond because it was not the ultimate
decisive possibility. It is a possibility expressed and then
put in parentheses. The way this possibility is understood
by each side may differ. The Catholic attitude is frequently
a feeling of superiority over Protestantism. The latter's
relation to Catholicism is seen as that of part to whole:
since anything contained in the part is also to be found in
the whole, there is no need for serious discussion. The
Catholic thinks back to the Donatist controversy and
Augustine's superb defense of the Church's universality.
He notes contentedly the ultimate fate of the schismatic
Donatist churches in Africa. There is no doubt that in
many Catholic circles intellectual apathy and indolence are
dominant; many feel it is better to know as little as possible
about Protestant theology. One could probably count on
one hand the number of Catholic theologians who regard
Barth's *Dogmatics* as compulsory reading.

These feelings of confident superiority are not to be
found solely among the dull witted, who feel that everything has been said already. They are also shared by many
agile and alert minds, who can carry out the debate on
any terms and thus feel convinced of their superiority. Is

it surprising that an adversary should lose his sense of humor when he finds himself boxed and classified before he even opens his mouth? We might well wonder whether such representatives of Catholicism really understand what the division between the Churches means. It is a yawning chasm which cannot be bridged by dialectics or analogy, a gaping wound which cannot be healed with theological formulas.

Now, after four hundred years, Catholics are beginning to realize that the part-whole analogy does not provide a full and satisfactory explanation.[1] According to certain theologians, the Reformation, which theoretically should have taken place within the Church, revealed certain values which might well be contained implicitly in Catholic teaching, but which could be expressed properly by it because of factionalism and the need for debate.

We also hear people talking about the end of the Counter-Reformation. The truths of Trent and Vatican I will never become outdated or antiquated, of course. But Revelation has other elements and aspects that were not brought out by these Councils. Throughout Church history, new statements are employed in the effort to do full justice to the inexhaustible treasures of divine Revelation. Catholicism can be regarded as the whole and total truth only after it has made every effort to incorporate the partial truths contained in other viewpoints. The Fathers of the Church tried to do this, linking the Logos of scripture with the *logos* of Greek philosophy and the *logos* of the Gnostics. Thomas Aquinas did this on a grand scale, taking account of both Christian and pagan schools of thought. Will today's Catholics wait for the work of modern philosophy and Protestant theology to be handed to them on a silver platter?

This brings us to another problem. Historical and cultural epochs are often characterized by distinctive styles and modes of thought. These modes can be neutral with respect to the thoughts expressed, so that the same basic truths can be couched in different terminologies. Yet, at the same time, these modes of thought have their own principles, which can perceptibly becloud their content. Temporal reality is created and, despite its participation in the immutability of the eternal, it has an historical dimension. Its fullness is expressed in a rich variety of forms and languages.

Anyone who wants to exist in the world has to learn languages. The person who wants to penetrate the intellectual world must learn its languages: the concepts and modes of thought that change with different cultures and with succeeding generations. Thus the Catholic, who feels a responsibility to preserve the deposit of faith intact, should make every effort to learn modern modes of thought. If he does not do this, if he knows only the terminology and outlook of the Middle Ages, he will not be able to give directions to his contemporaries.[2]

It has often been said that the Fathers of Trent gave a medieval response to a modern question. Their response was correct as far as it went, but was it a response to the question that had been asked, and could the questioners really understand it? And if there were a gap between question and answer then, how much more true that is today, four hundred years later. Matthew 28:19 and Matthew 20:27 suggest that we have to answer people's questions in a language they understand.

The Catholic's attitude, as he enters a dialogue with other denominations, is that he possesses the all-embracing truth. Aside from other considerations, this attitude is open to question on the objective level. As Augustine tried to show, every schism provides an occasion for deeper investigation into dogma; but for the Church it also represents an impoverishment. It represents a loss of members and a diminution of the full truth, because some part of this truth is carried out of the Church. Every heresy represents a one-sided emphasis, and the Church is forced to stress the other side of the coin. Here we might well note what Yves M.-J. Congar writes:

In response to such one-sided emphasis, the Church does more than stress the other side of the same truth; she stresses the total truth *vis-à-vis* partial truths and errors. Yet, in her contemporary pronouncements, she cannot help but stress those essential points that are being denied by the heretic. Her apologists cannot help but rehabilitate the truths that were missed. The theologians cannot help but spell out the related truths with full clarity. Thus heresy provides theology with an opportunity for further advances and also subjects it to the danger of one-sidedness.

When some error is formulated, the Church and her organisms steel themselves for a counterattack. To counteract the exaggeration of some truth, the Church spells out its exact dimensions. Usually, however, she does not run down the whole gamut of dogma; she is content to give more precision to the truth that has been misunderstood or rejected. The error is a partial one, and the contrasting dogmatic truth may be partial too, insofar as it maintains the contrary.

Many tend to pay more attention to official texts than to Christian life when they tackle an error. Some theologians are content to quote Danzinger instead of studying scripture, the Church Fathers, the liturgy, the living faith of the Church, and the clear testimony of Christian witness. Some apologists, whose job it is to combat the errors of their day, look at the Church's more superficial aspects. Many other writers and preachers do the same thing. They all quote formulas and combat the error with a one-sided, partial truth.

The reaction to dogmatic errors has led to greater precision and specialization. But it has also led to rigid formulations of the content of Revelation. Consider the condemnation of Baius, the determination that there are seven sacraments, the emphasis on tradition over scripture, and the condemnation of

Modernism. The attainment of greater dogmatic precision is worthwhile and even necessary. But it also has narrowed our perspective and our range of inquiry.

The condemnation of Baius, for example, has restricted theology's outlook on the supernatural and dampened its consideration of the relationship between nature and grace. The extensive work on the seven sacraments, and its canonical case, has made us forget the overall sacramental life of the Church and deadened our understanding of symbolism and liturgy. The anti-Protestant reaction that emphasized tradition was intended to counteract the false impression that the Church is founded on scripture; but it seems to suggest that scripture is founded on the Church. And the reaction against Modernism, which was necessary in certain respects, has in fact led to emphasis on certain aspects of the truth that are not the complete story. It has not helped us to understand the true meaning of life and historical development as they relate to the Church. Certain aspects of the truth have been overlooked or misunderstood, so that the authentic notion of tradition and dogma are placed in question."[3]

The Protestant partner in this dialogue has his own set of presuppositions. It is essential to realize that the Reformation was meant to be the restoration of "pure" Christianity, but it took the form of a protest against certain Catholic excesses. The qualitative "plus" in Protestantism is actually a process of subtraction—eliminating the excesses of Catholicism, purifying the temple, like Jesus did.

The Catholic tries to show that his position already contains within it the values of the Protestant side. And in doing this, he seems biased in the eyes of the Protestant. For Catholicism's claim to "comprehensiveness" is precisely the thing which the Protestant finds repulsive. The Catholic regards this comprehensiveness as the plus feature, as the proof that he possesses the total truth. He would be denying the Catholic view if he rejected this feature in approaching his partner in the dialogue. But what can be done when the very way in which he possesses the truth is an obstacle and a source of scandal to his partner?

The complaint that Barth made against Catholicism[4] is that the Catholic partner in the dialogue tries to do all the talking, assuming he is in the right even before the dialogue gets started. This complaint—that the Catholic does not obey the rules of the game—may well sum up all Barth's dogmatic objections and give them new weight. The Catholic approaches with the idea of being "ready to deal with" the heretic's concept of truth. The Protestant cannot help but feel that something is wrong with this approach. "If a person is absolutely sure that he will be vindicated in a confrontation with the other party, he will willingly accept the give and take of questioning without ever losing his certainty."[5]

The classical Protestant counterstance has been that the convinced Protestant could "deal cheerfully, resolutely, and finally" with the questions posed by Catholicism. Barth rejects this stance, and the reason he gives is hardly complimentary to us: "This stance is much too Catholic."[6] It is precisely what the Protestant should avoid: "I should say that Protestantism's greatest source of strength lies in the fact that it does not approach Catholicism in the same way that Catholicism approaches it—whether that is good one-upmanship or not."[7]

Now we have just noted that all truth formulated for polemical purposes tends to be partial and somewhat one-sided. Even though the Catholic may theoretically represent the "whole truth," he should never forget that any genuine faith, be it Catholic or Protestant, is to some extent implicit. It does not comprehend the whole content of Revelation; it accepts what God presents to it. The unknowable and the illimitable are of the essence of faith.

The true Catholic appreciates the infinity of Revelation, the living nature of scripture and tradition, and the development of dogma. He has no trouble, therefore, in seeing the partiality of his present position, the incomplete nature of the Church's present formulations.[8] He is open to everyone who, like himself, is seeking for authentic faith, who possesses faith as a subjective disposition (fides qua), and who therefore is qualified to make statements about its contents (fides quae).

What could be a more Christian attitude than the readiness to hear what one's fellow Christian has to say? Such readiness is an integral part of genuine faith and the best proof of it. True love of God reveals itself in love of neighbor, with which it is inextricably bound up. In like manner, the willingness to accept God's truth cannot be separated from the willingness to hear the words and the truth of one's neighbor. Most polemical confrontations are never real encounters, not because they are polemical but because they try to be encounters. Each side wants to meet the other; neither side lets itself be met. In many cases, we feel that Barth has not really sought us out, because he did not see where we are. But, on the other hand, I don't know of any Catholic writing in which Barth could really feel that he had been sought out either; and he surely tried to hear what we have to say. In a dialogue, willingness to listen is more important than talking.[9] It is part of our faith, part of our responsiveness, part of our prayer; and these three elements are indissolubly united.[10]

We shall proceed, therefore, on the assumption that something is really being said to us and that we can answer only after we have really listened. At Nicea, Ephesus, and Trent, the Church herself listened quietly at first and gathered her thoughts. Only then did she put forth an answer. Her answer was not a new truth, but a new declaration that had never been put quite that way before. Before the Council of Chalcedon, the Church did not have the conceptual armament to really move against Monophysitism. Before St. Augustine, she did not have the tools to face Donatism. So it might well be a mistake to assume that theology's present conceptual storehouse is equipped to handle all of Barth's questions. At any rate, it is our Christian duty to listen earnestly before we try to give a response.

There is no doubt, of course, that at present the Protestant enters the discussion without a grasp of the Catholic "plus" element discussed above. This "plus" may seem to comprise precisely those things which made the Reformation unavoidable, and whose rejection justifies the Reformation. We can thus understand why the Protestant accepts our invitation to dialogue with some hesitation. The Protestant cannot help but be suspicious when the Catholic offers to open the doors that were slammed shut long ago. He cannot help but wonder when the Catholic says he is willing to discuss the very questions that once caused schism. Any Catholic presentation that would be acceptable to Protestants presumably falsifies the Church's real position. Protestants are convinced that they have seen through Catholicism; and when a Catholic presentation does not strike them as absurd, it is because the Church's true face is disguised under some deceptive "jesuitical" mask.

How is the Catholic to counteract such deep mistrust? How is he to show that he cherishes no "untoward designs"?[11] Just listen to what Barth said: "The Catholicism that confronts us today is more refined and attractive than that of the sixteenth century. It has become jesuitical. . . . It talks better and it talks more boldly. It questions us with greater acuity and understanding. . . ."[12]

But Catholic inertia and Protestant mistrust must not thwart our commitment to reach an understanding. The

Protestant may not accept every Catholic doctrine, but he is not an unbeliever. He basically stands in the same realm of faith, believing in Jesus Christ, through the same sacrament of Baptism, and his faith essentially embraces all of Revelation, hence everything that is an object of faith. Hence our dialogue takes place in and around the content of faith; it is our common faith seeking understanding. The Catholic should not allow himself to be confused by his partner's suspicion; he will take it for what it is and try to understand it. The only way to dissipate it is to continue his own earnest search for understanding, to show his gratitude for any spark that helps him to gain a deeper, more authentic understanding of his faith. Genuine humility must mark his behavior.

One clear sign of this humility will be the Catholic's enduring readiness to acknowledge and admit his share of blame for the split. "At the time of the Reformation, the Catholic Church proclaimed its 'mea maxima culpa' through the lips of Hadrian VI."[13] This confession perdures so long as the split remains. The individual Catholic must join with his separated brothers in shouldering his share of the blame. There may be good reasons why the Church as a whole has not continued to acknowledge her guilt since the Reformation,[14] or why present-day theologians are more concerned with the relationship between sinfulness and holiness within the Church.[15] At any rate, the individual Christian will recognize that guilt is shared by both sides; when he comes to dialogue, he will openly admit this without damaging his obligations to truth.

A tinge of guilt surounds the whole question of divided Christendom. It is immediately evident that the heretic is tearing the seamless garment of the Redeemer and not less important that the split must have existed below the surface for a long time to have suddenly broken out with such vehemence. Later, it also becomes clear that elements of Catholic truth were taken outside the Church and continued to live there, without their full inner content of grace. As for us, can we sing *soli Deo gloria* and *sola fides sufficit* with unperturbed spirits now that the Protestant reformers have taken these words as their own slogans? Isn't it clear that both sides have been hurt?

Today, perhaps, we are beginning to move beyond the antithetical poles of Reformation and Counter-Reformation. We Catholics are trying to be primarily "catholic" and not "anti-Protestant," and Protestants are trying to be primarily biblical and "evangelical," not "protesters."

Montesquieu once made a shrewd prediction: "The Catholic religion will destroy the Protestant religion, and then Catholics will become Protestants."[16] There may be more than a grain of truth in this, insofar as reunion cannot be simply the external subjugation of one side to the other. This is the mistaken ideal often cherished by both sides, but authentic reunion must involve the humble submission of both sides to their common Lord and a common effort to make brotherly love a reality. That is how Newman envisioned dialogue.

Dialogue is the common need, but it must be a real dialogue, in which both sides recognize their guilt and search out the ultimate causes of division. With the help of God's grace, we may reach the point where we begin to wonder whether it is worthwhile to continue this split. Only very basic and important reasons, which may seem side-issues to one party, can permit Christians to surrender Christ's inheritance and reject His urgent commission. With an earnest desire to undergo self-examination, let us recall Barth's own words to himself and his Church:

With its doctrine of God's free gift of grace, the Reformation sought to preach the Christian's birthright to the world. It was with a heavy heart that it felt obliged to surrender its external unity with the Church of Rome. If this obligation seems to have passed . . . then it is time to wonder whether the restoration of external unity may not be worth the surrender of some small and inconsequential differences that still divide us from Rome.[17]

III · A DIALOGUE WITH BARTH

Why do we choose to approach Karl Barth in our desire to dialogue with modern Protestantism? Aren't there other worthy representatives of Protestantism, some of them even closer to us than he is? Wouldn't it be easier to start out with them? Why approach the very man who has set out to resuscitate the pure image of Protestantism, to take it more seriously than it takes itself,[1] and to "understand it better than it understands itself."[2] Isn't this a rather hopeless approach?

It is not because Barth represents one strong current in contemporary Protestantism that we are going to dialogue with him. Intellectual currents are transient phenomena, ebbing and flowing from age to age. Indeed some people claim that Barth's influence is already on the wane, but, then, there are certain epochs in which it is no disgrace for a person to lose influence. We must remember that in 1922, at the height of his career, Barth said his theology would be finished if it became a school of thought.[3] When *Church Dogmatics* came out in 1932, he suggested that people "would understand it better if they regarded it as a solo effort, not as the product of some particular school of thought . . . not as *the* dogmatic presentation of dialectical theology. . . ."[4] In short, Barth does not seem worried about the changing winds of popularity. For this reason, we must be wary of the notion that dialectical theology was entirely a product of the postwar period (World War I) and is now out-of-date.[5] Leaving aside the fact that Barth dropped the word *dialectical* (with all its corollaries) more than ten years ago, does a truly significant work of a past era lose its value with age? Are Leibnitz and Bach out of date? Barth will never be out of date for us Catholics so long as we have not confronted his ideas and found answers for the question he asks.

Barth was a representative of authentic Protestantism. The question he puts to us is not some vague current of thought, but a tangible reality, summoning us to dialogue. We must choose Barth as a partner for dialogue because in his work authentic Protestantism has found its full-blown image *for the first time.* Cutting through all the distorted developments of neo-Protestantism, he has gone back to the root sources of Protestantism, Calvin and Luther, and has even refined and purified these sources. He has modified or dropped certain points in Luther's doctrine, and he has done the same with Calvin. Calvin's doctrine is thought through to the end, spelled out more fully, and corrected where necessary.[6] Insofar as the early Reformers "are clearly guilty of inconsistencies and contradictions,"[7] we today must "do more than go back to the sources; we must move farther along the road they pointed out to us."[8] Barth veered away from orthodoxy as he veered away from liberal theology; that is why some want to lump him with the modernists.[9]

Barth desired to pursue the reformers' line of thought to the end, to follow the spirit, not the letter of Protestant tradition. This leads him to place the Reformation within the more general framework of the overall Church. As Calvin and Luther are toned down or corrected, the image of the patristic and scholastic periods come into sharper focus, which also have a right to be heard on critical questions of dogma:

We may see all too clearly the unsatisfactory traits of the Church during these periods, a Church which had not yet been reformed. But in Thomas and Bonaventure and Anselm and Augustine we are dealing with recognized teachers of the one Church, and it is our Church too, because in their day it had not yet rejected reform. They too have a right to be heard. Protestant dogmatics would profit greatly if it listened to them also, instead of regarding the Reformation as the beginning of all wisdom.[10]

The Church whose dogma Barth presented was not founded by the Reformers; only Christ can found the Church.[11] So Barth appropriated the Church's pre-Reformation testimony and teaching, feeling they were his just as much as they are ours. To him they were witnesses to the understanding of scripture and Revelation held by the one, holy Church, the perduring visible and invisible body of Christ. Catholicism and Protestantism both go back to the time of the early Fathers, insofar as they witness the enduring foundation of Christ in the midst of sinful men. Thus, in Barth's *Dogmatics* we find a theology that is coextensive with ours in history and subject matter.

Barth's work, then, has two features. It is the most thorough and forceful systematization of Protestant thought; and it is the closest approximation to Catholic thought. On the one hand, Barth developed the differences between us in systematic form, basing his discussion entirely on a *strictly theological structure* and set of principles. That is why a dialogue with someone else might appear to be more promising at first glance. On the other hand, his systematization of the differences in this way makes form and content seem to blend with one another; the Protestant element seems to be merely a dash of spice added to Catholic dough.

It is not surprising that Catholics may read much of Barth's work without feeling that they have to raise any serious objections to it, but to conduct a fruitful dialogue with Barth, one must take *both* features of his work into account. The Catholic reader may set aside the customary prejudices about Barth, that he is the purest embodiment of Protestant intransigence and hence dialogue is unprofitable; these prejudices focus on one feature of his work. But he may then overestimate the other feature of Barth's work, its approximation to Catholicism. Reading it, he sees citations from the Fathers of the Church and the medieval scholastics. He recognizes the questions being posed and is surprised by the similarity of views on such important dogmatic themes as the Trinity, God's essence, creation, Christology, and other subjects. He also notices that certain Protestant positions, such as Luther's stand on free will and Calvin's stand on predestination, are given a completely new and broader meaning; at first glance, they seem quite acceptable. We must make one point clear, however. Even though we may find ourselves in agreement with Barth on individual doctrines, the dialogue will not be fruitful if it is kept on that level. It must also take up the fundamental and formal set of theological principles that informs the individual doctrines and issues. If the dialogue does not tackle this, it will be a fruitless venture.

Having said that, we now seem to be faced with a new obstacle. Barth's theology grew and developed, even on essential points. The best proof of this is the fact that all the Catholic and Protestant objections raised against him between 1920 and 1930 now seem to be incomprehensible, misdirected, and out of date. Those criticisms have not made his work obsolete, far from it. He seems to have side-stepped them and moved on to his major work (*Church Dogmatics*), developing it far beyond their reach.

It is quite clear that the material content of *The Dogmatics* is quite different from that of Barth's earlier theological treatises. But did the formal principles of his theology change? This is a question we shall take up again, but let me say right now that the answer is "no." Despite the continuing development of his work, Barth remained true to his original intuition. To be sure, it found expression in different forms of thought and different words, but all these vicissitudes served to clarify it, purify it, and preserve it. If this is so, our first task is to look for the enduring constants in Barth's theology. We must search out the root intuition, the ultimate concern. Since earlier Catholic studies of Barth's theology stop short of the *Church Dogmatics*, we shall concentrate on these volumes in trying to present a new study of the formal principles underlying his whole work.

Only by doing this can we find answers to several important questions. Do his guiding principles represent the distinctive principles of Protestantism, a formalized statement of the whole Reformation that draws a hard and fast line between the two sides? Or are they susceptible to a completely different interpretation, one which might help to lead us beyond interconfessional antithesis? Obviously, this is no idle conversation; we are not just warming over questions that came to a boil four hundred years ago. We are dealing with a fresh, new question raised by Barth's original outlook and style of thought; we must do more than rummage through our stockpile of traditional answers. The dialogue is going to demand work on our part.

There is another reason why we are initiating a dialogue with Barth: his theology is a beautiful piece of work. I don't mean simply that it is stylistically beautiful, although he wrote well. The beauty of his style resulted from the fact that he combined two traits, enthusiasm and impartiality. He was enthusiastic about theological realities, and he approached them with the impartiality that is called for when dealing with such potentially inflammatory material. He was objective and totally absorbed in his subject.

What was his subject? His subject was God, the God who has revealed himself to the world in Jesus Christ, the God to whom the scriptures bear witness. Like Calvin and contrary to Luther, Barth turned away from the disposition of faith and focused on its content. He acknowledged his commitment to a strong theological objectivism: "Faith derives life from its object."[12] Thus he turned sharply away from the neo-Protestantism of Schleiermacher and did not engage in pastoral devotionalism. That is why he is so readable.

The subject matter provides its own splendor, but it is so overpowering and challenging to its author that his impartiality was combined with a deep-felt but controlled enthusiasm. Thus Barth's theological presentation differs markedly from the uncommitted objectivity that too often marks the work of Catholic theologians. The combination of enthusiasm and impartiality gives beauty to Barth's theology.

Who, in recent decades, has approached scripture the way he has? His work is not exegetical, nor hermeneutical, nor pastoral, nor inspirational. It is focused fully and exclusively on the Word, whose full splendor shines through its pages. Who but Barth has gazed breathlessly at his subject, watching it develop and blossom before his eyes? We would have to go back to Thomas Aquinas to find a similar spirit: free from the constraints of narrowness and tenseness, combining intelligence with just the right touch. In Barth the right touch is sometimes a spark of humor; usually, however, it shows up as a feel for just the right tempo, as a sense of rhythm.

Barth makes it easy for us to believe that he regarded Christianity as a triumphant reality. He did not write well because he had a gift for style. He wrote well because he bore witness to a reality that epitomizes style, since it comes from the hand of God. His attitude towards religious reality contrasted sharply with that of Kierkegaard. The latter regarded Christianity as an ascetical, polemical reality that is not of this world. For Barth, God's Revelation in Christ is God's perduring assent to himself and his creation.

Barth's symphonic style reminds one of Mozart. Indeed he spoke of Mozart now and then in lofty terms.[13] We cannot help but admire the orchestration of certain sections in Church Dogmatics.[14] Barth does not close in to focus on smaller and smaller details; he opens up a wider panorama as he proceeds.

This approach is not without dangers, of course, and Barth at times painted his frescoes in outsized dimensions and verbose strokes. Those superficial faults, however, never obscure his grasp of the proper internal proportions required by his subject matter. Theological realities always determined his method of questioning, his choice of problems, and the way in which he treated them. God's Revelation is the determining reality. Neither personal inclination nor the historical circumstances surrounding a question justify any departure from this guiding principle. Theology must focus on the same central things that Revelation itself focuses on. What is peripheral to Revelation cannot be made central by theology and studied as an independent issue.

Faith always means obedience, even when it is seeking understanding. It cannot pander to man's curiosity and desire for novelty. Many questions raised by man prove to be irrelevant and beside the point when seen in the light of Revelation. On the other hand, the topics posed and illuminated by God can never receive too much attention.

This was the guiding consideration for Barth, and this accounts for the purity and beauty of his presentation. Objectivity and beauty are tied together.

IV · BARTH'S STANDPOINT

Barth's basic position might be summed up as follows: 1. he took a stand midway between neo-Protestantism and Catholicism; 2. from there he believed he could expound Revelation objectively and pass critical judgment on the real thrust of neo-Protestantism, Catholicism, and modern thought in general; 3. the midpoint where Barth took his stand is to be viewed as radically Christocentric; in short, all secular relations and realities are to be explained in terms of the self-revelation of God's Word in Jesus Christ.

1. In the first volume of Church Dogmatics, Barth presents his work as a middle road between two erroneous lines of thought. It is not a compromise but a two-edged protest against rationalistic modernism on the left and Roman Catholicism on the right.[1] Thus he imitated the approach of Erich Przywara, who set the Catholic position (based on the analogy of being) midway between pantheistic naturalism on the left and theopanistic Protestantism on the right. But while Przywara drew sharp boundaries between the two extremes, Barth saw them as ultimately one, since both outlooks attribute to the "upright man" (Schleiermacher) or to the "holy, unspotted man" (Catholicism) a place that properly belongs to God alone, and

he invites them both to come to an understanding with each other, because nothing essential is keeping them apart. Both positions subscribe to "natural theology."

We can nevertheless say that Barth did take a middle road between them. Like Neo-Protestantism, Barth asserted that he was Protestant. "If I were to become convinced that the Schleiermacher-Ritschl-Troeltsch interpretation of the Reformation was in fact the *real thrust* of Luther's and Calvin's endeavors," he wrote, "I would not become a Catholic even though I should have to leave the Protestant Church; forced to *choose* between the two evils, however, I should prefer to become a Catholic."[2] His threat, in other words, was mainly intended to emphasize his hope that the real unity between Protestants can be brought clearly to light once again.

The same hope underlay his appropriation and use of Catholic tradition and dogma: that Protestantism can thereby become true to itself once again, truer than it may have been in the past. *Church Dogmatics* continually spells out how Protestantism strayed from its original path into the byroads of pietism, idealism, and other ideologies and is honest enough to show why this distorted development was almost inevitable.

Barth felt he was confronted with a superhuman task. He saw "how *formidable* the historical situation is . . . the unbelievable *chasm* and the enormous task confronting the Protestant theologian, the great temptation to throw up one's hands in despair—or become a Catholic."[3] One must stop a runaway horse; one must twist the rudder of history to prevent this four-hundred-year-old catastrophe from happening again. Even a pinch of acid must be used, if necessary, to rekindle a spark of life in a Protestantism that has become innocuous. Barth never ceased to denounce the now meaningless and ineffective protest of a Protestantism whose "toning down of Christianity" has far exceeded the jesuitical maneuvers of the Catholic Church.[4]

Is modern Protestantism anything else but a Catholicism disfigured by various and relatively insignificant heresies?[5]

How can we come to an understanding with Rome, if we have not yet agreed among ourselves as to what we stand for and represent as non-Catholic Christians?[6]

Seen from within, there is little reason to do battle with Rome; but there is much to be done in our own house.[7]

If Protestantism is nothing more than pious tradition, benevolent eclecticism, and individual spirituality,[8] if it is no longer the Church realm that truly embraces the principles *solus Deus, sola scriptura,* and *sola fides,* then one might well ponder whether Catholicism contains more of the original thrust of Luther and Calvin than the neo-Protestant heresy.[9] There at least one still finds "a strong awareness that the real and primary concern of the Church is God himself in Jesus Christ."[10] The Catholic Church lives "the notion of mediatorship and the concept of service."[11] On the basis of its belief that Christ is the subject of the Church, it dares "to claim *authority* for the Church . . . and authority is not a Catholic shibboleth, it belongs to the very essence of the Church. . . . Our protest against Rome's notion of authority is not akin to that of the modern intelligentsia, it is a quarrel between like-minded people."[12] "Protestantism protests for, not against, the Church. Protestant Church means *Church* even more than Catholic Church does."[13]

Here is not the place to ask how Barth could establish any real authority within Protestantism, or how he could speak of Church in the strict sense of the word.[14] These are serious questions, of course, but the important thing here is to realize that Barth's intent was to narrow in on the real substance of the Reformation, which in this particular instance has been better preserved in the Catholic Church than in neo-Protestantism.

Barth had no desire to cut all the ties of tradition that connected him with Schleiermacher and neo-Protestantism. He readily admitted his admiration of the latter's work and even went so far as to criticize Emil Brunner for treating it too lightly.[15] In his own discussion of Schleiermacher, he did more than criticize him. He brought out the points of contact between their ideas, showing the line that runs from Schleiermacher's theology through Wilhelm Herrmann's existentialism to his own theology of faith.[16] Barth was extremely critical of the turn taken by neo-Protestant thought, but he did not throw out the baby with the bath.

It is easy enough to see what Barth opposed; it is not so easy to see what he approved of. We shall discuss the first aspect here; the second aspect will concern us throughout the book. Anyone familiar with Kierkegaard and Hegelian idealism will readily see Barth's ties with these two factions. This should not surprise us. After all, Barth studied in Marburg under Herrmann, who took a middle position between them. Why shouldn't Barth's mental outlook have been closer to that of the nineteenth century than to that of a scholasticism which he discovered much later? One indication of this relationship is the fact that some people have unjustifiably accused Barth of being a philosophic idealist in disguise. The accusation will not hold up under scrutiny, but the seeming similarity of his mental outlook to the idealists does lend support to the charge. More of this later.

Barth's reasons for rejecting neo-Protestantism are clear enough: it had moved farther and farther away from Revelation, so that now nothing remained of Christianity but the name itself. God's Revelation, in which grace comes from outside and above us, had been put to one side. Man was to be elected, saved, sanctified, and re-deemed through a growing emphasis on religious subjecti-vism, through self-redemption (implied in pietism and fully developed in Feuerbach). Faith was reduced to the "highest potential" of reason, Revelation to the "highest potential" of history, and Jesus's awareness of God to the "highest potential" of human religiosity.

As Barth saw it, the course taken by German Christians led inevitably to neopaganism. Schleiermacher is the "Niagara" where two centuries of theological thought come crashing down with full force;[17] and the later conversion of Christianity into a nationalistic doctrine of racism was the last and ultimate stage of this rocky road traveled during the nineteenth century.[18] Since all this was clear to Barth, he rejected the spirit and the letter of this teaching: "the Protestant Church would do better to become a tiny remnant and flee to the catacombs than to make peace with this doctrine in any way."[19]

On the one side, Barth came to reject the whole content of neo-Protestant theology, while allowing for the possibil-ity of adopting certain formal elements in it (this we shall see later). On the other side (i.e., vis-à-vis Catholicism), Barth found himself in agreement with many specific teachings; but the mysterious formal framework of Cathol-icism precluded the possibility of a pact. As we shall see, this framework was soon designated as the analogy of being —as defined, depicted, and explained by Erich Przywara.[20]

It was Przywara's work on the analogy of being that led Barth to focus on this as the keystone principle of Cathol-icism. This is not surprising, when we consider the histor-ical circumstances and the great impact of Przywara's work. We shall have to examine the pros and cons of this partic-ular debate later on. Right now, let us just remember that Barth developed his *Church Dogmatics* midway between two unacceptable alternatives: the *content* of neo-Protestantism thought and the *formal framework* of Catholic thought.

2. Knowing that Barth had ties with the formal principles of modern philosophic thought (idealism in particular), and knowing that he rejected the apparent formal principle of Catholicism, we should not be surprised to learn that his own thought is set within the framework of formal principles. He was not a positivist, but a systematic, constructive theologian, even though he rejected the philosopher's notion of systematic.

Barth chose a standpoint way up on the heights, where faith can survey the meaning and purpose of the divine economy. It is a purely theological position but bears a formal resemblance to that of a Schleiermacher or a Hegel. Hegel set out to incorporate all theology into a comprehensive philosophy. Barth took a *purely theological* standpoint and set out to arrange the remaining types of human thought in concentric circles around it. Barth's thought was theological to the core, and he resolved to confront philosophy as a whole, as well as every variety of philosophical thought; *Church Dogmatics* gives extended treatment to major thinkers from Descartes to Sartre.

Barth's *Dogmatics* has a strict, formal structure and makes a claim to universality and "catholicity." In it the problems of faith and reason, of theology and philosophy, are pressing issues. The Catholic position is also formulated and tackled with a radically new approach.

3. The center where Barth stood is radically Christocentric. What this means will be spelled out more clearly in Part II. The important point here is that Barth clearly sets himself off from the two sides which he opposes; both seem to subsume Christ within some broader category.

For Schleiermacher, religious awareness was the central

category and Christ was merely the loftiest example of this awareness in action. Schleiermacher stopped short of being a real believer and remained a philosopher. Every system of thought that attempts to subsume God's Revelation in Christ under some broader category is betraying the faith. It does not matter whether you call it idealism, or personalism, or existentialism. That is why Barth felt obliged to move away from existentialist friends of his younger days.

Barth's objection to Catholicism should also be clear. Its underlying principle is not the belief that Christ is the Lord, but an abstract concept—the analogy of being. It approaches the question with a philosophical presupposition (in natural theology): that we can recognize the relationship between God and creation. Thus God's Revelation in Christ turns out to be the fulfillment of an already existing knowledge and ontology. Christ's place in the picture is reserved "in advance"; it is part of an ontology that exists prior to Revelation instead of deriving from it. In the Catholic system, Revelation and its claims are relative. Christ can still be the fulfillment of the natural order; he may even represent a breakthrough beyond it (*gratia perficit et extollit naturam*), but he cannot be the ultimate foundation of the whole temporal order.

This cursory sketch is based on the seven volumes of Barth's *Church Dogmatics* that have already appeared at the time of writing this appraisal. While much from the earlier stages of his thought may not be found there, it does represent the full-blown and definitive shape of his theological outlook.

Most of those who tackle Barth's work go back to his *Epistle to the Romans* and other early works. For this reason I shall devote subsequent pages of this book (in Part II) to the chronological development of Barth's thought. I shall also try to show that the same basic idea pervades Barth's work from the very beginning. We shall see him holding on to the same basic insight throughout his career, trying to find the proper way to express it, and discarding one form of expression after another. We shall see him coming into ever closer contact with traditional and Catholic forms of expression, until finally he stands before us as someone who has to be taken seriously.

V · THE CATHOLIC STANDPOINT

What is the standpoint of Catholic theology vis-à-vis Karl Barth? That is a complicated question. Indeed, one might well ask whether Catholicism as such has a standpoint in the same sense as Barth did. I am inclined to say it does not, but I shall explain my answer in a later section.

Barth was an individual theologian of great constructive power. The Catholic Church is primarily a church, not a system of theology. Catholic theology itself is not the work of a single thinker; historically speaking, it is a composite of successive thought systems that continue to coexist alongside each other. It is at least questionable whether one can extract a general "Catholic" thought system from this composite of varied systems.

That is why we must avoid putting too much stress on the work of Przywara. His discussion of the analogy of being is very enlightening, but it is not certain that this is the key to the whole problem.[1] We must not forget that Przywara formulated an answer to Barth's dialectical theology, and both were very abstract. But Barth moved on to *Church Dogmatics*, and Przywara's answer may no longer suffice. Even if it did, it could not be called *the* Catholic approach.

Let us assume that there is no single Catholic approach and that there need not be. The question still remains: What is our response to Barth's work? Here we have a thinker who tried to present the real thrust of the Reformation in a comprehensive, modern framework, whose outlook was not alien to that of the Church Fathers or scholastic philosophy, and who tried to incorporate their views within his own framework. Are we ready to dialogue with him, or must we prepare the groundwork for such a discussion? Is Robert Grosche correct when he says that Barth's "theology poses a question which we Catholics cannot evade; the old answers will not do."[2]

It would appear that the prospects for a dialogue are not too bad. Barth, the founder of "existential theology," did not continue to follow the direction taken by philosophical and theological existentialism. While they degenerated into "fads," he turned away to discover Anselm, Thomas, and scholastic theology. Says Barth: "Fear of scholasticism is the hallmark of a false prophet. A genuine theology will not hesitate to let itself be tested by scholasticism too."[3] Luther's "irregular dogmatics" seemed dangerous to Barth[4] when viewed in this light, and our modern efforts, he thought, cannot compare with those of medieval theology or the Reformation.[5] Catholic theology's return to Thomism was a healthy thing; internal consolidation is an acute necessity for a Church that must face challenges from without.[6]

While Barth was moving in this direction, most of the Catholic avant-garde was moving the other way. Its theologians were leaving scholasticism to explore modern thought. In Scheler they discovered the various categories of personalist ideals; in Husserl they discovered the relevance of phenomenology for religion; in Heidegger they discovered the radical historicity of finite existence. So deep was their veneration for Pascal, Kierkegaard, and Dosto-

yevsky—and even for Baudelaire, Nietzsche, and Rilke—
that these men were almost turned into modern Church
Fathers, and the teachings of tradition were viewed in their
light.

This countermovement cannot be regarded as a fruitful
complement to the direction taken by Barth or as the precondition for a happy encounter. The *theological* fruits
of this countermovement were meager. The trend between
1920 and 1933 can truly be regarded as a flight from
theology. Dissatisfied with their textbook theology, the
theologians fled from it, but they did not replace it with
anything of equal merit. Every attempt was made to avoid
the constraints of authentic theology. Serious Protestant
theologians were distressed by the trend of Catholic thought
during this period.[7]

That era seems to be coming to a close. Today's bolder
spirits realize that they can no longer evade the demands
of authentic theology. The task is difficult and almost
beyond man's powers, but the new horizons that have
opened up call for a dogmatic theology to match the challenge. They cannot overlook the fact that, while many fine
minds have devoted their attention to Rilke, Kafka, and
existentialism, Karl Barth persistently focused on the "one
thing necessary." He tried to speak about Jesus Christ in
clear and completely theological terms. His persistent pursuit of this issue continues to pose an urgent question to
Catholicism.

Realizing this, we can begin to consider a possible answer or approach to Barth. I say *approach* because we are
dealing with an ongoing process not a finished picture. The
development of this process will be described in Part II.
Here let us simply note that we are dealing with a process
shaped by individual theologians who far outweigh the
many in importance. Church tradition and Christianity
itself rests upon such individuals. While they may not

carry the same weight as the great names in theology, it is they who preserve and develop theological tradition.[8] It is they who have glimpsed the question posed by Barth, even though they found themselves compelled to give different answers.

My book takes its place among their efforts. Like every work of Catholic theology, it is the effort of one individual within a loosely organized current of thought that feels ready to dialogue with Barth. While it remains within the bounds of Catholic orthodoxy, it has grasped Barth's Christocentric emphasis and is prepared to follow it through. For it, dialogue is not only a possibility but a process already under way.

VI · OUR THEME IN FOCUS

It would be impossible to describe, analyze, and criticize Barth's entire *Dogmatics* (much less his whole corpus) within the covers of one book. So we shall limit our discussion to one of the two major thematic cycles in *Church Dogmatics*, since they offer the best prospects of a fruitful dialogue. The first cycle is to be found in the earlier volumes, and it centers around the treaties on creation, incarnation and redemption; here Barth's Christocentric approach is clearly evident. The second cycle centers around the themes of Church, sacraments, and Christian living. These themes flow from the first group, and Barth's remarks on them are greatly influenced by the decisions he arrived at in the earlier volumes.

In treating the first set of themes, Barth is creative, original, and very much at ease. In treating the second set of themes, he is rather ill at ease. His treatment of the Church (not fully developed) is rather pallid. His treatment of the sacraments is not very original. Only in his presentation of ethics do we catch a glimpse of the creative spark which pervades the earlier volumes.

How can we explain this unevenness? It may be due to Barth's own temperament or to his affinity to Calvin. If Catholicism wants to hold a fruitful dialogue with Calvinism, it would do best to focus on the first thematic cycle mentioned above; a dialogue on this second cycle is best held with Lutheranism. Hence we shall concentrate our attention on the first set of themes. At the close of our study, we shall bring up a few questions related to the second set of themes but based on Barth's conclusions in the earlier volumes. At first glance this may seem to be an arbitrary decision on our part or even that we are evading the most critical and important questions, but appearances are deceiving in this instance. If we tackle the problems of methodology and root principles spelled out in Barth's treatment of the first set of themes, we shall have gone a long way towards resolving the questions that surround the second set of themes.

When Barth tried to describe his differences with the Catholic Church, he always focused on the formal structures that make up the two positions. A given Church has a particular structure because it is required by a particular interpretation of Revelation, of faith, and of Jesus Christ. As a matter of fact, Barth felt that the difference in formal structure is what justified the Reformation. Because we are not one on this point, the schism remains to this day. It is for this basic reason that we shall focus our full attention on the first set of themes mentioned earlier.

In the course of our discussion, we may be able to show that, despite Barth's protestations, there is a real chance for dialogue and mutual agreement. This does not mean we would prejudge the specific issues connected with ecclesiology. It simply means that we would have cut through the formal, structural ties that support both positions. The question of ecclesiology would remain, but much of its theological weight would be siphoned off.

At this point one might well raise another question. In the light of the more recent volumes of *Church Dogmatics*, can we say that Barth's "structural ties" remained as rigid as they once were? The picture of the Church which Barth presented in his first outlines of the projected *Dogmatics* contains certain conceptual presuppositions that are no longer to be found in subsequent volumes.

In general, we find ourselves facing a paradoxical situation. In treating the first set of themes, Barth moved closer to the Catholic position; in treating the second set of issues, he moved farther away from the Catholic position. The reason for this will become a bit clearer when we examine the essential conclusions at which Barth arrived on the basis of his fundamental structural principle. We can say this much at least: if we can clarify or resolve the difficulties posed in his treatment of the first set of issues, then we shall have gone a long way towards eliminating the substructure that underlies the second set of problems.

VII · THE ROOTS OF CONTROVERSY

From the very first, Barth's standpoint vis-à-vis Catholicism was clear. Strongly influenced by Przywara, he was going to distinguish his position from that of Catholicism on the basis of a well-defined structural principle. It was not a question of holding *different doctrines*, but of having *different outlooks* on the same reality.[1] The main problem, as Barth saw it, was that the two sides gave different form and shape to the same reality.

Now form and shape do not exist in a vacuum, of course. They are concretized in some tangible issue, so that the two sides seem to hold different doctrines, but Barth regarded these doctrinal differences as primarily *symptoms* of this underlying difference in outlook. That is why our dialogue is uncommonly difficult. We are dealing with a difference in basic structure, but this difference can only be laid hold of in the content of some particular issue. We could clear up every specified issue without ever coming to grips with the underlying difference in outlook. The Catholic sees the world through Catholic glasses, and thus offends the Protestant.

On the one hand, the structural framework *can be grasped* at times *in the concrete issues*. The dogmatic differences may only be symptoms, but they do represent topics that must be subjected to theological investigation. The mysterious formal structure thus shows up as some kind of universal, some regulating principle that clarifies the nature and the arrangement of specific dogmatic issues. For this reason our dialogue about the two structures must involve a discussion of essential dogmatic principles.

Here again, however, we must make certain reservations. For the formal structure as such is *not* to be identified with the content of dogma. We face the same problem that we encounter in the natural sciences: general principles are encountered *only indirectly* in contingent realities. The "root principle" of theology is the content of Revelation; but it cannot be separated from its source, the sovereign God who chooses to reveal himself. Hence this principle is also a gandiose thing, over which man cannot exercise mastery as he does with the principles of natural science. It is *indirect* in these two respects.

Presuming that there is such a thing as theology, as both sides in the debate do, we can then ask: How do we encounter this doubly indirect principle? Here again both sides are agreed on the way in which the self-revealing God presents himself. He reveals himself in disguises, never in the way that purely temporal realities present themselves. He presents himself as a reality only to a self-surrendering faith. The understanding that comes from faith can never get beyond this indirectness, but it does get real insight into this principle.

We thus have a criterion for judging any system of dogma, no matter what it says or how it is presented. The critical question is whether the specifically theological principle, which serves as the root and source of the system, is recognized, respected, and preserved? This imponderable element, this formal principle, will decide whether a theology is authentic or not.

Now we can see what Barth's main complaint against Catholicism is, and we can understand why it is so important in his eyes. As he sees it, Catholicism has betrayed the specifically theological character of the root principle, believing it can be treated as a principle of natural science. In other words, Catholicism sees only one aspect of Revelation's indirectness. In drawing the line between his theology and that of Catholicism Barth had in mind the twofold indirectness of theology.

I regard the analogy of being as *the* artifact of the Anti-Christ. It is *precisely because of this* that one cannot be a Catholic. By comparison, all the other pretexts for not becoming a Catholic are shortsighted and negligible.[2]

This statement has aroused much unjustifiable surprise and ridicule. Such reactions would be understandable if it were a question of some particular Catholic tenet, not an attempt to formulate the distinctive formal principle on which Catholicism is based.

Protestant dogma, for its part, could hardly be called dogma if it did not try to describe and clarify its underlying formal structure. Barth spent his whole life trying to do this. Whether we call it *dialectics* or the *analogy of faith* does not matter. The important point is that we are dealing with a difference in formal structure. That is the focal point of our dialogue, even though formal principles only come to light in concrete doctrines. We could deny Barth's charge that the analogy of being represents an attempt to "take over God," to make him subordinate to a higher principle. We could argue that his counterprinciple, the analogy of faith or dialectics," actually tries to do the same thing. Both sides might also rebut these charges. No case could be presented, however, unless the debater stayed in constant contact with the whole range of concrete dogmatic doctrines. The dialogue can only move forward if we move back and forth between a *priori* principles and a *posteriori* doctrines.

Barth's attack on the analogy of being is only *one* expression of his basic objection to Catholicism. This basic objection can be found at every point where concrete doctrines clash. For example, Catholicism regards tradition as a second source of Revelation alongside scripture. In Barth's eyes, this tendency to juxtapose things in pairs was symptomatic of the underlying formal error in Catholicism:

The theology of *and* is rooted in one source. If a theology speaks about faith *and* works, nature *and* grace, reason *and* Revelation, then it must also speak about scripture *and* Tradition. This *and* is only *one* more symptom of a basic position worked out beforehand: God's lofty majesty has been compromised in his intercourse with men.[3]

In short, this passion for couplets is another expression of the analogy of being and its underlying presuppositions.

The same problem is evident in the doctrine of *sola fide*. Both Catholicism and Protestantism teach that faith alone gives us understanding. Yet, noted Barth, "a believing Catholic . . . and a believing Protestant cannot agree on these three words (*sola fide intelligimus*).[4] Why is this? Because the Protestant maintains that grace always remains grace, that it is a one-way street where man cannot "reciprocate," while the Catholic talks about "cooperating with grace" and holds up the ideal of Mary as Co-Redemptrix.[5] For Barth, the worst example of this attempt to "lay hands on God" was the whole notion of the *scientia media*:

It is an attempt to develop a system that embraces both God and man, to set them both on the same level and relate them to one another. What else is this but an attempt by the creature to take control of himself and of God too?

This very attempt is the basic thrust of the Roman Catholic system in its entirety and in all its details. It is the foundation for its teachings on grace, the sacraments, and the Church, on scripture and tradition, on the Roman primacy and papal infallibility, and particularly on Mary.[6]

What can one say of this approach?

It teaches the independence of free creatures *vis-à-vis* God. It is nothing else but man's hostility to God's grace expressed in theological form. It is the fall all over again. . . . We must remember that jesuitical casuistry has become the Roman Catholic brand of modern humanism; and the whole business seems to be aimed at *denying God*.[7]

Similar judgments are passed on other aspects of the supernatural Revelation is to incorporate the latter into the Catholic position. To distinguish between natural and former, because no one can serve two masters.[8] To talk about sacraments that work ex opere operato is to make the operation of grace an impersonal process, independent of God's initiative and man's faith.[9] Everywhere Barth saw Catholicism trying to control God. When the Church makes herself the authentic and infallible interpreter of scripture, "she stands over scripture and thus is no longer subject to its dictates."[10] She becomes a self-governing Church; and self-government is the prerogative of God alone.[11] It is an act of presumption and "flagrant disobedience." Her stress on formulated doctrines as such and all these other characteristics represents an attempt "to naturalize grace," to convert it into "a physical reality."[12]

No one would deny that some part of these objections *could* be valid. The Church would not be the Church of sinners and publicans if she did not daily experience this tendency to "lay hands on God." After all, this is only another way of describing sin, and she is a Church of sinners. As such, she can give way to this attitude of disobedience. Whether such possibilities exist in the Catholic "system," however, is not the real question; for these possibilities exist in every human medium that attempts to transmit God's Revelation. They exist in the Protestant "system" too, as Barth would have readily admitted. The real question is: do the specific doctrines of Catholicism, taken as a whole, *clearly* and indisputably represent the embodiment of a principle which itself is *clearly* and unmistakably a violation of grace, an attempt to lay hands on God? Barth's attempt to answer this question involves great difficulties, as we shall see in subsequent pages.

PART TWO

The Development of Barth's Theology

I · INTERPRETING BARTH

Before we attempt to consider the development of Barth's thought, we should bring up one point regarding the interpretation of his work as a whole. His work is so extensive, so varied, and so multifaceted that we cannot find our way through it unless we look for some guidepost and assume the existence of some overall design. At the same time, this guidepost must be flexible enough to account for the changes over the years in Barth's way of thinking and his manner of expression.

We are dealing here with a project that occupied Barth's whole life. How can we bring order into it? There are two basic alternatives: we can interpret and explain his later works in terms of earlier writings, tracing the former back to the root ideas from which they sprang; or else we can relate the earlier works to the later ones, regarding the latter as the full development and explanation of the former. There is no question of choosing one alternative to the complete exclusion of the other. Men build their thought in different patterns. Many produce one major work and spend their whole life explaining and interpreting it. Others pick up pieces here and there and try different patterns until they find the right one. Still others, like Goethe, seem to be beyond any clear and simple interpretation.

How are we to go about interpreting Karl Barth? Shall we explain *Church Dogmatics* in terms of *The Epistle to the Romans* or *vice versa?* Is his later project a sustained echo of his first flash of insight, or is the earlier work merely a tune-up for the great symphony to come? In other words, does the essential theme appear only in his later work and thus render the earlier work obsolete, or is it present from the very beginning, even if it be only in germinal form?

Any attempt to give a definitive answer to these questions would involve several presuppositions: that one was thoroughly acquainted with a work still unfinished at the time of this appraisal, and that an overall judgment was possible. Even if such a judgment were theoretically possible, it would presuppose long and intimate acquaintance with the whole Barthian corpus. So if we propose an approach here, we do so without trying to prove that it is the correct approach. Its validity must be judged in terms of the results obtained.

Having laid down this stipulation, we would propose this first tentative principle: any attempt to explain *Church Dogmatics* (and Barth's later writings in general) solely in terms of *The Epistle to the Romans* is really absurd; in fact, such an approach is an affront to Barth. For Barth moved away from the position he took in *The Epistle to the Romans,* as is quite clear in the Foreword to the fifth edition (1926). On more than one occasion he has cautioned readers against taking his words too literally.[1] Indeed he has given up the whole conceptual framework of his early work, including the term *dialectic*. Because he felt that the first version of *Church Dogmatics* contained too much from an earlier stage of his thought, he started all over again with a new version. In short, he deliberately abandoned the cryptic abstractionism of his earlier thought in order to lay hold of theological reality, in all its purity, at the place where it presents itself: in the Revelation of sacred scripture.

Yet, despite all this, there have always been those who have deluded themselves about the aims of *Church Dogmatics*, who have seen it as nothing more than an extension of the *Epistle to the Romans*. Between 1920 and 1930, the *Epistle to the Romans* gave rise to a lively philosophical debate among theologians (e.g., Tillich, Reisner, Althaus, Heim, Oepke, H. W. Schmidt, Messer, and Siegfried); their positions were quite understandable for that time, but one begins to wonder when one finds Friedrich Gogarten writing from this viewpoint as late as 1937 (*Gericht oder Skepsis*) and using Barth against Barth because his position has changed. The situation is even more ridiculous ten years later (1947), when Cornelius van Til (*The New Modernism*) tries to explain the whole theology of Barth and Brunner on the basis of their earlier positions and in terms of the philosophical principles that are supposedly at the root of their system.

On the Catholic side we find this same backward glance adopted by Barth's would-be critics. Jerome Hamer, O.P., wrote a small book about Barth (1949), an excellent effort in many respects, but he too focused on Barth's *Prolegomena* and tried to interpret it in the light of his earlier works, disregarding the fact that later volumes of *Church Dogmatics* contained much that developed or went beyond the methodology and the philosophical premises of the *Prolegomena*.[2]

We would also propose a second principle: any attempt to bypass Barth's earlier thought, to regard it as a thing of the past and to concentrate solely on his later works, can only lead to a very incomplete understanding of them. There is no doubt that Barth's later works are, in a real sense, his earlier works as well, that the intense radiation of *Church Dogmatics* represents the explosive unleashing of an intellectual power that was there from the very beginning. We can understand the whole process only if we regard the *Epistle to the Romans* and related writings as the first symptomatic formulations of a deeper intention.

Many people have referred to the "metaphysical cast" of the *Epistle to the Romans;* Barth himself has spoken about its "crust of Kantian and Platonic concepts"[3] and the need to strip away this crust in order to unearth the book's real aim. In 1938, he readily admitted that he had to probe still deeper. This probing would involve throwing off the last vestiges of a philosophical and anthropological framework in the elucidation of the Christian message. It would involve a "Christological emphasis" that enabled him "to express everything more clearly and more simply, more unambiguously and more religiously, more freely and more comprehensively." In all this he felt that he "was merely moving further along the road he had set foot on."[4]

Looking back on that sensational first edition of *Romans* today, the reader will be astonished to find that the real concern of Barth's early years was the same as that of his mature work, all appearances to the contrary. To be sure, *Church Dogmatics* sets forth its concern in simple, classical German rather than in the abrupt, expressionistic terminology of "dialectical theology." But this only means that the reader, in all fairness, should assume that dialectics was not the end itself, but only a means and a method to arrive at the "real thing." It served its purpose at the time, but then it was confused with the end itself and became expendable.

Yet here again we must not jump to conclusions. The expressionism of *Romans* is more than a stylistic form of expression, and was not chosen arbitrarily. Perhaps buried in this expressionism is the plaintive cry of a man who has seen something that no one around him has seen. Perhaps it is a truly existential attempt to express the inexpressible, to "catch the movement of a bird in flight," knowing full well that "motion itself, apart from the thing moved, turns into a topic, a thing."[5] *Romans* did have its own wellsprings and its own problems. It was an attempt to use a conceptual framework, which might be somewhat awkward, but in which words with some consistency might point to the pure *happening*, the pure reality that Revelation essentially is.

At that point the analogy of being (*analogia entis*), of course, already was the archenemy, but that is not to say that we can describe Barth's development as simply a transition from dialectical theology to the analogy of faith (*analogia fidei*). This line of movement is correct, and indeed it is central to an understanding of Barth. But we should not forget that his early dialectics has not spent its force. When we interpret his *Dogmatics*, we must remember that Barth has never abandoned that first flash of insight, his desire to create a theology, not of being but of "happening."

We must agree with Jean Louis Leuba when he warns against static, "systematic" interpretations of Barth's *Dogmatics*. As he points out, such an approach leads to absurd conclusions and disappointing results; "prophetic" interpretation is the only legitimate approach. If Leuba is correct in asserting that a "decisive happening" (not a being) lies at the root of Barth's theology, then we must interpret

Church Dogmatics on the basis of this root idea, not on the basis of the *Epistle to the Romans* itself.

At this point we can say little more. We shall follow the chronological development of Barth's thought from dialectics to analogy, and then try to show to what extent the former has been preserved in the latter.

II · DIALECTICAL THEOLOGY

---

1. *Epistle to the Romans*: FIRST EDITION

When the first edition of the *Epistle to the Romans* came out in 1919, no one could have predicted what the second edition would look like three years later. Only now, looking back, do we see that the first edition announced the same theme that was hammered home in the second, even though the conceptual framework was different.

The theme is dynamic eschatology, the irreversible movement from a doomed temporal order to a new living order ruled by God, the total restoration (*apokatastasis*) of the original, ideal creation in God. This movement of a doomed world, which still knows its true origin but cannot get back to it on its own, is due solely to God, who shows his mercy in Christ. In Christ he implants life in the dead cosmos. In Christ he implants a seed which will sprout and spread overpoweringly until everything is transformed back into its original splendor. All this will not take place in plain view but will work itself out eschatologically.

Undoubtedly, this is a message that proclaims the "good news." An enthusiastic vision, depicting how the salvation economy unfolds according to its own laws, it is dressed up in a conceptual framework deriving from Plato, Hegelianism, and religious socialism, not from scripture, Luther, or Calvin.

According to Plato, the world displays a threefold movement: existence in the Idea, break-off from the Idea, and return to the Idea. Christianity (Origenism) took over this schema and modified it in two ways. Existence in the Idea becomes "Spirit"; break-off from the Idea becomes "psyche," the "realm of the soul" in the (supposedly) Pauline sense of that word. Remembrance of the original homeland, by itself, does not have the power to restore the lost soul to its rightful place; in itself it is a "yearning," a "void," a "crisis"; religiously speaking, it is an "inferno,"[1] from which the lost psyche is saved by the descending Logos.

These Christian modifications of Platonism, however, do not tackle the root issue: the notion of "existence in the Idea," for authentic and real existence can only be "existence in God." This existence is "immediacy,"[2] "direct relationship,"[3] "direct unity."[4] At the very beginning God was open and communicative; he was not a secret mystery. Only the fall "made a secret out of the divine";[5] and to those who have been reborn in Christ it is "no longer a secret."[6] Only the fall, "the flesh, turned humanity, which was supposed to be one with the divine, into something merely human."[7] The "divine in me,"[8] the "pristine divine nature in humanity"[9] makes it a divine race with a divine viewpoint; it establishes an ultimate *identity*. Humanity is a "particle of God's universal power."[10] "It is not we who are at work; it is God who is at work in and through us."[11] Goethe's world-soul is invoked at this point.

When God sets out to restore mankind, "his own good Spirit steps in to take the place of the flesh."[12] The redeemer becomes the foundation for the life of each and every individual. Thus, man, who had broken away from

God, recalls his origins once again; and, at the same time, he recalls his own transcendental being and God. He is summoned to become what he really is.[13] A real "happening" takes place from above. What was once idea without power and logic without dynamism, what was once the hollow shell of religion and philosophy, is now filled with vitality once again. Possibility is transformed into reality.

What constitutes the fall, the breakaway? "There is only one sin: man's desire to establish his independence vis-à-vis God." Man breaks away from direct existence with God. He resents living directly in the Spirit as a child. He wants to be like God, to be self-important in his own right. Sin is reflection—the turning in upon oneself, and reflection is sin. St. Thomas' definition of sin (conversio ad creaturos) and of reflection (conversio ad phantasma) are equated with one another. The desire to exist of oneself means separation from God, and this move is sin. Distance between the creature and God represents the creature's separation from God. Hence the principle of analogy, which expresses this distance, is equated with the breaking away.

The man who is separated from his (i.e., God's) Spirit becomes "flesh." His new condition (katastasis) is an offense in itself. It is the root of multiplicity, "the splitting up of life into two types of existence, the divine and the temporal."[14] It sets up opposition between life and ideal and is the source of time. Since this condition drains away life, it is death, illusion, untruth, nonbeing, chaos.

This theology does not possess one concept clearly included in the principle of analogy (and of distance): the concept of nature. Nature, set at a distance from the creator, teeters between two, and only two, possibilities. Either it is total identity with the creator or separation from him into absolute nonbeing. Pantheism dissolves the creature in God and in nothingness. In this theology God is "the innermost but disarrayed 'nature' of all things and all men."[15] Hence the grace of Christ is a process which "is not external to us; it is natural, not alien to us."[16] It is our natural law, the natural foundation of all existence, our "nature in God,"[17] For this reason "nature," which is now our nature and which is totally alien to that other nature ("as water is to fire"), can only be "unnaturalness."[18] The pantheistic concept of nature necessarily becomes dialectical.[19]

Now at this point the platonic and oriental Christian concept of "identity" necessarily turns into the Reformation concept of "opposition." Here Origen and Dostoyevski encounter Luther, Calvin, and Kierkegaard, and the details of this struggle are spelled out in the second edition of *Epistle to the Romans*, as we shall see.

Theological Hegelianism does not inject any really new theme into the Platonic scheme of Origenism. It underlines the notions of restoration (*apokatastasis*), dynamism, and vital function as historicotemporal or "protohistorical" lines of movement. It also underlines the switch from religious subjectivity, from romantic pietism, to objectivity. Subjectivity, reflection, and psyche represent the "breaking away." The journey through the "hell of interiority" and the "inferno of pietism," whose last agonizing cry echoes in the second edition of *Romans*, reads like a page from Hegel's phenomenology.

Turning to Christ means turning away from self. It means forgetting oneself and abandoning the attempt to live in and of oneself. It means living within the "enduring objectivity of the true and the good,"[20] and the "objective Spirit" is the Holy Spirit, who leads us into "the realm of absolute spirit."[21]

Finally, this whole picture is tinged with the distinctive brushstrokes of religious socialism. Subjectivity is "individualism." To turn one's back on the accursed isolation of individuality is to find salvation "by attaching oneself to the new humanity which has appeared in Christ."[22] God expropriates our "private property" and our unholy individuality. The variety to be found in individuals is only the surface of existence. Kenosis really means "the elimination of the personal element."[23] This is the authentic revolution, and it has been the message of all the great human spirits from Moses to John the Baptist, from Plato to the Socialists.[24]

These great spirits were truly free. They stood above other men and pointed the way ahead, but instead of exercising their power as some brand of rugged individualism, they used it to sustain weaker souls. Weaker spirits still need religion, piety, and, most of all, churches; the great spirits have long since discovered that these things are not authentic. Leaving behind such supports as religion, church, school, Judaism, Christianity, morality, and idealism, they exercise patience even as God does. They let the kingdom develop organically, acting as midwives with the help of God's grace.[25]

What a startling book it is! Barth's opening chords reverberate throughout. It chants of a radical, philosophical mysticism, of a radical historical outlook on the world, and of a powerful universalism deeply tinged with liberalism and socialism.

The Foreword to the second edition of Romans claims that the whole edifice has been razed from the ground up, so that not one stone has been left standing on another.[26] Perhaps Barth should have been more careful and selective in his revisions; could such overpowering themes be done away with so easily?

2. *Epistle to the Romans:* SECOND EDITION

In the fire of Overbeck, Nietzsche, Dostoyevsky, Kierkegaard, and the Reformationists (now somewhat strange to the eye), the spark is lit. The possibility of contradiction, which was latent in the notion of "identity," now breaks to the surface. The second edition is like dynamite, it revolutionizes religion and drives us to the abyss.[27] We are dragged through the heights and depths in order to be convinced that our existence is not our natural selves, but the deep-felt contradiction that we feel in the core of our being, the impossibility that we ourselves are.

The Romans to whom Paul wrote his epistle appear to have been "very free and expansive spirits";[28] Barth's book, too, is for free spirits who, like Nietzsche, are beyond liberalism. They look for untruth in everything,[29] and thus they are able to unmask every untruth. They are nihilists in theology and, for that very reason, omnists also. "The strong man, precisely because he is strong, does not stand against anyone; he stands behind everyone. . . . He does not criticize (being too critical for that). . . . He doesn't step to the forefront, he moves to the back. He is nowhere, because he is everywhere."[30]

As a pure eschatologist, he stands on the far side of all human possibilities, without falling into the dangerous Titanism of freedom. Deeply antireligious, he realizes the necessity of religion for all (even himself). He is a question mark and an exclamation point, standing on the border line. He is no longer a man, he is simply a signpost, a raised finger; for this reason he is unimportant and unheralded. He is "this extreme, extrapolated standpoint which is *no standpoint at all.*"[31] He does *not* place any value at all on his radical words or his radical image. "He is truly special because he does not come forward as something special."[32] This self-effacement is the real test of example, and it proves his earnestness.

But what is left for us? Nothing, it would seem—or else, God. As the totally imperceptible, he should become visible in this groping. The "infinite qualitative dissimilarity" should be demonstrated. Distance and room for transcendence should be created. It should mark the end of every attempt "to divinize man and to humanize God with romantic formulations," "to wipe out the distance between them."[33] Every attempt to relativize the relationship between God and man must be seen for what it truly is: sin.

Religion is the creature's attempt to "lay hands on God," to draw the boundary line between God and man. It is the law of which St. Paul speaks, and it steps beyond the proper bounds in its very attempt to define them. "The religious man is a sinner in the clearest sense of the word,"[34] for he does what he cannot and dare not do. He establishes a relationship between himself and God, and thus he sets himself over against God. He is on the heights and in the depths at every moment. "At every moment he must be both Moses and Aaron, Paul and Saul, prophet and pharisee, priest and parson; at every moment he is the loftiest indication of the positive divine element within human realities, and the clearest example of man's negativity towards the reality of the divine."[35]

The ultimate cry of religious pathos is: "You shall be as God." When we experience the deep-rooted questionability of our existence, we cannot help but be religious men. We are all religious. This being so, why not step to the very edge of this possibility, where, from a human point of view, only the question itself remains? Here is the diacritical point where man is nothing but a hollow cavity, a minus sign, where he is on the verge of recognizing God as God. "The one and only possible presence of God

in the world reveals itself in the recognition of the fundamental separation between God and world."[36] But even
this point is not salvation. Our recognition of privation,
our awareness of hunger and thirst, can lead to the triumph
of a new pharisaism; it can tempt us to a new type of
haughty pride. "Shall I not rest content with the fact that
I am discontented?"[37]

We can easily spot blurred traces of the first edition of
Romans behind this dialectic. The pathos of the absolute
distance between God and creation, which seems to be a
new Kierkegaardian or Reformationist notion, involves a
latent presupposition. It is none other than the notion of
original identity, which we encountered in the first edition.
Once again we encounter the notion of "remembrance,"[38]
of our "lost intimacy with God," of our "eternal source,"
our "existence in God," our "direct unity with God."[39]

Once again we read of man's breaking away as the
creature's acquisition of self-awareness. "Man was not
meant to be, in his own eyes, a second reality alongside
God. He was not to know the secret which God knew
and mercifully hid from him: that he is only a man."[40] The
moment of eternal creation is gone and it cannot be called
back. Gone is the moment in which God as God and man
as man are not two but one.[41]

Here again the law of distance, the law of analogy, is
sin. To be a creature means to be guilty,[42] but here again
salvation in Christ means return to unity. In Christ we
see clearly what being a man represents in God's eyes:
death, hell, abandonment of God.[43] Christ steps in Adam's
place, and Adam is each one of us. "The Adam-Christ
dualism perdures only in that it neutralizes itself. It is the
dualism of a thrust."[44] It is the mystery of a single predestination "which hides itself in the duality of Adam
and Christ in order to reveal itself in their unity."[45] The

fall into the abyss is supralapsarian, but even here it has a dynamic relation to redemption. "There is no fall from God in Adam, no sentence of death, that does not originate from the point where man, reconciled with God in Christ, is granted life."[46]

Only against the backdrop of a presupposed original identity does the whole dialectic of *Romans* become possible. The pathos of distance, which resounds through the pages of the second edition, does not change that fact. Once again identity results in the elimination of the concept of nature. On the one side, nature again coincides with grace, since they are of one and the same origin: "where everything natural is holy by that very fact, because *the Holy, too, is natural*."[47] On the other side, the very personality of man coincides with the Holy Spirit, the new man in Christ;[48] it is the new "I" of man, standing before the face of God and beyond the psychological reality visible to us.

For these very reasons nature again coincides with the state of sin as such, since sin "signifies the timeless, transcendental disposition of the human world."[49] Naturalness and creatureliness are the same as transitoriness. *Natural* means "within the world, profane . . . materialistic."[50] In this realm spirit and personality are actually illusions of the flesh, in Feuerbach's sense of the word. They are ideological projections of the flesh, which strives to be flesh no longer; for "flesh means unconnected relativity, nothingness, nonsense."[51]

The coincidence of the two concepts, nature and grace, leads necessarily to the coincidence of nature and sin. The road leads straight from Baius to Jansen. The law of life, the entelechy of nature, is eros, concupisence. Here again eastern gnosticism converges with the Reformation. They become one in the concept of *pathos*, which signifies both guilt and nature, stress and decadence. Once again only one ethic remains: "Move on! Come out of yourself! Give up the lofty ideal which religion offers! Become transparent! Give up the attempt to set yourself over against God! Return to being what a creature is supposed to be: a shadow following the light of God."[52]

When the opposition and contradiction is drawn in such radical terms, there is no longer any room for the relative continuity of socialist concepts. Overcoming the visible Church (as impossible as it is necessary) through the invisible one is no longer represented in terms of the mystical body. For all organic concepts of community derive from below, from the realm of eros. The intangible ego, agape, the Holy Spirit is "pure act"; hence it is a purely qualitative unity. Our neighbor is *neighbor* only through his qualitative otherness. It is only as a *person*, not as an *individual* member of the race, that a human being enters the authentic, intangible Church.

Yet socialist notions only seem to recede into the background as Kierkegaardian "pathos" takes the center stage. Fall and salvation are total, universal happenings. The *individual* cannot be the ultimate reality in a scheme where the unity of predestination establishes him in solidarity with all men. Here we have a dialectic thrust which carries everything along with it, a thrust in which God consigns "all men to disobedience, that he may have mercy upon all" (Rom. 11:32).

Our brief sketch of Barth's second edition has been harsh and even somewhat unfair. We have isolated certain ideas and thoughts that were originally meant to illustrate Paul's theology, but our purpose was not to show the agreement between Paul and Barth; it was to show where Barth diverged from Paul and to give the reasons for this divergence. His Christian radicalism is super-Christian and therefore un-Christian. It is "reflection" through and through, since it absolutizes a methodical thrust and turns it into a standpoint, and hence it truly is a *conversio ad creaturam*. The ultimate result is that all the divine mysteries are stretched taut on this methodological rack, ripped apart by the blazing shafts of the dialectic, and given a paradoxical immediacy that demolishes their mysteriousness. Here we see the Hegelian influence at work.

The critical point, however, is that the hardcore center of Christianity, the Incarnation, now becomes impossible. If the divine touches the world only tangentially, if the only relationship between God and the world is that of an infinite qualitative difference, then there can be no such thing as a *life* of Christ. All there can really be is a *death* of Christ; this alone can be the meaning and the substance of the Incarnation. "Christ's life becomes tangible solely and exclusively in his death on the cross."[53] "Dying must be the meaning of Jesus' life, because on this side of death the only possibility for man is the possibility of sin. . . . The meaning, the ultimate, the death in this death is God."[54]

3. *The Uses of Dialectics*

If we try to evaluate all this, our first impression is one of great ambiguity. It is plain, of course, that a powerful and explosive philosophical spectacle has been introduced into the realm of biblical Revelation. But the question is: Is it merely a new *form of expression*, a new way to clarify the truth of Revelation, or is it an attempt to subordinate Revelation to a philosophical system? Is it to be the servant or the master of Revelation? Is this Platonic cast of thought, with its mystique of "identity," a means to an end or an end in itself? Is it, in short, a prophetic utterance or a systematic philosophy?

If we subsume the philosophical elements under the term *dialectic*, then it is a question of determining the proper meaning, the proper role, and the proper limits of this dialectic within theology. Much has been said along these lines from many different viewpoints.[55] We can take a shortcut here by gradually unfolding its full range of possible meanings in theology and then determining its meanings so far as Barth is concerned.

The word dialectic (*dia-lektikē*) refers to a process of setting one word against another (*dia*, apart, over against) in order to point out a direction or find a way through this unavoidable *vis-à-vis* (*dia*, through). If we stress the first stage of the process, we come up with a more static and dualistic dialectic (e.g., Kierkegaard); if we stress the second stage of the process, we come up with a more dynamic and tripolar dialectic (e.g., Hegel).

Dialectic confrontations involving statement and counterstatement are common in the sphere of purely temporal realities. It is worth our while to consider the makeup and impact of such confrontations. Three stages may be discussed.

1. There is the *subjectivity* of the one participating in the dialectic, the one who is seeking knowledge. There are limitations on human knowledge, which is abstractive rather than intuitive. It does not possess its object as it really is; it catches fragmentary glimpses of the object through the dualism of precept and concept. Insofar as it tries to obtain an objective knowledge of the object, to know this object as it really is, it must try to fill out the concepts it has gained. The human mind cannot rest content with the concepts it has formed. As Hegel put it, "the known, as such, is the unknown."

Thus thesis gives rise to antithesis, as we test and probe

our assertions. Since our thesis offered only one limited aspect of our object, our antithesis may add some essential and necessary element. From Heraclitus and Zeno to Abelard, and from Abelard to Kant and Hegel, this process of dialectic is a common procedure and of itself involves no prejudgment on the nature of the object.

2. The inadequacy of human knowledge *vis-à-vis* the object has its counterpart in what we might call the superiority of the *object* itself. When a thing becomes an object of knowledge, its true nature is hidden. Objective knowledge gives us the object, but not in all its fullness. What we see is some aspect of the object, a signpost pointing towards something we can never fully grasp. Knowledge, however much it may give us, is essentially open-ended and incomplete. There is always something new to be learned about a thing, and nothing can alter that fact.

3. The impossibility of grasping an object fully becomes more pronounced as the thing itself ascends higher on the scale of being, as it becomes a real *subject* itself. To be an individual is to be beyond full definition, not only because individuals cannot be compared fully with one another, but also because they are free and self-determining. We cannot predict all their potentialities beforehand.

If a subject is to become the object of another's knowledge, he must freely reveal himself to the other. He is a person not a thing, even though he may possess the characteristics of a thing insofar as he is a member of a cosmos, a species, or a race. At this point the process of knowing necessarily changes from a monologue by the knower into a dialogue with the other subject.

Here we deliberately exclude a problem which will have to be discussed later: the possibility and necessity of adding a fourth stage to the process, where the person opens up to the divine and the dialectical dialogue takes on its fullest dimensions. In such a case, relationship to God would be the supreme and utmost instance of personal relationship, along the lines indicated by Scheler and his disciples.

Included in this problem is another one. Can creation be interpreted as "God's personal self-revelation," objectively effected and subjectively grasped independently of his personal self-revelation in Jesus Christ? However we may answer that question, it is clear that when we leave the three stages discussed before and enter the field of Revelation itself, dialectic becomes a necessity.

1. God's Revelation to man in Christ is an event in which God pronounces the decisive Word about himself. Hence it includes his decisive Word about man and the world itself. It is a Word which only God can utter. Even though this Word comes into the world (Jn. 1:9) and takes the form, the likeness of man's word (Phil. 2:7), it does not appear simply as the word of a man or as one human word alongside others. It is the distinctive Word that was with God in the beginning and, indeed, "was God" (Jn. 1:1).

This Word takes on the likeness of man, it becomes flesh; but it does so in order to reveal the God whom no man has ever seen (Jn. 1:18). In the commensurability of the human word appears the incommensurability of God. What cannot be seen is made visible.

This Revelation of the hidden God, his merciful self-disclosure, finds no adequate possibility of response in man. Man, who hears this Revelation, has no natural capability of accepting it. He possesses merely a "potentiality," itself a grace: faith. God's revelatory utterance cannot be related to man's other types of knowledge. It is its own foundation and justification. Thus man's acceptance of it cannot be based on any other motive except the very act of hearing and accepting it.

To be sure, the Word of God comes to man in human form. It takes the form of concepts and percepts. These things are suited to men, and therefore his faith, too, takes on the form, the likeness, of his human reason. As believer, man can "understand" and try to deepen this understanding, but insofar as the Word he hears is God's Word and God himself, man's understanding of concepts and sentences is not of itself an understanding of the Word of God nor an understanding of God as Spirit; as such, reasoning is not faith. The Word of God *shines through* man's words on God, *concealing* itself at the same time. God becomes *flesh*, but the flesh itself is not God.

Man, then, is one who hears and believes the Word of God. But he is also summoned to proclaim this Word to the whole world. He must reiterate it in additional human words and use additional human concepts to understand it. This task is *theology*. As a human activity, it is not Revelation, but it does derive its life from the Word of God, which is its object in the objective order (*fides quae*) and its source of understanding (*fides qua*) in the subjective order.

Here we face the paradoxical situation of theology, the "enigma at the heart of theology":[56]

⟨Its criterion is *the Word of God*. But it cannot exercise control over its axioms as other sources do. As Revelation, it is a personal action of God. He testifies to himself in an act from which the content can never be abstracted.

⟨Its criterion is *contingent*, temporalized, and historical. Hence the obedience of its faith is radically transformed into belief in Christ, in the Church, in scripture, dogma, and tradition.

([Theology is a science of *faith*. In other words, it operates through an act from which it can never fully separate itself. This act is wholly other, yet remains a human science.[57]

([If theology abandons its objective and subjective criterion, or one of them, then it abandons its authentic nature. The hidden root of theology is faith, which cannot be set forth in scientific terms. Faith is its source of life and its justification, and theology reverts back to faith once again. But the root of faith is not found in faith itself; the root of faith is to be found in the Word of God, which is the criterion of faith. And God is the one who hides himself beneath his revelations, else he would not be God and faith would not be faith.

Here *dialectics* steps in as a theological methodology. Theology needs dialectics to serve as a continuing warning sign and corrective. Dialectics reminds theology that it is talking about God in Christ, through the divine power and mandate conferred on Christ, and hence that it stands at a distance from God in Christ. This function of dialectics is analogous to the *first* function described earlier, but far transcends it.

Dialectics, then, is not a new theology. It is primarily a source of light shining on theology from without,[58] a siren warning theology not to take things for granted. In theology we cannot come to rest on a "yes" or a "no." We must shift from one to the other, gaining illumination from both and thus moving closer to the intangible heart of the matter. To put it another way: "Dogmatics is a process of dialogue, of question and answer, answer and question. Only through this continuing process do we gain understanding. It is using thesis and antithesis to reach a synthesis. It is, in short, dialectical thinking."[59]

2. Thus dialectics serves as a *pointer*; it becomes the Lord's precursor, paving the way for his message. Its purpose is to call men to attention, to open them up to God's message.[60] It operates indirectly, but this does not mean that its answer is ambiguous or ambivalent. It simply means that its answer points towards the message of someone else.[61] This function of dialectics is analogous to the *second* function described earlier, but far transcends it because of the transcendence of the object involved.

That object is God's message in a human form. As such it is not a contradiction but a genuine possibility emanating from God. The affirmation and negation of the dialectical process must be patterned according to this possibility. If it does not do this, if it tries to make itself the guiding norm, then it will prevent God from truly taking on human shape and human forms of speech. From the viewpoint of the object, the dialectical method has something to offer only insofar as it lets itself be ruled by this object. It has something to offer only insofar as it becomes *objective*, while fully realizing that man can never be completely objective, that "existential thinking" is an indispensable requirement of theological reflection.

This ingenuous attitude is, in a way, the ultimate thing demanded of us in the Church. The dialectic becomes hushed and quiet, enabling us to tread the silent pathways of the Lord. It becomes a form of service; it becomes God's theology. It becomes the angel with the flaming sword who stands before the aseity of God.

In discussing St. Anselm, Barth speaks of God's aseity with exemplary theological objectivity.[62] He returns to the threefold approach of traditional theology (*via positionis, via negationis, via eminentiae*), although he has certain reservations about it.[63] Here the important thing to note is that the *via eminentiae* cannot be regarded as a synthesis that moves above and beyond the countercurrents of affirmation and negation. The *via eminentiae* is essentially an attitude of openness to thesis and antithesis, and it shows the priority of negation in this inquiry.

Theological dialectic continually calls out for further completion. It is essentially a stance of openness, a web of incomplete thoughts and sentences that points beyond itself to the inexpressible fullness of the divine message.[64] The methodical use of contradiction points towards God, who contains within himself no insoluble paradox and no logical contradiction,[65] even in the mystery of his Trinitarian nature; for God is a mystery, not a paradox. The dialectical method, then, may be applied to any aspect of dogmatics, whether it be part of a negative or a positive theology:

Dialectical thinking is a process of statement and counterstatement, of question and answer. Essentially, it never breaks off . . . and there is no final word. Both sides are always there—irreconcilable yet inseparable . . . standing over against each other: Faith and obedience; heteronomy and autonomy, or, authority and freedom; the Holy Spirit talking to us and in us; the Incarnation of the Word and the outpouring of the Holy Spirit; reconciliation and sin; primeval history and Revelation history; God's Word and man's word in the bible and the pulpit.

The prototype for everything, the thing that makes dogmatics necessarily dialectical, is the reality of God and man in the person of Jesus Christ. Only those who take away this "and," only those who picture one thing when they say God-man and can replace "Jesus Christ" with one name, only they can afford to be *nondialectical* theologians.[66]

The prime target here is, of course, Schleiermacher, with his "forced and ambiguous formulations." For him the opposition between sin and grace is only relative; one can stand above it and see the whole picture. Dialectics is really the intellectual form that obedience to faith takes; it is respect for the transcendence of the object being considered, for the superiority of God's thought over that of man's. The "and" which Barth uses time and again[67] is the hallmark of dialectical thinking, the shibboleth of a theology for people "in via." "God's Word, God's theology is not dialectical . . . but we are men."[68]

God manifested his incomprehensible mysteriousness most clearly by becoming man and showing that the human was compatible with him. Insofar as it points towards this God, dialectics will reject the negation of finiteness as the most suitable way to knowledge of God. Instead, reversing God's downward movement of kenosis, it will make a bold ascent upward, stripping off every vestige of anthropomorphism. Here Barth deals a death blow to many vestiges of Neoplatonism that still adhere to Christian theology.[69]

God stands on the far side of our notions of finite and infinite. The temporal-finite can take on the image of God, as the Incarnation shows. But this stress on the "via positiva" does not represent a diminution of the "via negativa" and a consequent short-circuit of the dialectic. We must recall once again that God's self-revelation in faith is the revelation of his nature, of his aseity and perfection. Every attempt at affirmation is an assertion of negation.

3. Dialectics will try to protect the divinity of God and of his Word. God's Word is the objective reality, because it is God's subjectivity. God's Word is God speaking, and nothing could be more concrete than that. But precisely because it is the concrete reality of God, it cannot be predicted beforehand or repeated afterwards. What God says is never known apart from God himself.

Theology tends to forget this time and again. It siphons off the content of Revelation and sets its form to one side.

In so doing, however, it also sets the content aside; for form and content cannot be separated in this case. Revelation ceases to be revelation when it is presented to the bar of human thought as some universal truth.

Repeating the *third* function of human dialectics presented earlier, but on a much higher plane, dialectics here must defend the divine quality of Revelation. It will remind every theology that the infinite subject shines in and behind every objective element, that purely "objective," uncommitted examination is a disobedient flight from the subject behind it. The response that God demands for Revelation is faith, total commitment of one's existence to the truth of Revelation.

However existential dialectics may be, it cannot take the place of faith. "Considering its object, dogmatic thinking is a living process fraught with responsibility . . . the object of this science leaves room for only one thing—*service*. . . . To make reservations, to create a dichotomy between one's life and one's thinking is, in this case, to opt out of the process."[70] When it is consciously employed, dialectics can all too easily become the opposite of what it purports to be. Instead of being an earnest commitment, it can become a playful game that is not taken seriously.[71]

The allusive function of dialectics is fulfilled only if it is utilized in a specifically *theological*—that is, a Christian and ecclesial—sense. It must *bear witness*. In the testimony offered by Christ we encounter a miracle of grace, where Christ's witness must be distinguished from his person. As witness, his whole life is dialectical. He is a person, of course, but it is not as a person that we regard him. As Spirit, he is the "matter," the staging place, of Revelation. This type of existence is the opposite of a dialectical game when no decision is called for; thus it directs any authentic theological dialectic towards a definitive commitment, a "yes" or a "no." This type of Christian existence remains the measuring rod for Christian reflection and its methodology.

4. We have found that the three functions of human dialectics crop up once again in theology. Have we then discovered the full shape of theological dialectics? Indeed, have we touched upon it at all? Don't our previous remarks apply to any philosophy that tries to discuss the relationship between the absolute and the relative?

Actually, we have not yet spelled out what Karl Barth regarded as the distinctive theological mark of dialectics in its early days. Two things radically distinguish Christian Revelation from every philosophy about God or creation. These two things are radically different, even contrary, yet they are closely related to each other and set each other off.

The first thing is the pure actuality of God's Revelation. It cannot be compared with any actuality in the temporal world for, scholastically speaking, it is the presence of *actus purus* in the act of Revelation. For Barth, the actuality of Revelation means this: everything in it is pure act, pure decision, pure creation, pure sovereignty and freedom; hence it is the revelation of the divine in God. Whatever a person may think about the similarity or dissimilarity between God and creatures, one thing is certain from Revelation: divinity, pure act, is not one of their analogous traits; it is the incomparable prerogative of God alone.

The sharp edge of pure absoluteness, which is not brought out by the concept of being (as applied to God and creature), invades the world of man in Revelation and takes possession of it. And this invasion brings the second point to light: that man is a sinner, totally alienated from God and bound for damnation. Whatever he may possess of worldly goods, he, as sinner, is found to be deficient. Against him is his unbelief, his disobedience, and God's condemnation.

The blazing fire of God's aseity does not encounter a neutral creature; it encounters a creature who opposes its own holiness, a creature who chooses not to know God and to flee from him. It is a creature who has nothing to say about the Revelation-event, not only because God's incomparable nature is involved, but also because his opposition to God has deprived him of the possibility to make any response to God's Word.

And so the two aspects of the Christian event stand out sharply against each other. God's infinite holiness comes blazing into the realm of sinfulness, like a red-hot iron into a pool of water. The total ungodliness of the world is brought to light in God's self-revelation. In its encounter with the world's total sinfulness, God's incomparable perfection, which already stands beyond any possibility of similarity (because it reveals the dissimilarity in all its fullness), is removed far beyond any possible or conceivable attempt at contrast. The encounter itself is not a neutral event, given meaning only later by something else. From the very first, it is the encounter of infinite grace, of infinite pardon and justification, with creation. In this act of God, the abysmal sinfulness of creation is unmasked, and creation is carried to the precipitous heights of divine adoption.

One will grant that this description of the event (which of itself does not raise confessional differences) makes the use of sharp dialectics understandable and even mandatory. Both the acute reality of the event and the grace-sin dichotomy would seem to justify it. For every created word seems too common to handle the incomparable nature of the revelation-event, and every human word seems totally incapable of expressing the opposition between grace and sin, between God's "yes" and creation's "no."

For Barth, Revelation raised the elementary question of style and form in theology. He wanted not only to say something proper about the content of Revelation, but also to convey the stupendousness of the dramatic event being unfolded. Here the style is a necessary ingredient of the truth of what is being said, and the style that Barth chose is dialectic in two ways.

First of all, it resembles Kierkegaardian dialectics, focusing on the "infinite qualitative difference," and highlighting the aseity of God. It uses every means to set God and the creature off from one another by picturing the holiness of God in all its loftiness and the sinfulness of the creature in all its lowliness.

This brand of dialectics was rediscovered in the hectic years following World War I, in the era of expressionism. This partly explains Barth's second edition of the *Epistle to the Romans*. In methodology, it is theological expressionism. The problem, as Barth put it so eloquently, is this: "Is any word of mine *the* Word, the one I am looking for, the one which I, in my distress and longing, would like to utter? Can I speak without having one word cancel out the other?"[72]

The inquirer is faced with a tragic situation: "He has to speak about something of which no man can speak."[73] His starting point is "not a *standpoint* at all, but a mathematical point on which one cannot stand."[74] How can he compel people to listen to something which God himself cannot compel people to hear? Caught on this rocky crag, he is overcome with dizziness and beset by a temptation: to consider his impossible position as the definitive state, to consider dialectics as the *essence and nature* of theology instead of its corrective, to make a standpoint out of the mathematical point to which he clings. He thrashes about in despair, and what he cannot show us is to become visible in his despair.

But how can this emptiness be a real signpost? Why can't it signify the opposite, nothingness, just as well? Here a second type of dialectics comes to his aid, the dynamic dialectics foreshadowed by Hegel and Idealism. If Revelation truly is the point where the whole world is shown to be guilty and worthy of damnation before God, if it is the act in which God releases grace in Jesus Christ and restores the sinner to righteousness, then Christianity is the miracle of complete reversal and transformation. It is, then, the ground of all being and all history, the unique once-for-all event that decides everything, the movement of God from "no" to "yes." It is the "self-movement of truth" to a degree that not even Hegel was given to know.

This raises a question that brings us to the limits of the dialectic method used by Barth in the second edition of *Romans*. Does this twofold process of static and dynamic dialectics suffice to bring out what happens in Revelation? Or, strange as it may seem, does dialectics fail just at the point where it boasts the failure of other methods and proclaims itself to be the only method of inquiry and expression? At the point where dialectics regards itself as the absolute, we find absolute identifications (static or dynamic) taking place: God (in all his aseity) is identified with his Revelation; creation is identified with pure opposition to God, with nothingness; and inasmuch as creation is retrieved by God in Revelation and brought back to Him through God's dynamic movement, creation is then put on a par with God, at least with regard to its origin and end.

This leveling off is to be found in both editions of *Romans*. Where Barth tries to engage in pure theology, where he tries to leave no room for human ways of thinking that are not transmuted by dialectics, we encounter the invasion of a very unbiblical, philosophical pantheism (or theopanism, if you will). This becomes evident in the very use of dialectics itself; its very exclusivity renders it void.

"The dialectical approach is by far the best,"[75] says Barth, yet "the dialectical thinker is no better than the dogmatic thinker or the critic."[76] By pushing dialectics to its limits, the second edition of *Romans* proves that dialectics, presumably the best method, is actually inferior to dogmatics and critical analysis. It actually betrays its mission to speak only of God and focuses attention on itself instead. In protesting its limitations, it turns them into absolutes, and employs the very cleverness for which it berates religion. Its self-flagellation is guilt ridden.

The annoying reality of which it speaks cannot be exploited in language; it is a divine mystery. There is no suitable way to illustrate "the infinitely qualitative difference between God and man." Dialectics cannot replace theology, it must be content to serve as a corrective.

To express what he really wanted to say in *Romans*, Barth had to find a new way of expressing himself. He had to change his form of expression, his style of thought, and even the content of that thought. Although he had wanted to produce pure theology, his product had ended up as philosophy. To make it theology, he would have to introduce something else into the picture: analogy.

Dialectics, of itself, dissolves the subjects involved in the theological event: God and the creature. God's aseity dissolves in the Revelation-event and fades out. The creature has no permanent place of its own; it either coincides with God (in origin and goal) or becomes pure opposition to him and fades into nothingness. No wonder then that the identity of creation with itself, in the justification-event, is vigorously affirmed at one point,[77] and vigorously denied at another point.[78] Creation, too, is thereby nullified.

Although Barth made his way to analogy slowly, it was a continuing and irrevocable process. He focused on those elements which were necessary to preserve the basic insight of his first work and to answer its many critics. His later efforts are a paradoxical attempt to rehabilitate *Romans*; in them it becomes clear what *Romans* was *trying to say*.

We learn that Romans was not meant to be a philosophy dressed out as theology, but a theology dressed out as philosophy, yet distinct from the latter.

With the introduction of analogy into Barth's theological thought, the whole question of dialectics and its uses is reintroduced on an entirely different plane.

III · THE SHIFT TO ANALOGY

---

1. Previews of the Future

Between 1922 and 1932, Barth gradually made his way from Romans to Church Dogmatics. Looking back on this period now, we can see that the most important work of this transitional period was published in 1928. The Prolegomena to Christian Dogmatics (1D) was the first draft of a projected series, which never went further. Even though Barth later became dissatisfied with it and started over, it is an important transitional document since it tells us where Barth is heading, and serves as a prelude to the expanded Prolegomena, which will come later. Clear, concise, lively, and unpolemical, it remains one of the best introductions to Barth's thought.

The reader must stick close to what Barth actually says. We find Barth trying to pinpoint and expound plainly the principle that sets off Christian theology from philosophy, metaphysics, and religion on the one hand and (within the Church) from the Word of God, scripture, and the proclaimed message, on the other. Having been entangled in complicated methodological questions by Romans, Barth now moved away from his former bedfellows and headed right for the main object: the real content of dogmatics.

Rejecting philosophy and metaphysics in all its guises, Barth focused on the one and only object: the concrete Word of God, become incarnate in Jesus Christ.[1] Here we are not dealing with a law but with a unique miracle that breaks all laws. It is a pure "happening," beyond man's ken. Everything centers around this point and moves out from there. The triune God becomes visible to the world in this happening. In Christ, his Word makes contact with history and enters it; yet it remains a decisive event, ever new and present, through the activity of the Spirit and through scripture. "The Word of God is still happening today in the bible; apart from this happening, the bible is not the Word of God."[2]

In the Word of God, God is the subject—free and supreme, beyond man's ken, beyond human presuppositions and controls, outside the sway of nature and history. In the act of Revelation, his sovereignty is set forth as triune; God himself is a Thou, and in no way is he directed toward any created thou.

Why did Barth introduce the doctrine of the Trinity into *Prolegomena*? Because there is then no need to introduce any created consciousness into the picture. Because he can then meet and vanquish the note of "consciousness," which plays such an important role in the theology of Schleiermacher. In his Revelation, and nowhere else, God becomes accesible to man; but because he is three in one, he remains totally free. God is wholly revealed in his Revelation; no secret is left hidden.

Noteworthy is the fact that Barth used this line of thought to launch an attack on the possibility of a second, "natural" kind of Revelation. Revelation must be all or nothing; and since we have one total Revelation already, there can be no other.

On the other hand, room is left for the Protestant but extra-Calvinist possibility of a creation revelation outside that to be found in the Revelation of the incarnate one. This extra-Calvinistic notion finds approval because

it thus becomes evident that the Word of reconciliation is also the Word of creation, and that the latter is renewed and confirmed by the former. The realm of nature is also the kingdom of the Son, not just the realm of grace. In the realm of nature, as the Word of creation the Son is not yet the incarnate one. . . . the logos asarkos, however, is not a secondary (although primary), natural, partial revelation. There is only one total Revelation, through the logos ensarkos, but the preexistent Logos, as the creator's Word, is the necessary antecedent of it.[3]

This total Revelation, of course, takes place within the veil of flesh. Hence it is indirect and screened from mankind, because it can only be laid hold of through hearing, believeing, and obediently responding.[4] Although Revelation comes from above, it appears actually in incarnation and in its concomitant economy. The assumed body of Christ is truly flesh. His kenosis does not indicate any alteration in his divinity, but it does indicate that he truly took on humanity. Instead of taking a position over against God, however, he stands as the son of God himself.

As Paul tells us, Christ was "made sin" for us. He subjects himself to the contradiction of human existence and suffers the punishment. But since he is God, he does not commit sin or further the contradiction in which he is implicated. Thus we cannot say that divinity and humanity are merged in Christ as thesis and antithesis; if this were true, sin-laden humanity would not be redeemed through his Incarnation. To speak of a dialectical unity in Christ is to speak "of unity in diversity, of a unity that comes about in the activity of Revelation."[5] Barth makes explicit reference to the Christology of Chalcedon and expresses his agreement with it.[6]

The unity of divinity and humanity in Christ brings up

another question: Is human nature a suitable medium for God's Revelation? Barth says it is. Genuine human encounter of the I-Thou type offers two things: 1. a real I, a subject, which we cannot fully penetrate; 2. a real encounter, where each person pierces through that impenetrability to comprehend a Thou who is like himself. Barth will later say that this possibility of an I-Thou relationship in man bespeaks an "analogy" between God and man and hence the possibility of a Revelation. This is the basis on which Barth will later build his notion of "the image of God," the starting point for establishing contact between Revelation and man (image).

The incarnation event becomes alive for man through the work of the Holy Spirit on him and in him. Through the Spirit, he becomes capable of accepting the Word of God, of believing and understanding through his belief, of living and behaving in accordance with it. Barth places great value on the activity of the man who has thus been blessed. Encounter with God involves a claim on our own life, and it stresses the interconnection (not identity) of faith and obedience, or faith and works.[7]

Here again he challenges Schleiermacher, maintaining that genuine thinking and willing (not emotional feelings) by man are the bases of faith and obedience. "Thinking and willing are part and parcel of human life. If there really is a relationship between man and God, it must involve thinking and acting."[8]

By centering the whole of Revelation, and indeed the whole God-man relationship, on the self-revealing Trinity, Barth clearly indicates that the real antagonist here is not Catholicism but the idealism of Schleiermacher. He attacks it at length in the chapter on religion ("the great mistake").[9] Here we find in embryonic form, however, all the objections which Barth will later raise against Catholic thought as well, since it is infected with the same idealism that he attacks here.

Insofar as it is a human *a priori*, religion is the arch-enemy of Revelation. It makes men false because, instead of highlighting their sinful condition in God's eyes, it tempts them to lofty flights of fancy and idolatry. It betrays God, making him a projection of man's religious potential and rendering him accessible through religious emotionalism. It dulls the sharp edge of Revelation, as a real action between God and man; instead of dialogue and dramatic encounter, it offers the nebulousness of mystic contemplation. Everything is dissolved in a pantheistic soup, where there is no longer any I-Thou.[10] Man's consciousness is made one with God's being; and although room is left for a certain amount of tension, the sin–grace opposition is not provided for. Religion, insofar as it is man's occasion to neglect and disobey Revelation, is the ultimate act of human opposition to God.[11]

Nonetheless religion is man's ultimate potential, and it too is open to redemption:

If the human sinner can obtain justification and sanctification, so can his religion. Of itself it may signify the most radical revolt against God; but it can also signify communion with God. As a human reality apart from God, it is the pinnacle of sin. Through God's grace, however, it can be the concrete actualization of Revelation. . . . Religion can become acceptable to God, human piety can become faith, obedience, and genuine reverence.[12]

In contrast to Barth's wholesale condemnation of religion in *Romans*, the *Prolegomena* offers the possibility of salvation to religion within the precincts of faith.

Nevertheless, certain themes and motifs from *Romans* crop up in the *Prolegomena*; their presence eventually from scratch once again. Barth's concentration on the forced Barth to reject his new formulation and to start Revelation of the Word as an action carries a twofold danger. First of all, it does not really overcome the old dialectic between identity and contradiction. God in his activity is identity; man, whose created nature is not clearly distinguished from his sinfulness, is the realm of contradiction (or opposition). As a preacher or hearer of the Word, man finds himself called to judgment by it because he experiences his existence as a "contradiction."

Kierkegaard is thus invoked against Hegel. Even as the Hegelian dialectic is resolved in Christ, the existential dialectic takes on new force and inevitability: "Revelation brings the dialectic of our existence to the fore."[13]

Barth had not yet freed himself from the notion that existentialism is a precondition, or at least a correlate, of Revelation; that it is the modern face of "natural theology." Toned down though it be, the keen edge of contradiction is still the herald of the salvation reality.

The second danger is tied up with the first. Barth's concentration on the reality of the Revelation-happening is not matched by a corresponding emphasis on the Christological motif; the doctrine of Chalcedon is not allowed free play, as it is in subsequent volumes of *Church Dogmatics*. Full emphasis is placed on the activity of the Word, not on the fact that Christ actually *became man*. The divine side of the picture is stressed; creation, however, is in danger of being dissolved within this divine bath.

The necessary correctives are mentioned clearly enough, but they are not developed adequately. Barth does not point out clearly that creation of itself is not contradiction to God, that of itself it is a legitimate, divinely established counterpart to God. From Christ he will eventually learn that to be a creature is not a bad thing.

In the *Prolegomena*, Barth endeavors to eliminate all the hidden roots of philosophy from theology, but he realizes full well that every man brings some sort of philosophy along with him:

No one has the right to boast that he has fully renounced Greek philosophy, that he has not diluted the New Testament with his own outlook on the world. It is simply untrue. Luther and Calvin had their own philosophies, both sharing different brands of Platonism. Zwingli's thought is heavily reliant on the pantheism of Pico della Mirandola.

Recent New Testament exegesis has been influenced by phenomenology, and Kierkegaard's anti-Hegelianism is a philosophy too. . . . We all wear our own special pair of glasses, without which we would see nothing at all. We must use some framework to unlock the biblical message. We do not intend to save theology by waging war on a particular philosophy. . . . Using the same philosophical presuppositions, a man can hear the Word aright or wrongly. Philosophy does not threaten theology because it is philosophy, or a particular brand of philosophy. It becomes a threat only when its relative influence on our hearing of the Word is not taken into consideration.[14]

Over against such philosophical frameworks, Barth set a "biblical outlook," calling for the obedience of the dogmatic thinker to the Word of God. It is the attitude of the prophet and the apostle, of a man who starts from the fact that God has spoken and acknowledges his primacy. This is an outlook that we learn, just as we learn to walk and talk. Barth's subsequent thought was motivated by this desire to comprehend biblical revelation in all its purity.

2. *Breaking New Ground*

There were two critical turning points in Barth's life. The first, his conversion from theological liberalism to radical

Christianity, took place during World War I and found expression in *Romans*. The second was his emancipation from the shackles of philosophy and his quest for a genuine theology that could stand on its own feet. This latter process lasted about ten years; it found expression in his little book on the Anselmian proofs for God's existence (A), published in 1931.[15]

The most important document leading up to this second conversion is the *Prolegomena* we have just been considering. If Barth's intellectual development during this period is to be seen clearly, however, we must also take into account some of the articles he wrote around this time. Here again we see Barth aiming right for his main object and leaving behind the pitfalls of *Romans*; here again, however, philosophical vestiges from *Romans* prevent him from fully exploring the content of his newfound starting point.

At this stage, his theology was a dynamic theopanism— God stands at the beginning and the end—and it embraces and encroaches upon a real temporal order which is viewed in a dualist-dialectic perspective. This theopanism of the Word of God, expressed in the terminology of philosophical Idealism ("mediate" and "immediate," and the like), threatens again and again to swallow up the reality of the temporal order. Though the world may really be something (as opposed to nothing), it looks so hopeless and forlorn that one might well wish it did not exist.

Barth sensed the un-Christian terror of this panorama and strove mightily to move beyond it. We might well classify his attempts to bring salvation to the temporal order under three categories: 1. the attempt to save culture and philosophy; 2. the attempt to save ethics; 3. the attempt to save the Church.

1. *Culture and Philosophy*. Two highly informative articles by Barth should be considered here: "The Church

and Culture" and "Fate and Idea in Theology."[16] Both
pick up early ideas and pursue them further.

In Barth's outlook, monism embodied a tendency
towards universality from the very beginning. In the first
edition of *Romans*, Barth stresses the service character of
the Church, the terminology of socialism, and the notion
of human solidarity. The Word of God does not shine
down on a select group of faithful, it illuminates all. Here
Barth is in agreement with the final outlook of Schleiermacher.[17]

"The Church and Culture." Barth sought to examine
the cultural work of the former and the theological aspect
of the latter. The Word of God becomes a "happening" in
the Church, and the Church makes this Word the alpha
and omega; it becomes the primary legislation event, governing all other sets of first principles. Fichte and Idealism talked about the real but intangible first principle; in
Barth's work it is the Word of God, the first and last legislation over nature, which, by means of the Church, breaks
in upon all other temporal principles. Between the alpha
and the omega stands the world, established, qualified, and
addressed by the Word. The world is established as a
creature and defined as Christian (and hence human); it is
set within limits and then accosted by the Word.[18]

Limits, however, is a positive concept in this perspective.
Set over against the Word, it implies something more than
mere deficiency; it implies a capacity *vis-à-vis* the Word, a
chance to share in the promise offered by the Word. This
holds true even if this intermediate sphere of nature is
painted in dualistic strokes (body and soul, Spirit and
nature, object and subject, external and internal) and cries
out for a unifying, synthesizing principle.

Here again we hear the underlying drumbeats of an
anthropological existential outlook. But we hear a new
note also, borrowed from extra-Calvinist thought: "the

kingdom of Christ does not begin with the Incarnation, and it is not restricted to the Incarnation; the divine Logos (*logos spermatikos*)[19] fills heaven and earth" Barth goes on:

This does not mean that there is automatically a real relationship between God and nature, God and history, or God and human reason. It does mean that when the Word is spoken in the world of sinful men, it strikes against a possibility that sin has not destroyed. It rests on a legitimate claim, God's claim on man, which gains power through his work of reconciliation. The kingdom of the Logos perdures above the fall–redemption antithesis, and it is a necessary presupposition for the presence of God's kingdom among sinners.

In the Incarnation of the Word, this presupposition takes on new vitality. Revelation and the reality of divine grace preserve and reveal natural theology and the reality of divine creation. In this sense, it is quite right to say that grace perfects nature rather than destroys it. The true nature of creation is brought to light by Revelation.

Bound up with the true nature of creation is the Promise. God promises man a life of union with him, a life that does not preclude the unified existence he is looking for. Human sin has not distorted God's image in man to such an extent that man has ceased to be a beloved creature of God.

Even as a sinner, man is still man; and God speaks to him in Jesus Christ. Humanness is the promise which is restored to life through God's assertion of his claim in Jesus Christ. The Promise offered to man is precisely that which the word *culture* signifies: fulfillment, unity, totality in the human sphere, even as God possesses these things in his sphere.[20]

The line of thought is clear and consistent. The only difference from the ultimate formulation in *Church Dogmatics* is the lack of a clearly formulated Christological foundation. If he had maintained this position unswervingly, the break with Emil Brunner might have been forestalled, and his debate with Catholicism might have taken a different turn.

For here we find him talking about natural theology as a legitimate entity buried in revealed theology and brought to light. He is saying that the nature of creation is reestablished by salvation. He speaks of the undestroyed image of God in man, who is still capable (by virtue of obediential potency) to respond to the Word.

To be sure, these themes are still buried under the monistic framework of his thought. Once again the realm of culture is equated with that of the law.[21] and the "commandment of natural law," which Barth calls humanity, coincides with the positive law contained in the Word of God.[22] Culture, along with nature and law, remains tied up with something "beyond" to which it owes its existence, something which enters the world as a promise through the Church.

Despite his introductory statement, culture winds up as the "untheological external aspect of the Church."[23] Barth concludes by drawing sharp attention to the eschatological limits of all culture; but he does not present it as being in the service of this divine–human confrontation, which still is defined solely in terms of the worderworking Word.

The second article tackles the relationship between philosophy and theology in greater depth than before. Because the Word of God enters the world, and because the kingdom of the Word as Savior reveals the kingdom of the Word as creator, culture is the external side of the Church; for the same reason, theology lives within philosophy.

Theology is the entrance of the revealed Word into the realm of human thought, hence into the realm of human problems and human ways of thinking. Like culture, philosophy does exist; and it, too, is conditioned and set within limits by theology. Insofar as philosophy is man's necessary way of conserving the world, theology must grow and develop in a philosophical way.

Philosophy mirrors the dualism of temporal reality in the contrast between realism and idealism. The ultimate reality may be viewed (in a realist philosophy) as a reality which is there and which cannot be manipulated by human thought; or it may be viewed (in an idealist philosophy) as a reality which is there and which cannot be manipulated by human thought; or it may be viewed (in an idealist philosophy) as something upon which the human mind reflects in order to reach the pristine idea which lies above and behind it.

In the long run, these two forms of human thought cannot survive without each other; they reveal the inconclusiveness and creatureliness of human thought. Barth's conclusions here are quite similar to those of Przywara, but Barth radicalizes this situation in two respects.

❲On the one hand, it is quite legitimate for human thought to strive for unity, trying to subsume one form of thought into the other. On the other hand, it is not legitimate for man to anticipate the unifying Word, which can only come from God above. The decisive stage is set only when the Word comes.

Before God revealed himself as the unifying Word, man tried to anticipate it. He fashioned a concept of God, equating the real or the ideal with God himself. This step reveals and embodies the presumptuousness and the radical sinfulness of man.

This does not mean that philosophy is necessarily an expression of this sin. So long as it leaves empty the spot that only God can fill, it is the friendly ally of theology. But when a philosophy seeks to be a theosophy, then philosophy and theology must necessarily be at each other's throats.[24] Theology must utilize the concepts and thought categories of philosophy—how else could it think about Revelation? But it must avoid equating the content of Revelation with the content of philosophical concepts. It must try to understand the God of Revelation by using realist and idealist notions, but it must always remember that the object of its concern is not the object of the philosophers.

The living, triune God is not to be identified with the concept of being, however loftily it may be conceived; nor is the Christ-event to be identified with the philosophical concept of history. The nonobjectivity of the God of Revelation is not the nonobjectivity of which idealism speaks. But since theology must utilize philosophical concepts and categories, it must critically examine its content. Is it the living Word of God or some philosophical first principle?

([Behind the first radicalization (with which Catholic theology could agree) stands another: philosophy's open-endedness, its refusal to formulate a complete synthesis, can only follow upon the communication of God's Word. So we encounter the notion that philosophy basically derives from theology: "All philosophy has its origin in theology."[25]

Here again Barth's monistic framework weighs down his thought. Philosophy becomes nothing but a theology that has been alienated from itself and grown weary of remaining loyal to its true source. It is up to theology, therefore, to heal the breach that has been created.

Once again everything is dissolved in the notion of "identity." Theology and philosophy become indistinguishable in the temporal sphere, and the Word of God hidden in Christ becomes indistinguishable from human history. Theology depends on the presence of a faith that cannot be really diluted; faith depends on a free divine choice, which cannot be really detected. All we can do is join in a chorus of praise for predestination.[26]

As before, what is lacking is a developed Christology. To be sure, it is laid down as the foundation in the last sentence but is not really present in the framework. Barth's ultimate word of praise for philosophy[27] has a hollow ring.

2. *Ethics.* Four articles mark Barth's progress from the ethics of *Romans* to the ethics of *Church Dogmatics:* "The Problem of Ethics Today";[28] "Keeping the Commandments";[29] "Justification and Sanctification";[30] "The First Commandment as a Theological Axiom."[31] The articles present the same basic doctrine in three different types of dress. First we encounter the anthropological and existential orientation that characterized *Romans.* Then we encounter the emphasis on theological actualism (i.e., on the Word-event) which characterized Barth's period of transition. Finally we encounter the Christological orientation that was to become the definitive framework.

"The Problem of Ethics Today" has the same framework as *Romans* itself. The problem of ethics is the critical question confronting man's whole life and existence.[32] Assuming for a moment that the question of truth can be isolated from that of ethics, we can say that truth is a question which man may view as a spectator on the sidelines. He cannot do this where ethics is concerned.

In the question of ethics, man is the one who acts and makes decisions; at every moment he is challenged and forced to choose. He cannot stand on the sidelines and treat ethics abstractly. The ethical imperative breaks in upon temporal existence irresistibly. On the one hand, we have the real world of men, where people eat, drink, procreate, and die, with its thin layer of cultural breeding. On the other hand, we have the concrete reality of a commandment, which Kant and others tried vainly to analyze.

And where do we find ourselves? We find ourselves in a utopian nightmare from which we cannot escape. We find ourselves caught between the absolute "thou shalt" of the commandments and the absolute "I can't" of mankind, and because it is a question of ethics, we can't flee to the two-edged razor of dialectics.[33] This predicament can only be understood by man as a judgment upon him. This is the sinful fall that precedes and determines all history.[34]

Yet this must be so, if there is to be a real encounter with God. "Would there be a source of all being, a creator of all things, if, over against him, all things were not non-being alienated from him?"[35] It is in the shipwreck that a sailor finally clings to the rock. In the splintered fragments of our existence, we glimpse the critical reality of our twofold predestination; it is then that we learn that we have not been cast aside but have been chosen.[36]

In "Keeping the Commandments," this existential outlook is no longer to be found. Barth does not start from the impossible situation of man and move to the reality of grace that makes all things possible. He starts from the other direction: in the light of grace we come to see the impossible nature of human existence.

Here again concrete reality is inescapable, but now it is the concrete reality of God's commandment under which man lives. That this is where man stands is a simple fact, as in the content of the divine commandment. And a problem arises only when man tries to put distance between himself and this commandment.

The Word of God and man himself are concrete realities. The Word of God is not an empty dictate to which man adds meaning and content. The moral law or the notion of good itself is not God's commandment. They are, as it were, the essence of his commandment, just as the categorical imperative signifies simply the unconditional nature of its dictate. They themselves are not the specific content of God's commandment. Man's conscience can flesh out the content of his awareness, but this is not the commandment either.

The commandment is the Word of God. It is absolutely concrete because nothing is more concrete than the living God. It asks something very specific of me because God's love shines through it, choosing me and conferring on me the promise of love and salvation along with the commandment itself. "Apart from the gospel, I do not hear the commandment as such. Apart from the gospel, I do not hear it as a Word that binds me. The divine commandment summons me to be what I am; it summons me, not to choose, but *to be chosen*."[37] And in the light of God's love and election, I see myself for what I am: disobedient, insufficient, traitorous.

Every commandment is based on God's absolute love, hence it can only demand love. Here we come to the paradox that the men of the Reformation brought out: our decisions do not bear witness to this election, they do not indicate that we wish to be with God as he has chosen to be with us.[38] Our election in faith is God's work entirely, and our own actions do not measure up to this calling. In terms of God's election, we are righteous; in terms of our own deeds, we are sinners.

"Justification and Sanctification," written in the same year, does not get beyond this same paradox. Barth rejects the quasiquantitative solution proposed by Catholic moral thought: as grace increases, sin decreases.[39] The paradox becomes bearable only by considering the overlapping eons in which mankind takes part. Man's justification can be perfectly accomplished in one era, while in another his sanctification is just begun. But authentic sanctification must involve man's conscious awareness. He must know he lacks it, he must thirst for it, and run to meet it. In their own way, both sin and grace are eschatological concepts.

The final article mentioned earlier moves us farther along the road. The concreteness of God's commandment is no longer based solely on the reality of his election. It is also based on the fact that God speaks to the believer in the precincts of the Church; and he speaks as the God of the covenant and the Father of Jesus Christ. The commandment cannot be separated from its Christological ties;[40] this gives it its concreteness, which stands within and brings fulfillment to the course of history.

From start to finish, Barth's ethic has been "situation ethics." In the first stage, it was an existential ethic of crisis, in which everything was ultimately reduced to the divine. Later, he tried to make his way forward by stressing the absolute concreteness of God's commandment: the concrete individual must give concrete obedience to God. But dialectics continued to play their part; man was sinful and righteous (simul peccator et justus). Moreover, the concreteness of the whole situation was based entirely on God's Word alone, because Barth had not yet gotten around to basing his ethics on Christ and his twofold nature.

It is in in his 1933 article that we glimpse the formulation of a new principle, whose implications will be spelled out in the ethics of Church Dogmatics. In the meantime, Barth's position on ethics remained similar to his views on the relationship between philosophy and theology:

"Christianity is not a system of ethics and has no special ethics of its own. The Christian can only ponder the same questions that every man must ponder."[41]

3. *The Church.* In the transitional stage between *Romans* and *Church Dogmatics*, Barth's most important pronouncements deal with the nature of the Church.

During his years in Münster (1925–30), Barth was in close contact with Catholicism. He wrote three articles to clarify his concept of the Church over against that of Catholicism.[42] To these we may add the ecclesiological doctrine of his *Prolegomena* to dogmatics and another article: "The Problem Facing the Protestant Churches."[43]

It is worth noting that all these pronouncements[44] derive from a period when Barth had not yet found the ultimate basis for his theology. They stand or fall with the premises on which they are based, and these premises are rooted in *Romans* and his subsequent emphasis on the concreteness of God's Word. They are superseded to a large extent by the foundation which he would later develop for *Church Dogmatics*, but they stand until he gets to that point.

In *Romans*, the Church was necessarily the razor's edge of dialectics. Seen from God's point of view, it is the realm of God's Revelation, the "invisible church of Jacob." Seen from man's point of view, it is the "visible church of Esau," the realm of sinful pride when the divine is anthropomorphized and viewed subjectively. "The Church is the great negation of Revelation";[45] "Atheism is the authentic essence of the Church."

The Church's guilt is immeasurable because she knows what she is doing; she is the realm of divine Revelation. Yet, for the very same reason, the Church is a necessity. Outside the Church there is no salvation because in her we discover what we all are: sinners and darkness. The

Church is the incarnate image of *homo justus et peccator,* the living embodiment of the self-contradiction that mankind is.

When Barth began to dialogue with Catholics, he moved away from this tragic ecclesiology. Another solution suggested itself. He would accept all the essential characteristics of the Catholic Church, reworking them completely and moving beyond them in the framework of theological actualism (i.e., putting emphasis on the concreteness of God's Word).

In "The Concept of the Church,"[46] Barth accepts the four characteristics of the Church. It is *one,* even as a visible entity, and its authority depends on this. It is *holy,* and this is the basis of its "essential infallibility and durability." It is *catholic* in terms of its virtual universality and the priority of its body–head union with the individual members. And it is *apostolic* in terms of the authority which it exercises; indeed, Barth did not hesitate to say that this is documented in Matthew 16 and that people need not be upset by Rome's use of this text.

As for the authority of the Church, it is a relative, delegated authority; Catholicism says the same thing. The Church can only be a vicarious subject; it truly is such, and there is no comparable authority on earth. The Church's authority comes from God, however, and the best way to underline this is to view the Church as the medium and instrument of God's free activity.

With the injection of this notion, we are back to the outlook of Romans. The Church is a "channel." Her relative, temporal, formal authority cannot be set over against God's claims. Her essential notes revert back to God in the last analysis, for it is he who uses the Church as his instrument. Barth by no means pinpoints the Church's specific and peculiar role; everything ends up in the all-embracing activity of *pure act.* There is no room for any other center of activity; over against God there can only be passivity.

The Church is holy insofar as she obeys, not insofar as she commands. She is infallible insofar as she listens to what God has told her; what she says cannot lay claim to divine authority.[47] We are back to the diabolic dualism of *Romans*. On one side, the Church coincides with the Word of God; on the other, she feebly attempts to express this Word.

Nevertheless, in these articles we see Barth trying to get beyond this perplexing dialectic. Without fully realizing what he is saying, he points out that such concepts as Revelation, Church, and faith introduce a third level, a *middle ground*, between God's eternal truth and man's religious opinions. Barth was not yet prepared to deal with this middle ground, however.

The old themes crop up once again. The Reformation represented the reinstatement of God's authority over the authority of the Church; hence it represented the reinstatement of freedom of conscience.[48] In the Protestant Church, the four marks of the Catholic Church are little more than tinsel decorations. The Church can only serve; she cannot rule. She searches for visible unity but she has never found it. She lives on God's promise, never enjoying its fulfillment.[49]

The situation is clear enough. So long as the Christology of Chalcedon does not have the last word, a Church with the four marks of Catholicism is meaningless. Only from Christ will Barth learn that there is room for a genuine and *active* human nature alongside God, and this human nature of Christ will be active even though it is grounded wholly on the act of Revelation and sent from above.

What did this discovery do to Barth's ecclesiology? Ought he not to have altered it completely, making his earlier thought obsolete? In truth, Barth was compelled to establish the relationship between God and the world on an entirely new footing.

Some might object that such a radical step was unnecessary, that certain notions already spelled out by Barth could have formed the basis for his Christology. Couldn't the *anhypostasis* and *enhypostasis* of Christ's human nature have served this purpose? In the *anhypostasis*, they would say, we find a basis for a "body" whose head is God, for papal authority, for sacraments that work *ex opere operato*.

Barth would not permit this, however. He regarded *anhypostasis* as Christ's exclusive prerogative. Any attempt to attribute this prerogative to redeemed men would be, in his eyes, an attempt to erase the *distance* between God and man. Christ's hypostatic union stands apart from every other type of unity with God. The redeemed man and the Church do not enjoy it. Because it is the prerogative of Christ alone, the Church cannot take a stand of her own alongside him.[50]

This brand of ecclesiology forgets that the Church is not only his "body" but also his "bride," that she has a personality of her own. She does not exercise sovereignty independently of Christ, but in her dependence she does have a freedom of her own.

A doctrine which focuses on the sovereignty of scripture alone cannot preserve the *distance* between God and creature. Such a flaw in the framework, which cannot be eradicated, finally forced Barth along the road to the doctrine of analogy, to the analogy of faith.

3. The Analogy of Faith

Barth did not suddenly replace dialectics with analogy. The change cannot be isolated in any one passage, for it took place gradually. Hardly noticeable in the first volume of *Dogmatics*, Barth takes note of it in Volume 2 (1938); by the third volume, it has taken real shape in his thought. Analogy develops more and more with each succeeding volume, to become the central theme in his treatment of creation (1945), human nature (1948), and providence (1950).

One will look in vain for a fully developed version of this doctrine in the earliest stages of *Dogmatics* (1932). The first volume does move far beyond the existential–anthropological cast of the *Prolegomena*, seeking a purely theological foundation in the Word of God; but Christology remains in the background. Yet even in this volume we see the analogy of faith emerging within his discussion of the Word of God, as yet unrelated to Christology.

At one point Barth is talking about the possibility of man's predisposition to faith. There is no question of man having some innate, natural, *a priori* disposition that favors his acceptance of faith; it is a gift from God.[51] Only by virtue of God's gratuitous gift of grace does man become receptive and obedient to the Word. In contrast with the analogy of being, the analogy of faith involves two things:

[It is not to be regarded as a typical process of analogy, which moves from observation to synthesis. It is not a characteristic of being which the creature shares with the creator despite their dissimilarity. It is an *action*, a happening, which makes man's decision in faith similar to God's.

It is action, not being. Being is a vague general category, while action is a concrete reality that cannot be boxed into some abstract pigeonhole. God himself is pure act; it is he who makes the critical decision. Through his action, creation is set in motion; and the only way to describe the process is through the concept of analogy.

"All we can do is call it 'analogy,' because we are talking about a resemblance to God."[52]

This brings us to the classic formulation of Barth's concept of analogy:

In man's profession of faith, God's Word becomes man's thought and man's word. The dissimilarity is total, but there is not a total strangeness between them. The human counterpart of the divine prototype is a real counterpart.[53]

⟨[Creation's likeness to God is a one-way street. It is fashioned from above by the Word, which lays hold of creation. It is the action of God upon creation.[54]

The third volume of *Dogmatics* spells this out more definitively. The concept of analogy cannot be avoided, because the relationship between God and creation can never be one of equality or identity. Equality would mean that God had ceased to be God or that man himself had become a God. It cannot be pure and total dissimilarity either, because that would mean we cannot know God at all. If we come to know him, it must be through our human concepts and words.[55]

Thus the relationship can only be described as some *middle road between* the two above extremes, and this middle road is analogy. It is not to be described as a relationship of partial identity and partial dissimilarity. The fact is that creation is actually dissimilar to God in every respect in which it is also similar to him. Analogy is a relationship which cannot ultimately be explained by any underlying similarity or dissimilarity.

The words we use to speak of God are not independent of the relationship *which God establishes*. This relationship is grounded on Revelation, not on some law of nature or natural occurrence. The truth contained in our concepts of God is created, finite, and relative. To latch onto God, our temporal truths must be brought into relationship with God himself. He chooses to make our truth an expression of his truth. And his choice is not a random thing, because our truth does in fact belong to him, even as our being does.

His truth is not our truth, but our truth is his truth. That is the oneness which truth finds in him, who is Truth. What we do in our truth through concepts and words, trying to come to a knowledge of his creation, finds its real truth in him as the Creator. The truth we express is first expressed by him. He is the pristine, self-evident truth; ours is a derived, dependent truth.

We are part of his creation, but we have fallen away from him through sin. Our concepts and words cannot claim that God is truly their object. But he can lay claim to our concepts and words; he can claim to be their true object. In doing this, he is not abolishing his truth or setting up a double set of truths; he is merely acknowledging *himself* in our concepts and words.

Our words and concepts are concerned with his creation; indeed, they are part of his creation. He recognizes himself in them. They proclaim him, as does his whole creation. In Revelation he, the creator, lays claim to us and them. It is not a miracle, but a work of restoration. . . . Our words really belong to him. In taking charge of them again, he places them at our disposal once more. . . . We misuse our words, if we restrict them to creatures. If we apply them to God, we relate them once again to their pristine object.[56]

Now this highly Platonic talk about the authenticity of all truth in God is theological talk for Barth. Why? Because the relationship of analogy is established from above, by the appropriative action of Revelation. This theological talk cannot help but refer back to the *creation relationship* in order to demonstrate the legitimacy of the appropriation. But this reference to creation does not make God's Revelation dependent on something else; for creation itself gives God claims upon the existence and truth of his creation. If Barth went so far as to use scholastic terminology and to speak of the analogy of attribution,[57] we must note that the ultimate foundation of this analogy is the act of grace embodied in Jesus Christ.[58] More of this later.

Sticking to the Protestant doctrine of justification, Barth insists on talking about an *extrinsic* analogy of attribution. Why? Because the relationship which grace establishes between God's Word and creation is not an intrinsic one. This insistence leads to conclusions that contradict the facts. After all, if the authentic truth of creation resides in God, then it is God's truth; for it was created and established by him. That being the case, its relationship to him is not extrinsic but intrinsic.

The concept of analogy, as spelled out in volume three of *Dogmatics*, leads Barth to another interesting conclusion. Over against God he must posit a creation that is good in itself even though it is not God. For the first time he has to give serious attention to the notion of *creature*. No longer need creatureliness be moved out of the way, as it was in 1919, in order to make room for Revelation and the divine life. It is no longer the creation-event alone that is blameless, that brings man and God together. Now Barth can say that creation itself is blameless in its freedom, its self-awareness, and its position vis-à-vis God.

Sin may indeed enter the picture, latching onto this freedom and self-awareness. Herein lies the possibility and the temptation to lay hands on God. Sin surely *presupposes* freedom and self-awareness, but it is not to be equated with them. Thus sin does not plunge the creature into chaos and nothingness, as would be the case if creatureliness were equated with sin.

The existence of a reality distinct from God cannot be a source of embarrassment solely because of its distinctness from God. There is no problem in positing a world over against the absolute reality of God, a world that is given reality by God is designed to give glory to him.[59] God's absoluteness is inherent in him, and his freedom is not threatened by the existence of the world. He can leave room for another being to exist alongside him. He can exercise his will over this other being in such a way that it is protected rather than threatened.[60]

Creator and creature exist together, totally unequal, the latter subject to the former; yet this coexistence is far beyond any sort of pantheism. When we talk about God the creator, we affirm not only his transcendence but also his *immanence*. God is *present* to the world he has created; he is free, but *closely tied* to his creation. He sustains and controls the finite world without ever taking man's freedom away. Because he is present to his world, we cannot make the world into an idol; but neither can we talk about divine enmity for the world or God's alienation from it. In the world he makes himself visible as the creator who transcends the world. And, by the same token, he reveals his nearness to man in the very fact of his transcendence.[61]

Having come to this positive outlook on creatureliness, Barth can later discuss divine providence in these terms:

God sustains the reality of his creation, distinct as it is from his own. Finite and dependent, it stands on its own feet alongside him because it has him to thank for its existence. . . .

Freely created by God, it cannot dissolve back into him nor lose its proper independence. When we say that God will become all in all (1 Cor. 15:28), we do not mean that eventually there will be nothing around but God. We simply mean that eventually his purposes and plans will take definitive shape in all creation. Pantheism in any shape or form does not do justice to God or to his creation. . . .

When scripture talks about Wisdom "playing" before God, we do well to take note of that word. It is a game for two, originated by God, in which both have something to do. Man must toil and calculate, eat and drink, sing and dance, laugh and cry, love and hate, grow up and grow old. With his head held high, with a clear conscience and an open heart, he must be a man to the fullest possible extent. Only a false god degrades man. The true God allows man to be what he has made him.[62]

However dependent creation may be, ontically and no-etically, on God's Revelation in Christ, the fact is that *in* this Revelation we glimpse a *presupposition* lying at its foundation and making it possible:

God's Revelation presupposes the existence of a world, distinct from God, in which he can reveal himself; it also presupposes the existence of someone to whom he can reveal himself. . . . Revelation testifies to the coexistence of God and man, and it bears witness to the reality of God's creation. . . . In Revelation, God addresses himself to man, affirms and approves man's existence, takes man in as his partner, and honors man's active role.[63]

The reality of creation finds its high point in the fact that it is free and aware, even in its complete subjection to God and his grace. The goodness of creation resides in the fact that its obedience and blessedness is not meant to be the automatic working of a natural process; that God's goodness and grace are to operate through the freedom which creation enjoys. The play between man and God is to be an *active* process on *both* sides.[64]

This also means that man is made a partner in the process of Revelation. He is brought into the Revelation event, even though it is a new creation and even though God may have to give him the freedom required to accept it. Our faith is a grace to which we can lay no claim; but it is also our decision, and it calls for the exercise of our intellect and will. Besides God's fidelity there is man's faith. Besides God's commandment there is man's trust and obedience. To respect the notion of distance, as we must, we shall have to talk about a "secondary subject"[65] in the grace–bearing event.

Mutuality and reciprocity are involved here, even though they ultimately rest on God's one-sided activity of creation and sanctification. Creation is so much God's handiwork that it must respond as well as receive. Indeed, it must accept in order to respond, and its response should ever remain an act of acceptance as well. That is what theological analogy is all about.

IV · ANALOGY IN FULL BLOOM

---

1. The Christological Foundation

As the doctrine of Church Dogmatics unfolds, the central notion of God's Word is gradually replaced by another: Jesus Christ, God and man. It becomes clear that God's Word is not the most comprehensive designation for the nature and content of Revelation. Word is only one designation for the Son, and it is the Son himself in whom God has chosen to bind all things together in heaven and on earth.

Because the Son becomes man within his creation, created reality has an essential relationship to him, even as he has an essential relationship to Creation. No longer need Barth work his way around extra-Calvinist doctrine in order to prove that the Redeemer is also Lord over this (contradictory) creation. The whole perspective has changed. Because the Word, as Redeemer, becomes man in time, all creation is thereby good and justified; for the same reason, it is only right that God take man for his partner.

Already the notion of analogy has brought God and creation together. Now the ultimate basis and proof for their unity is made plain in the miracle of Christ's Incarnation. What better foundation could there be! Insofar as Christ is the measure of all things, no contradiction between God and the world can break in upon their compatibility. We have now gone beyond the *Prolegomena* and its talk of "opposition and contradiction" between God's Word and its formulation in the bible, in preaching, and in theology. The new focus on Christ's Incarnation supersedes and replaces all such ideas, and their accompanying methodological framework.

The clearest possibility for any talk of opposition between God and man now resides in the portrait of the suffering Son of Man in the Garden of Olives, where he cries out to the Father. But Barth consistently interprets this scene as the loftiest example of filial obedience, in which the God–man opposition is done away with. If it were otherwise, then Christ would no longer be the measure of all things.

The new Christological foundation begins in earnest in Volume 2 of the *Prolegomena*, where a provisional Christology is formulated;[1] it is developed systematically from Volume 3 on. Volume 2 begins by strenuously affirming the doctrine of Chalcedon and the concept of nature (*phusis*). Without doing away with the perduring mystery of Revelation and the Incarnation, this concept can focus on the mystery and describe it in greater detail.

In considering the whole human nature of Christ, both the physical and ethical aspects of the mystery should be considered. Nature here is not, as in most modern Protestant thought, to be set in opposition to spirit, thereby disdaining the being of God as it appears in his Revelation.[2] In shunning the physical in Revelation, one rejects the realism of the biblical message.

Christ's human nature is real only in the actuality of his godhead; it is the potentiality to become a man, which every human being has, but his is an authentic human nature just as it has become since Adam's fall. Christ wore this nature without sin, learning obedience through what he suffered. But Revelation nowhere seeks to spell out this learning process (Heb. 5:7ff.) fully, and we would do wrong to try to reconstruct it somehow.

If Christ is a man, we cannot deny his human nature nor his human will. "In its clash with monotheletism, the primitive Church knew what it was doing when it distinguished and juxtaposed the divine will of Christ and his human will. . . . His free response to God is authentic obedience. . . . It is thus that he fulfills the commandment. . . .[3]

When we say that "the Word was made flesh," we are saying two things. We are talking about a being (or a particular nature), and we are talking about an event (or a part of history). Faithful to the Calvinist outlook, we should remember the event when we look at the being; this reminds us of the freedom which Revelation enjoys. Faithful to the Lutheran outlook, we should remember the being, the once-for-all union, when we look at the event. In Christology, the concept of nature obtains equal status with the concept of actuality.

The nature of Christ is the authentic *truth* of human nature in God's eyes. His human nature is the ground and justification for all human nature. By accepting us as we are, God sustains us. "Because man has the man Jesus Christ as his head, because he shares Christ's battle and triumph, he is as protected as he can be without being Christ himself."[4] It is the sinless nature of Jesus Christ which provides human nature with unbroken continuity, over and above the discontinuity caused by sin. Because of Christ's human nature, the sinner does not fall into the bottomless pit.

At creation a promise was given to human nature. In Christ human nature is so blessed that it can never be totally engulfed. Whether man in his perversity chooses to realize it or not, whether or not he can realize it, the fact is that what he is and what he does in accordance with his nature points towards redemption and signifies it. While sin may indeed represent total opposition to grace, nature itself cannot possibly be such because it is grounded in Christ.

Barth has taken an important and decisive step forward. All human relationships may indeed be affected by sin, but their basic structure is not *altered* by sin. The underlying substance of these relationships is the created nature of man which we have just been discussing—the being of man that is not disturbed by the sin-reconciliation-redemption antithesis. Because of Christ, we must talk openly and unashamedly about the "necessary and *constant* destiny" of human nature. It is the task of theological anthropology to shed light on this unassailable constant.

In the course of developing this theological anthropology, Barth saw that he had parted company with the traditional Protestant doctrine on man. He did not follow the usual Protestant approach—denigrating human nature as much as possible in order to highlight what God's grace accomplishes in man. A rapprochement with Catholicism and the natural theology of human nature becomes inevitable. It is not by nature that man is hostile and antithetical to God's grace; he becomes so in the rejection and misuse of his nature, which is all too real.

But all man's perversity cannot undo God's work on his nature.
. . . Despite the havoc which man causes by sin, his sinfulness
never becomes a natural condition for which he is inculpable.
. . . Sinful man does not become a stranger to God. . . . His
position vis-à-vis God remains what it was by God's creation.
. . . To deny this would be to deny continuity to man as
creature, sinner, and redeemed sinner.[5]

Even when he takes a stance against God, man retains
an indestructible nature and will. By virtue of these, he is
essentially ordained to remain united with his fellow men,
joyfully and willingly. By nature, he has no real possibility
of an alternative choice. We cannot overlook the fact that
many men, who are evil and sinful from a Christian viewpoint, are still capable of readily dedicating their humanity
to others and of putting Christians to shame in this
respect.

Barth thus moves beyond the strict either-or of eros and
agape. There is a third element in the picture: humanitarianism. Humanitarianism and Christian love are two
different things: "What benefit would the Christian derive
from his knowledge of God, from justification and sanctification, from devoted service to God, if he lacked the
quality of humaneness?"[6] Agape is "the love in humanitarianism."[7]

Humanitarianism and eros are two different things also.
A culture based on eros, such as classical Greek culture,
retains the quality of humaneness in large measure. It shows
us at once the essential quality and nature of man, the
pristine motive underlying all subsequent choices: the
desire to join together with one's fellow men.

The adverse reaction of some recent theology to Greek culture
was not a good thing. With its emphasis on eros, Greek
culture realized that man is a free, open-hearted, spontaneous,
cheerful, social being. Nothing could be more important. . . .

No other nation of antiquity, not even the chosen people of Israel, was granted the privilege of displaying so fully what humanity as an unbroken reality means. . . . Many elements in the theology of the New Covenant are cast in Greek forms and hues, transformed by the light of truth but basically undisturbed. . . . The *agape* of the Christian may not be what it claims to be if it remains hidden to the Greek; in encountering the Christian, he should feel a sense of solidarity.[8]

Here, then, we have Barth's new portrait of human nature. Good in itself, it is thoroughly abused by sin but not disrupted; and grace confirms human nature once again, even though it also loses some of its luster in the radiance of grace. It is only logical that natural law should now emerge with new and stronger meaning.[9]

All these statements, so thoroughly Catholic in outlook, are possible only because Barth saw in Jesus Christ the "real ground of divine creation" and regarded this as the strict teaching of scripture. Text after text in scripture designates Christ as the alpha and omega, the first-born, the head of all, and the one through whom and for whom all things were made. Because of these texts it is impossible exegetically to talk about the eternal Son of God or the Logos in the abstract; we must talk about him in his union with the man Jesus. That is what Saint Paul tried to tell us and that is what Saint John, too, tells us in the prologue of his gospel.

Jesus Christ was there before and during the foundation of the world. His eternal presence guarantees that the world is good and that its nature cannot be destroyed. He guarantees the fidelity of creation and its continuity, its maintenance and its preservation. There is no Origenist bias in the following remarks:

In accordance with God's will, the Son, the Word of God, humbled himself and gave up the trappings and the exercise of his godhead. From all eternity—that is, even before the creation of all things—he chose to become flesh, to become the Son of Man. In his person he chose to bear the curse of sin for all men . . . even to the cross. . . . In view of his Son's decision, God loved mankind and the world from all eternity. even before he created them. . . . He created the world and man because he loved them in the person of his Son, who stood before him, as an outcast and a dead man, on account of their sins.[10]

Precisely at this point, however, the major difficulty of this whole viewpoint comes to the surface. In this scheme Christ the god-man is the authentic prototype upon which creation is based. In him becomes visible the authentic shape of pristine human nature. But Christ is not purely and simply man; he is God. So the idea of humanity as such cannot be deduced or extracted from Christ's Incarnation; it can only be presumed at the start. In other words, because God became one of us, humanity must have already been a real possibility at the start.

A being to which humanity were alien would be a being of a different nature than the man Jesus. If man were such a being, then we would have to say one of two things: either the man Jesus has been the only true human being as God created him; or else Jesus was not really a human being at all but a completely different type of being.

If there is a similarity between Christ and us, despite all the dissimilarities, then something in us must correspond to his being-for-others. At the very least, at its roots our being must be a free being with other men.[11]

Here we have come to the core problem of Barth's theology as it exists in its latest form: the fact that something is presumed, presupposed in God's primeval act of determining the order of things:

Where the salvific work of the man Jesus on behalf of other men becomes possible, we must look for some sort of unifying correlation between him and this other being. This correlation between them cannot be based on their communion; it must be presupposed as a possibility from the start. We must look for some basic trait of humaneness in other men, in mankind generally, which clearly makes it possible for Christ to be a man-for-them.[12]

The ultimate mystery of man's destination presupposes another mystery buried in his created existence as such. In Jesus Christ, who is the Truth, "the truth of our being, of human nature as created by God, comes to light."[13] At the same time, we cannot equate the truth of our nature with his; through Christ we can distinguish what truly belongs to our nature (death as the end of a finite creature, for example) from what does not authentically belong to our nature (death as a punishment for sin). In the light of Christ we can separate what necessarily belongs to our nature from what de facto belongs to our nature.

The methodological problem, then, is clear. To clearly comprehend what is presupposed, we must view it in the light of God's action. But we must scrupulously avoid equating the two. "Christology cannot be anthropology."[14] We cannot come to a direct knowledge of man's nature in general on the basis of Christ's human nature; but through Christology we can set forth some minimal characteristics which would have to be present in any theologically useful concept of man. It would serve both as a negative and as a positive norm, because in its light we would investigate man's nature.

When Barth says that Christ determines who and what man really is, this does not mean that Christ is the only true man. When Barth says that the ontological determination of man is grounded in the fact that the Man Christ exists among men, this does not mean that "determination" and "original constitution" are to be equated.

Two alternatives must be rejected. We cannot deduce

the nature of man from the humanity of Christ or the natural order from economy of salvation. Nor can we sharply separate the two orders, deducing the ultimate shape and meaning of nature without considering the Incarnation. Between these two alternatives, another program is proposed: a theological doctrine of creation and anthropology.

This program simply proposes that the natural order has its own proper, even though finite, place within the order of grace; that the two orders must be respected and distinguished if they are to be correlated with one another. The relationship of human nature to God is not the same as Jesus's relationship to the Father, but the former cannot be clarified without the latter. Human history is not simply prehistory or the history of the god-man; but it is ultimately grounded in the latter. The uniform notion of *presupposition* embraces within itself a duality of orders, and this duality of orders actually insures its unity and coherence.

2. Creation and Covenant

In the doctrine of creation, this duality finds expression in a weighty formula. Creation—that is, the order of nature—is the exterior ground of the Covenant;[15] the Covenant—that is, the Incaranation and Redemption—is the interior ground of creation.[16]

Here again the two orders are clearly distinguished from each other, as is evident in the following passages:

Revelation is not creation nor the continuation of creation. It is a mysterious new work of God upon creation.[17]

Grace is truly a new twist. Through it God erects an order which was not there before. Man has no claim to its work or its benefits, no power to receive or accept it. All he sees is that it is something special that has been brought into the picture.[18]

How could grace come to man as grace if it were coincidental with nature, if nature as such were grace? In reality, grace is a *mystery*. It is the *hidden* meaning of nature. When grace reveals itself, nature does not cease to be. How could it cease to be, since God does not cease to be its creator? But now there is something more within nature. Now nature itself becomes the showplace of grace. Now the freedom of grace and its mastery over nature becomes visible.[19]

Through this new reality, creation acquires a deeper perspective. Everything is carried over into a new order, but this new order plunges into the realm of nature as well. The nature of creation does not necessarily imply that it *must* have this perspective, but in the work of reconciliation and revelation what becomes evident is that it actually *does*. God's response to the fall was not simply a work of restoration; instead, he revealed a fullness of perfection that lay hidden in the original integrity of creation.[20]

In short, we should not equate what creation does have with what it must have. Nature and grace are two of the concepts which dogma has to separate. When we talk about the outpouring of the Holy Spirit, we are not talking about the participation in God's Spirit which makes man himself spirit. We have to talk about another prior presence and activity of the Holy Spirit in creation, one that is presupposed in Revelation.[21] In the same manner, the Incarnation ratifies the reality of the creature as distinct from God; but insofar as it makes God and the creature one, it also reveals that they in themselves are distinct and separate, that the creature has its own reality alongside God.[22]

There is also an analogy between nature and grace. It is not a question of continuity, even though the *de facto* oneness of the supernatural end allows us to say that "something in the analogy points towards continuity."[23]

Grace is a *special* work . . . that does not simply coincide with the work of creation. . . . Nor can it be regarded simply as the continuation and crowning phase of creation [though it is that, for in it God the creator carries on and completes his work] . . . .[24]

The productions of the Holy Spirit are productions in another being who already exists. Birth in the Spirit is a *new* birth, a rebirth, and the man reborn to God is already there when this happens to him.

On man's side, this happening comes from outside himself. It presupposes creation as God's basic foundation for man's existence, renewing and perfecting this existence. Revelation, then, is really something new, something special, something more than nature and creation; it elevates and transforms nature. The created world as such is the realm of the Logos; but the fact that the Logos became man goes far beyond this:

The pageant of creation itself is not just the story of man's genesis and the world's genesis. It is also a promise of Revelation and reconciliation, a sign that the world is good and that it can be the setting for Revelation. Thus it clearly indicates that God's Revelation will mean something special, that it will be a free gift of grace, that it will turn out to be Jesus Christ.[25]

Barth's distinction between the two orders lead him to say:

The Covenant and its history is not the goal of creation itself, according to the bible. Rather, it is the substance of the divine work of reconciliation which is separate from creation. But this substance is made possible by creation. . . .

We can say that creation points towards this other work. . . . But we cannot say that the work of creation is the cause of this other work, or that this other work is the purpose of creation.[26]

In short, both works are reflected in each other, and they are antitypes of each other, but despite their relationship, we do well to maintain the distinction between them, even when we make the second order the prototype.

One example will serve. The creation account indicates that plant life is to serve as man's food, while meat becomes the sacrificial repast of the Covenant. The new arrangement, culminating in Christ, does not erase the natural arrangement. It presupposes a pristine natural arrangement. The new divine arrangement stands out against the natural backdrop, superceding it and confirming it at the same time.

The order which is presupposed is also oriented towards the order which comes after it; Covenant history follows upon creation, but not from creation. Coming first as it does, creation serves as a model for the other history which comes after it. Creation aims toward history, as Cocceius and his followers saw so clearly; the concept of history is immanent in creation:

Creation is not an atemporal truth, even though time begins with it and even though it stretches across the whole expanse of time. . . . Scripture tells us that there are no atemporal truths, that all truths are specific actions of God in which he reveals himself. These actions are eternal and encompass the whole expanse of time; but they also have a concrete temporal character. . . . The definitive commentary on the biblical account of creation is the rest of the Old Testament.[27]

The Old Testament sets up the arena in which this history is played out. Creation is already an event produced by the Word of God: "Let there be. . . ." In creation, God's blessing is imparted to his creatures. New as it is, Revelation is not a complete novelty; it is the same Word of God, with a new shape and intensity.

The nature of creation is its preparation for grace. Its

creatureliness is a promise of, and a plea for, the things which God has in mind for man. Hence at certain points in the work of creation, the hidden roots of Covenant history come to the surface, such as in references to the Sabbath and in the second account of man's creation. We come upon two viewpoints, two lines of movement, which stand over against one another without being in opposition.

This relationship shows creation to be one vast symbolism of grace. Here Karl Barth provides logical justification for the symbolic outlook of Alexandrian theology. Everything in the bible, the great moments in particular, symbolizes and express the salvific event which takes place between God and man. Creation is "a unique symbol of the Covenant, a true sacrament."[28]

The relationship between God and man is most clearly depicted in the relationship between heaven and earth and in the decisive action of the Word, which lays the basis for creation and brings order to chaos. God's coexistence with man is prepared and made possible in the symbolism of man and woman. Light, water, air, and the alternation of day and night all serve to symbolize this relationship. In the lights of creation we glimpse the light which is God himself, the light which breaks in upon the world with Christ.

In the display of created realities and in the account of their creation, we find the real meaning of any authentic theological outlook. It is not simply a matter of drawing comparisons between the work of creation and God's work in the old Covenant; for the Old Testament, there is a real existential connection between them. The animal world, too, serves as a mirror for man. In it he sees reflected the real purpose of his existence. Adopting a Platonic line of approach, we can formulate an authentic theological interpretation of creatureliness. The concept of nature is *formally* presupposed at the base of what is to come; but it has a *material* aspect as well. The whole content of creation is polarized positively towards grace; from God's Revelation it will receive its fullness and its truth.

3. *The Partner of God*

In the work of creation man is made ready for grace, if he is capable of becoming God's Covenant partner, but he is capable of this only if he himself realizes what it means to be a responsible party in an I-Thou relationship.

The analogy between God and man, put very simply, involves existence in an I-Thou relationship. This relationship is what constitutes the godhead, first of all [the Trinity] . . . and then human life [primarily in the male-female relationship]. . . . To dismiss this relationship is to deprive God of his divinity and man of his humanity.[29]

In both instances, we have distance for the sake of nearness, selfhood for the sake of intercourse and love, otherness for the sake of genuine oneness. The polarity of two human beings, in the sexual relationship and in all forms of human communication, is the authentic and basic image of God in man. The totality of what man is becomes operative through this polarity.

Before we attempt to delineate man's nature in detail, however, we must take note of our precise point of departure. Since it is a question of theology, our view of man's nature will be molded largely from Revelation; that is, from Jesus Christ. Barth is trying to depict man's nature, as a created being, from without and within. In short, we must expect to find a twofold viewpoint at work, involving both creation (the external ground) and reconciliation (the internal ground). It is extremely important that we keep this in mind, particularly if we are wont to operate from a different starting point (e.g., scholastic philosophy).

Man has his own created nature, his own proper analogy to God. It proceeds from grace, insofar as creation is grounded in Christ. It also points towards grace, insofar as creation itself is not the Incarnation but the presupposition for it. It is from this viewpoint that Barth begins his discussion of man's nature:

From the start man must be regarded as a being who stands in some relationship to God. . . . It is a relationship that differs from the one we found in the man Jesus; but in its own way, it is no less radical or basic.

We cannot regard man as a closed circle of concrete realities nor as a creature open solely to some or all of the cosmos. We must regard him as open to God and related to him. And we must interpret this relationship to God as a necessary and constant constituent of man's nature.[30]

In a philosophical framework, we would be tempted to interpret this quality of transcendence as an *a priori constituent* of man's nature. We must be careful, however, for we are really starting from the fact of Revelation in Jesus Christ upon which creation is grounded. We can only talk here about a theological presupposition, about the orientation of man's nature to this *de facto* Revelation. Once this is clearly understood, we can say certain things about man which differ greatly from the statements of Barth's earlier years.

Man is not a closed-in creature, a being of hopeless immanence, overwhelmed by the dialectics of grace. He becomes explicable only in terms of transcendence. Man is truly man only insofar as the god-man is his brother, only insofar as he already stands in a relationship to God. "To be man" means "to be with God." "Thus godlessness is not one of man's potentialities. It is an ontological impossibility for human nature . . . an attack upon the fabric of his creaturehood."[31] All this clearly holds true for man, because Christ is a man; and since mankind has ties of solidarity with all creatures, it holds true for them, too, in some mysterious way. Fundamentally and ontologically, man is a being who, along with the Son of God, is the object of God's personal election and lives out his life listening to God's Word.[32]

These two characteristics are proper to man as such, as a being distinct from God. Hence he cannot flee from God into himself to avoid encounter. As man, he is already involved in an encounter with God. If Christ is God's chosen one, God's beloved, then every man is chosen too; from the very start he is ordained to belong to the body of which Christ is the head.[33] The Word of God is not addressed to him as an outsider but as a partner of the Incarnate one; in his very existence as man, he is addressed and summoned.

When we say that man's existence is a history, we are not talking simply about a human condition. What Christ alone is, man is too. The light of Christ is not simply something external in which we stand; it is the internal reality which we essentially are. The likeness between Jesus and us is revealed and made clear only in the historical reality of God's Incarnation.[34]

Only now can we spell out what the immanence of man involves: existing with other men, in an integral composite of body and soul, as a finite creature in time. To be all this, man is first and foremost a thinking subject who is responsible for his own actions; but he is also challenged and encountered by God's Word and God's commandment. He is a free, thinking being, bound up in a relationship with the freedom of God's Word and God's Spirit. He is a spirit because he is vivified and accosted by the Spirit of God.[35]

Man's immanent freedom and spirituality perdure as his constant attributes, but they are founded on a transcendent determination which is the gratuitous work of God. In this sense, it is not *natural* for man to be tied to God, because God is in no way obligated. It is God's gift and God's grace; this becomes apparent in man's death. Man lives and dies experiencing the living reality of God.[36] Thus Barth is led to reject all the classical philosophical statements which attempt to define man in terms of his immanent nature. Such statements touch upon certain aspects and potentialities of human nature, but they do not lay hold of authentic man.

At this point a question may arise: Did Barth remain true to his decision not to deduce the nature of man, as a natural, created reality, from the economy of salvation? In the precarious integration of these two orders, we certainly do find nuances and shifts of emphasis; and once the doctrine of creation has been formulated in the fifth volume, we cannot get away from this pendulous correlation. Any step beyond this, however, any attempt to deduce nature from grace systematically, would be a step backward to the monism of *Romans*. Barth's own admonition in the first volume of *Dogmatics* must be kept in the forefront of attention:

It is not permissible to make this a two-way road. We may try to recognize the creator once again in Revelation. But if we are not content with this, if we try to deduce creation as such from Revelation, then we are indulging in unwarranted speculation. . . .

If we ascribe the Church or Revelation to creation or the creative design of God, then we are forgetting that the Church and Revelation can only be a response to man's sin. Or else we must include man's sin in the work of creation. In that case we are forgetting the gratuitous goodness of God or making it a necessary component of a dialectical process.[37]

We have every right to say that nature is the wherewithal of grace and that this makes it real and meaningful. We have every right to look here for the ultimate meaning and reality of all natural conditions. But, on the other hand, we must not forget the other side of the coin: the innate properties of nature that permit it to be the wherewithal of grace.

If Barth gave nature short shrift, if we perceive a tendency to lose the material aspect of nature within its formal aspect and to immerse nature within grace, the underlying reason is clear enough. For aside from the influence of earlier stages of his thinking, Barth clings to the *Augustinian concept of freedom.*

In this view, freedom is essentially and primarily a process of living and making decisions, a process of moving about in the intimacy of divine freedom. It is not a neutral stance vis-à-vis God, operated by a neutral free will. If it is real freedom, it involves dwelling within the mysterious realm where self-determination and obedience, independence and imitation, act upon and clarify each other. It is the realm of the Trinity revealed by grace.

This concept of freedom, which leaves every philosophical notion behind it and challenges their claims to definitiveness, is to be the ultimate foundation of Barth's anthropology. To salvage the loftiest and most authentic freedom, he will give little attention to immanent freedom and its prerequisites. To make clear that immanent freedom is a secondary, derived phenomenon, he will put all the emphasis on the primary freedom: man's participation in the internal freedom of God.

For it is this which reveals the loftiest point of the

God-man relationship, the point of mutual influence. When man really hearkens to God, then God reveals himself as the being who is so free and so much in control that he can allow himself to be influenced by man's faith in him.

But again we are confronted with questions. If man looks back on the immanent, presupposed condition of creation from the vantage point of this higher freedom, what does his *natural* freedom really mean? Is it to be reduced to purely internal decisions, or is it to be regarded, as it should be, as a *formal* element in these transcendental relationships also? If it is not this, how can we talk about real creaturely freedom *vis-à-vis* God?

When Barth is discussing God in Volume 3, he calls the believer's influence on God "the novel and distinctive element in the order of grace."[38] Paul's words about reigning with Christ (2 Tim. 2:12) apply only to the friends of God. It is not by virtue of their creaturely freedom, by virtue of some vague rivalry with God's omnipotence, that good men may exercise this influence on God. It is in the freedom of their friendship with God that they are permitted to influence him through prayer, in which they actively confront him.

This line of thought runs parallel with Barth's attack on Molinism, which allows the creature as *creature* to intrude into the precincts of God's eternal truth. It permits the creature, by virtue of his creatureliness, to exert influence on God's will and hence on predestination from all eternity. Why? Because through *scientia media*, God knows all the possibles, all the would-be decisions of creation, without having any influence on them; and foreknowing these creaturely decisions, he then makes his own.

Rejecting this outlook, Barth has words of praise for the Thomists, who do a better job of preserving God's freedom and absoluteness in this area. He goes so far as to say that here Catholic theology has done a better job of preaching the gospel's doctrine on grace than orthodox Protestantism, for the latter succumbed to Molinism. The only thing he wonders about is whether Thomism is being consistent with its own basic principles, whether this specific doctrine accords with the notion of the analogy of being. For according to this notion, God and creation are fitted into a philosophical ontology, under a neutral concept of being, before theology enters the picture. The Church, after all, never settled the issue between the two schools, and it may well be that she is still hobbled with the underlying premises of *analogia entis*.

Barth's concern here is to keep God's absolute being and absolute truth from being mixed up with the realm of created being and created truth. He does not want creaturely freedom to gain any foothold within the realm of eternal truth. Molinism "denies the sovereignty of God, sets limits on his omnipotence and activity, and challenges his godhead."[39] Creation as such, as nature, does possess its own relative freedom within its own proper sphere (both before and after the fall); but influence on God is something which, as Barth saw it, comes about only within the order of grace.

Here as elsewhere, Barth wanted to preclude the ever present threat of philosophy's encroachment into the realm of theology. If he rallied behind Thomism, it was on two specific issues: (1) authentic creaturely freedom does exist; (2) however, it remains subordinate to the sovereign freedom of God, which determines everything. But he broke away at the point where these notions purport to be philosophical, indicating the intrusion of philosophy into the realm of theology. At that point, they become anticipatory determinations on matters which can only be established by Revelation and the order of grace.

Here we are dealing with something more than methodology or epistemology, but with a question of being itself. Man's freedom, rationality, and spirituality are to be understood in terms of the creation in Jesus Christ. Only on this basis can we come to know what created spirit really is; in encountering this event, we come to know what *real* freedom is.

Barth's point of departure, then, was quite different from that of Thomism. Moreover, his persistent distinction between the two orders—creation and reconciliation—did not allow him to settle the question of creaturely freedom once and for all. Creation is not an intrinsic, essential ingredient of the Incarnation economy, but its "external ground." This fact, however, should not be allowed to obscure the truth of the order of creation. Hence when Barth treated the doctrine on redemption in Volume 7, he is forced to reexamine the nature of creaturely freedom and its relationship to God.

Here again Barth's discussion of the relationship between the creator and creation as such is a purely theological inquiry. Faith in the redemption is not a common denominator, a meeting ground, where Christian faith joins together with any and every ideological system that treats of God and the world. Just as faith forms the distinctive, unique foundation of this theological outlook, so too its object is a unique event which is not to be confused with some more general, neutral contact between God and the world. Moreover, Barth is not talking here about God's special presence in Christ, the Church, and the Covenant; he is talking about "God's universal presence and dominion in world events."[40]

The Christological point of departure, however, is not abandoned. God's universal presence in world history is grounded in his special salvific design for the world, a design which is hidden in world history and revealed openly in the Church. The special history is inseparably intertwined with general history, and history as a whole participates in salvation history proper. In its special realm, faith looks openly at the work of God, and its light casts an illuminating glow over the shadowy meaning of history as a whole. We come to understand general history properly when we look upon it as the companion, the orbit, the preparation for and working out of salvation history.

Here again we must consider the activity and freedom of creation and its collaboration with God's work of reconciliation.[41] It is at this point that we encounter something which seems to run quite contrary to what has already been said. It is tied up with the demands of Protestant doctrine, however, and, paradoxically enough, it provides us with the element that was missing in Barth's discussion of God (Volume 3). We now learn that the real sphere for the creature's activity and collaboration is the realm of nature or creation, that the realm of grace is reserved for divine activity alone.[42]

While there is real collaboration in the realm of nature, this is ruled out in the order of grace. In the realm of nature, the creature can truly collaborate in maintaining, propagating, and shaping creation. In the order of grace, however, the creature cannot operate or mediate actively. It can only be a witness and a sign, a liturgical assistant, testifying to God who does all the work by himself. There is a connection between the two spheres, however. Because creation, as nature, truly does operate, its activity is related to the work of grace which God performs alone. Creaturely activity is the servant and tool of God, the mirror and showplace of his activity.[43]

However this may work out in practice, it is certain that creation, as nature, is truly active and hence collaborates with God. The notion of *concursus* is unavoidable. It maintained its validity in the teachings of Lutheran and Reformed Protestantism, which took over the concept of

cause from Catholic theology and made it their own:
The concept of causality does not derive from the bible, but this does not mean that its adoption by theology was an error. It can help theology to express what it must in spelling out and applying the biblical message. One would have to prove concretely—and it cannot be done—that we could avoid the use of this notion or a similar one in talking about the activity of God and the activity of the creature and their interrelationship.[44]

The notion of *concursus* (concurrence) is logically sound and still useful today. Through it we have won clarifications that might not otherwise have been gained.[45] The conditions that Barth set down concerning its use would also be accepted and taken for granted by Catholic theologians:

¶There must be no talk of a causality that operates mechanically.

¶There must be no talk of "things"—a fatal danger for theology.

¶There must be no development of an all-embracing concept of cause, under which God and the creature would be subsumed.

¶There must be no slipping back into philosophy. The attempt to interpret Revelation must remain theological.

¶Thus the whole matter must be developed within the first article of the Creed, which necessarily involves the second and third articles as well. God, the creator, sustainer and companion of his creation, operates as the first cause in a way that integrates the activity of the secondary cause with his own salvific activity. He correlates creation's activities with his own special deeds that make up the history of the Covenant.[46]

The doctrine of collaborative activity is presented, along the lines of Thomism, as the doctrine of God's *prae-cursus*, *con-cursus* and *suc-cursus*; but it is presented from the vantage point of the biblical God, who lovingly grants freedom from the unfathomable depths of his own freedom and love. This vantage point prevented Barth from going into a serious question that emerges for Thomism at this point (according to its opponents, at least): Is creaturely freedom really possible under this type of divine sovereignty?

For Barth, the possibility and the reality of creaturely freedom is simply and obviously a fact, and he proceeded from there. Once he adopted a positive outlook on the notion of creature around 1930, he never again entertained the slightest doubt about creaturely freedom, and in trying to explain the coexistence of absolute freedom with a finite, relative freedom, Barth was not disturbed by the fact that we have no concept or percept for it.

The first thing to do is simply to set aside any and all false conceptions. We cannot say that God is the stronger (or the strongest) force to which creaturely activity, as a weaker force, must necessarily submit. We cannot say that God's activity is actual, while the creature's activity is only potential (e.g., motor versus gears). We cannot say that God's activity is the first in a series, pulling the activity of creatures behind it as a locomotive pulls a train. We cannot say that some divine quality is conferred on the creature by God, because the creature's nature is not touched or altered. Nor can we say that God's activity is some broad undifferentiated thing to which creation, through its subsequent collaboration, provides differentiation and diversity.[47]

To move in the right direction, to avoid confusing detours for which authentic theology cannot assume responsibility, we must try to see and comprehend God's activity as it is presented in the Covenant and in Jesus Christ. If we do this, we can express our findings this way: "God acts by speaking his Word to every creature, and his Word possesses the power, the wisdom, and the goodness of his Holy Spirit."[48]

The only question left is this: Is every creaturely activity to be regarded as the activity of God in, with, and upon his creatures? The answer is "yes." God is secretly at work everywhere, as he clearly is in the Covenant. Because he himself lives a triune life, he can confer true freedom and allow the creature to have its own standpoint. Only the abstract bent of philosophy could inject a note of anxiety at this point, regarding God's infinite freedom as a threat to finite freedom. For in reality it is only God's infinite freedom that can create and protect creaturely freedom.

When this anxiety shows up in theology, it is a sign of fear and unbelief, not a sign of love and faith. The summons of God's Word is always a summons to responsibility. The conferral of the Spirit is always a conferral of selfhood. To be sure, this freedom entails obedience, but it is a bond forged by love, and that is what real freedom is.

In seeking to explain creaturely freedom within the general boundaries of the salvation economy, Barth is led once again to interpret it in terms of the special freedom we exercise in the order of grace. Over against this authentic freedom, there can really be no other. The light of Revelation not only clarifies the structure of our freedom in the obscure realm of nature; it is actually the hardcore substance to be found in this realm. In the realm of the Covenant we see clearly what lay hidden in the realm of creation. Our one and only freedom is the *holy* freedom which derives from God's love and is offered to us in Jesus Christ.

Thus Barth's teaching in Volume 7 hearkens back to his teaching on man in an earlier volume (Volume 6). But now we are faced with an orphaned notion, the concept of secondary causes in the realm of creation, for the note of discrepancy breaks out into the open. Creation, in its creatureliness and its individuality, is a secondary cause; but its freedom must be interpreted in terms of the economy of grace. Contrary to Protestant teaching, we are forced to conclude that creaturely causality achieves its real character and fullest scope in the order of grace. The full reality of this notion (secondary cause) is not to be sought in the natural realm of creaturely activity, however much it may be a part of this realm; it is to be sought in the ineffable mystery of "influencing God" which was mentioned as early as Volume 3. The discussion of reconciliation in Volume 7 culminates in a hymn of praise to this possibility: the possibility of ruling with God through obedience, prayer, and supplication:

There really is such a thing as the imitation of Christ. There really is such a thing as faith in him (and hence in God himself) and obedience to him. There really is such a thing as praying with him and through his intercession. There really is such a thing as a participation in Christ—in his prophetic, priestly, and royal offices.

In him God really did cross over to our side and descend to our lowliness; and in him we really did cross over to God's side and make the ascent to the lordly throne where all decisions about created reality are made. . . . To deny or doubt this would be as fatal as to deny or doubt the humanness and creatureliness of the Christ-event.

The Christian stands on the side of God—not by himself but in Christ. In Christ he has a say in the decisions which are made . . . as a member of Christ's body and Christ's community. . . . It is a personal role, not insofar as the Christian is a private individual but insofar as he has been summoned to God's side and endowed with it. . . .

Where the Christian believes, prays, and obeys, there we find creaturely activity—and something more. There we find the finger of God at work, hidden within this activity—and something more. There we find the heart of God at work, there we find ourselves at the seat of power and government which gives meaning to world history.

This subjective image of abject petition, this portrait of an empty hand reaching out to God, conceals the most objective reality there is. For it embodies and actualizes the lordship of Israel's king, who holds the whole world in his hands and brings good out of world history *per Jesum Christum Dominum nostrum.*[49]

It may well be that in our presentation here we have not paid due heed to the advice of J. L. Leuba, who suggests that Barth should be interpreted "prophetically" not "systematically." If Leuba is correct, Barth took these truths for granted at the start rather than trying to explain them or prove them. What we have, then, is a description of things as they appear in the light of God's Word, not as they are in themselves.[50]

If this is the case, Barth did not try to describe the essential nature of creaturely freedom and creaturely spirituality. He took these things for granted in order to describe the high point of their operation: their confrontation with the Spirit of God. That is why he defined created spirit almost exclusively in terms of this confrontation: "Man is man because he *has* spirit. . . . We cannot say simply that he is spirit."[51]

We must move on from this question, even though many obscurities remain. The exact nature of the relationship between God and the creature is not spelled out. Barth affirmed it and approved of it, but he did not say what it is exactly. The order of grace presupposes the order of creation. The latter is distinct from the former, but all too often Barth seemed to reduce it to the former.

4. Faith and Reason

Epistemologically, the problem of the relationship between nature and grace (i.e., between the order of creation and the order of divine reconciliation) becomes the problem of faith and reason. Here we determine, once and for all, the value of man's natural knowledge of God and the significance of the analogy of being; hence it is important that we pay close attention to what Barth really says and really means. Too many ridiculous notions have been imputed to him in the past.

Ever since Barth turned his attention from dialectics to the concept of analogy—it is only this latter stage we are interested in—he expressed his views at great length. There can really be little doubt about his line of thought.[52]

Man, as the partner of God, derives his reality from the fact that he is the brother of Jesus Christ and lives in the same realm as Christ. In like manner, man's knowledge of God finds its authenticity in the act of faith, where man comes to know God as God has revealed himself: as the true, living God, as the Father of Jesus Christ, as the creator, redeemer, and sanctifier. We can say that faith is the medium of absolute truth (veritas increata) and that there is no other medium for it.

Why is this so? First of all, because the Absolute can only be perceived through the Absolute. Concretely, we can only come to know God through his self-revelation. This self-revelation finds its foundation and its acme in Jesus Christ, the Word of God, who sustains the whole of creation, who is absolute because he is God, and who becomes comprehensible to man through Revelation. It is also true because man is not God. He cannot start out from some innate form or idea of the absolute that he himself possesses and thus come to know the living God.

Nor does he become identical with the Word of God when he encounters it, sharing its outlook as soon as he begins to do theological thinking. Man can only come to know the living God by opting wholly for the Word. This option is a gift from God and a decision made by man; we call it faith.

As we noted in the previous section, any reflection on man apart from his grounding in the Word is purely abstract in Barth's view; and if it presumes to be the last word on man, it is simply false. The same thing can now be said about our knowledge of God and man. It is a false knowledge if it claims to be the last word, without taking into account the encounter between creation and the living God and creation's response of obedience. The cohesion and reasonableness of nature derives from creation's freedom in the world; so, too, the cohesion and reasonableness of all thought depends upon the gratuitous Revelation of the Word. The Word is the Logos; he embraces and establishes whatever there is of logic.

In Barthian terms, we can regard faith as being a *priori* to any knowledge of authentic reality, so long as we do not attribute anything to nature in the abstract. In short, Barth posits faith at the start, at the precise point where Fichte posits the active ego (prior to discursive thought) and where Schleiermacher posits an intuitive feeling for God (prior to reflection). But it is not an a *priori* which belongs to reason, nor an innate constituent of the human spirit; it is something established by the concrete, authentic Word of God. Only then can we say that reason is truly reason, that knowledge is truly knowledge.

What we are talking about is the creator's self-revelation. It is not a further development of our consciousness; it is something that our consciousness runs up against and from which it derives new knowledge once it adverts to it.

The reality of the creator differs from all other realities in that he alone exists of himself. In like manner, his self-revelation differs from the self-revelation of other beings and spirits in that he alone is capable of proclaiming his existence with authenticity and truth. For this reason, any knowledge of existence that actually takes place outside of him depends on this condition: that he has made known his infallible knowledge about his own existence. . . . The self-revelation of the creator makes it possible for created things to know about existence and reality outside of God.

From the knowledge of God's existence, we can come to knowledge of our surroundings and our own being. . . . Because God first says, "I am," we can and must say "Yes, you do exist . . . and so do we!" The ontological order holds its own in the noetic order. . . .[53]

Clearly, it would be ridiculous to label this position as scepticism; for it derives from the certain knowledge of God's Word through faith. It would also be ridiculous to dismiss it as irrationalism; for it derives from the unmistakable revelation of the Logos, who embodies rationality itself. Finally, it is not ontological idealism, since it talks not about some image of God buried in every process of knowledge, but about our recognition and acknowledgment of God in faith.

We cannot speak of Fideism here either, at least not as the term was used in the nineteenth century and at Vatican I, but we can see a legitimate relationship between Fideism and Barth's position. Abbé Bautain was greatly influenced by Kant's philosophy; it led him to deny to reason the capability of reaching God on its own. The same conclusion is reechoed by Barth, but they do not share the same starting point. Bautain is speaking as a philosopher about the natural capabilities of created nature; Barth is speaking as a theologian about real human beings, for whom this supposition has no real meaning. Our purpose here is not to evaluate his position but simply to spell out exactly what it is.

What, then, is faith? We can begin by saying what faith is not. Faith is not some magical ability ennabling man to do something that lies beyond his created nature (in the Augustinian sense of nature), nor is it an activity that man performs through his natural capabilities. Faith proceeds from the Word of God. As a real happening, it is a determination made upon human existence in history (in salvation history).

Faith does not invade man's concrete nature as an alien force from without, however. Instead, it awakens him to an action that is *truly proper* to him. This action is not only within the scope of his created nature; it is actually the loftiest natural definition of his creaturehood (here again, we are using these terms in a concrete, Augustinian sense). Similarly, "the Incarnation of God's Son is the prototype for the genesis of faith. It represents the wholly gratuitous deliverance of human nature and hence the restoration of its loftiest creaturely orientation."[54]

This means we must reject two extreme interpretations of faith:

On the one hand, we must reject the notion that faith is simply blind *subjection* to a law imposed on our mind and will from without. On the other hand, we must reject the notion that faith is simply a matter of human *conviction* about the legitimacy and importance of an objective situation.

Contrary to the second notion, it imposes a bond and an obligation on man. Man must surrender his own desires, subject himself to a light which falls upon human life from without. But, contrary to the first notion, this light does not shine wholly from without, but also illumines man's mind and will from within. It does not blind man, it opens his eyes. It does not destroy man's intellect nor does it force him to sacrifice his mind. Instead, it frees his mind and sets his will in motion.

The Incarnation of God's Son epitomizes the nature of faith. It becomes real and concrete in the total obedience and total sovereignty of Christ's actions. The reality of faith stands above such oppositions and subsumes them within itself. Faith is wholly God's work and wholly man's work, wholly a binding and wholly a loosening. Roused to life by the Word of God, it lives and breathes within this integrated totality.[55]

When we read this description of faith, we can hardly accuse Barth of presenting a one-sided definition. Faith is supernatural and positive, but it is also in conformity with nature. It engages our natural capabilities, our mind and our will. It does not derive from our nature, but it is adapted to our nature and it perfects our nature according to the creator's plan.

On the one hand, faith lives wholly from the Word of Revelation. It helps to fulfill the divine decree, reflecting and echoing the "yes" that God uttered in raising Jesus Christ. Thus it is a participation in this divine activity and its thrust, an effort to follow Christ. Faith is not a mere spectator of God's deeds; it is caught up in the drama of God's activity in the world.[56]

It is also a summons sent out to man, to his whole nature and life, to his whole body and soul. Though it is grounded wholly in the Word of God, it is also our own action as well. How could the sovereign action of God's Word find fulfillment if it did not reach us in the work of the Holy Spirit, if it did not summon us to personal decision and action? It is a gratuitous grace, but that does not alter the fact that it calls for the conscious response of our own intellect and will; without our response, it could not be God's gift to us and for us.[57] As man's act, faith is a radical decision in favor of God; but it is not a blind, irrational decision. It is a decision made with absolute certainty, as a result of our encounter with the Word.

Barth lays great stress on this rational aspect of faith,

so much so that he has often been accused of rationalism by Protestant spokesmen. Lutherans, in particular, have accused him of betraying the element of simple trust in their notion of faith. Barth acknowledges the element of bold trust, but he sees it primarily as the obedient response demanded of us by the Revelation-happening. For him it is the created spirit's act of self-surrender, the decision to live in and by God's truth, the act of adoration which is at the root of a vital faith, and in its origins this act is lit up by God's Logos.

Christian faith sees and knows what it is holding to. Its trust is not a vague boast, an idealistic dream, nor simple resignation to the inscrutable and insoluble. To be sure, it does not see its object directly. Instead, it peers through earthly reality and glimpses God, who hides and reveals himself therein. The incomplete and imperfect nature of created reality does possess an aura of completeness and perfection, not of itself, but insofar as God has destined it in Christ for his own image and nature. In the gospel, we do not find faith and knowledge separated from each other. It is through both taken together that we made a positive decision with regard to Christ. The reason for this is that Jesus's participation in the divine and his human nature are not counterbalancing realities; it is his participation in the divine that grounds his reality as man. "To hear God's Word means to know God."[58]

Before we proceed, let us recall that Barth sees a fundamental parallelism between the order of being and the order of knowledge: "The ontic order is maintained in the noetic order."[59] That man is a reality, not a figment of the imagination, depends "ontically and noetically on the fact that he cannot exist without God."[60] The basic ground of human knowledge is that man can come to know the living God only through Jesus Christ; and it is tied up with the ground of his being: namely, that Jesus Christ is the real ground of creation.[61]

For Barth, human nature derives from that primeval grace; it can be understood and appreciated only in the light of that grace. So too, reason derives from God's self-revelation in Jesus Christ; if it is viewed apart from its origin there, it cannot be understood correctly. That is why Barth rejects the position of Catholic theology regarding reason. To preserve the notion of grace in all its purity, Catholic theology maintains that reason can exist and be understood even without faith. Barth regards this as an absurd position because it overlooks real beings to examine nonexistent possibilities. It is also a shameless position because it tries to prove that something has meaning apart from grace, when in fact it only has meaning within the framework of grace.

We must be careful not to equate Barth's position here with that of Baius. Barth would not dream of claiming that grace was an integral part of human nature, but he would say that nature, with all its needs, does rely upon something beyond its natural freedom and its natural necessity, that it relies upon the freedom and "necessity" of grace.

Keeping this point clearly in mind, we can now follow Barth's train of thought more easily. Man's understanding of truth derives wholly from God's gratuitous self-revelation in his Word. Essentially, neither the creator nor creation is hidden from us; only evil is. The encounter of being represents the openness of one being to another. Obscurity and untruth appear only when this essential openness is rejected, only when the creature seeks to obtain truth and certainty on his own apart from the self-revelation of God's absolute truth.

That is why Barth railed against any and every attempt

to ground truth on a philosophy which would sharply and expressly delimit itself from theology. Barth did not deny the existence of created truth in the world, in the realm of reality and the realm of knowledge. Nor did he deny that this created truth is grounded in the world's openness to uncreated truth. What he does deny, unfortunately, is that God's revelation in nature is truly *natural*, that it is an inherent property of nature rather than a supernatural gift. God is never an *a priori* imbedded in nature. If we contrast Barth's view with that of Fichte, Schelling, and Schleiermacher, then we can see what position he is really attacking and why he rails against the analogy of being.

His definitive position is first spelled out in his analysis of Anselm's *Proslogion* (1931). We are not concerned here with the validity of his analysis. We are more interested in the personal view he expounds. The core of his analysis is his argument that the notion of God itself forces us to recognize the real and specifically divine existence of God:

Anselm starts with a word, but it happens to be the Word of God. As such, it is tied up with his Revelation; and part of this Revelation is the revelation of his existence. In uttering the name of God, Anselm is not trying to deduce his existence from it; he is pointing out the impossibility of his nonexistence. Our belief in the existence of God can thus be acknowledged rationally.[62]

Fidens quaerens intellectum is Anselm's starting point. When a believer utters the name of God, he utters it within the context of his encounter with God; and the same holds true for a nonbeliever who utters this name from the standpoint of solidarity with a believer. The context of encounter makes this problem different from any other. We cannot utter the word *God* in this context and then conclude that he does not really exist.

The ultimate conclusion of a proof for God's existence is a negative one: a purely notional God is a manifest impossibility. Only on the basis of Revelation can we make a positive, unassailable affirmation of his existence, and only in conjunction with the self-revelation of absolute truth can the relative truth of creation be known and appreciated.

As the existence of all things depends on God's existence, so their truth and knowability depends on his absolute truth. "Everything that exists outside God, does so only under the umbrella of his existence. And they can be conceived as existing only insofar as we contemplate his irrefutable existence."[63] Finite existence and finite truth exist only because absolute truth and absolute existence do. The former is real and authentic, but it is analogous.

So the question is: Can analogous being and analogous truth ascend of itself to absolute being and absolute truth? Taken in the abstract, they are not sufficient by themselves; they make the grade only on the condition that absolute being and absolute truth reveal themselves in these analogous realities and that this Revelation is accepted in faith. Man can recognize God in the visage of the world, but only where faith resides—in the Church.

This brings us to the ultimate problem of Anselm's work and the position adopted by Barth with regard to it. If this parallel does exist between the ontic and noetic order, if man's knowledge and being is grounded on the Revelation of the Word, how is is possible for man not to have faith? Is it really possible for man to deny the existence of God? How can the fool say in his heart that there is no God, when he cannot really entertain such a thought?

Barth did not answer the question as he would have answered it in his dialectical period, referring to the self-contradictory nature of creaturely existence. Instead, he

asserts that the affirmation and the denial of God's existence take place on two separate levels.[64] On one level,
where God's Word and self-revelation accosts man, he
cannot really deny God's existence, but when he abstracts
from this experience of encounter and handles the idea
conceptually, he can deny God's existence. Conceptual abstraction is the culprit and the source of the big lie:

The authenticity of man's thought and speech depends on its
ties with the being that stands over against that speech. . . .
Abstracted from the being that stands over against it, man's
reflection must be labeled false.[65]

What, then is the exact nature of the fool's unbelief?
It is simply that the fool disavows his faith; he chooses not
to believe what he cannot help but believe. This ultimately
ties in with the whole question of predestination, which
is a topic to be treated later on. Here we shall simply
carry on with Barth's exposition.

In *Church Dogmatics*, Barth grounds the possibility of
finite existence on God's omnipotence and fidelity. The
noncontradictory reality of created being and created truth
is rooted in God's absolute being and his absolute truth.
The latter is the source of its legitimacy.[66] Relative being
can only provide relative assurance; only absolute being
can provide absolute assurance. The potential of created
reality finds its valid worth in the freedom and will of
God the creator. If our relative assurance in the truth and
consistency of creation is not grounded on the absolute
assurance of faith, it will sooner or later lead to contradiction; the history of philosophy bears eloquent testimony
to this fact. In the light of God's self-revelation, we know
that he cannot act contradictorily; and we also know that
only his self-revelation guarantees the impossibility of contradiction.

Barth's extensive treatment of Descartes' *Meditations*

in his *Church Dogmatics* (5:401–415) leads to the same conclusion. What has Descartes ascertained for sure? Directly, only mathematical truths, says Barth. Descartes has not directly ascertained his own existence or the existence of God. All he can ascertain is the existence of an *imagined* perfect being, which is not enough to insure the validity of my thought process. How can the existence of the ego in Descartes' third meditation and of mathematical ideas in the fifth meditation be dependent on this type of demonstration of God's existence? Is finite thought bound up in a vicious circle?

It is a circular process, said Barth, but it is nothing for human reason to be ashamed of. The demonstration can only succeed when it is God's self-demonstration breaking through the circular process of finite reasoning; and, on the other side of the coin, we must have man's obedient response to this demonstration in his own process of reflection. This is the kind of demonstration which Anselm of Canterbury gave in the eleventh century. Descartes, too, speaks of believing by faith. But unlike Anselm's demonstration, Descartes' faith is operating outside his philosophy and eventually turning that philosophy into theology.

Once again we come up against the relationship between philosophy and theology. In the last analysis, both can only point the way; they cannot provide proof. Both must proceed from the pristine openness of absolute truth and presuppose that at the start. We can mount from the world towards the Absolute, but only insofar as we presume the priority of the Absolute over the relative. Descent must come before our ascent; Revelation must come before the view opens up to us.

If philosophy wants to get back to the ground of things, this is the course it must take. In this respect, it is a thrust and a methodical movement in a certain direction, and Barth regarded it as a real possibility, but this thrust is not self-contained because the last word can only come from God, that is, from a theology that obediently listens to him. Theology holds the place to which philosophy must ultimately point.

It is certainly true that philosophy can raise the question of God and consider the authentic created nature of the world. This problem lies within its scope, at least as an unsettling question at the boundary of its potential, but the theologian knows that this uncertainty can only be dealt with insofar as God's revelation is a fact. So it is quite conceivable that philosophy could pose its questions from the point where God supplies an answer, particularly if it chose to speak about God's openness as a Christian philosophy. In this case philosophy would lean on theology and become an unconscious theology. From the very nature of his notion of faith, Barth has to leave the door wide open for this possibility.

Romans 1:19 is reclaimed for theology by Barth, but it is also reclaimed for philosophy. What man can know about God is plain to him, because God shows it to him. God's invisible essence is made plain to man in the light of his works. It is a real light for man, even if he misconstrues it and tries to turn it into "natural theology."

The Thomistic proofs for God's existence seek to move from the world to something beyond it. If this effort is to succeed, however, it must involve more than an attempt at self-transcendence by the world. God himself must transcend the world from his side and show himself; and the testimony of the bible is there to tell us that this actually happens. The bible's testimony justifies every attempt to demonstrate God's existence, making them partial efforts and first steps in a theological explanation.

It is in the sixth volume of *Church Dogmatics* that Barth began to deal seriously with this possibility. There he considered the different forms of philosophical anthropology and came to a reconciliation with Emil Brunner. Various philosophical views on man do draw close to the truth and can be used by theology.

Barth came to see some merits in the anthropology of materialism, naturalism, ethics (Fichte), existential philosophy (Jaspers), and Brunner's religious outlook.[67] Idealistic ethics sees man as the active subject of his own life; existential philosophy sees man already open to something outside himself; theistic anthropology moves on from existential philosophy and relates man to a transcendent God, who is man's origin and ultimate goal. This theistic anthropology does indeed describe man's potential to become God's partner. If it focuses on this point and does not try to say what turns this possibility into a reality, then it is a legitimate procedure.

These forms of philosophical anthropology do not derive their knowledge of man from God's Word or his Revelation. They represent the general science that deals with man's attempt to know himself. Theology knows that man can be known in the light of God's Revelation, and hence it can derive insights from the various forms of philosophical anthropology. In this context, the relationship of philosophy to theology is that of the abstract to the concrete, of possibility to actuality. So long as the two poles are tied together, philosophy is valid and authentic.

Thus abstract reasoning does not necessarily lead us into a blind alley, as Barth had suggested in his analysis of the Anselmian proof. It can put us on the right track, provided that it knows it is not the ultimate concrete reality. Brunner is thus correct in talking about the legitimacy of a proto-insight. Did not the Church Fathers feel justified in expropriating pagan philosophy?

When theology does move into the realm of philosophy, however, it should proceed boldly as the Israelites moved into Canaan. After all, this is the land that belongs to its Father. In fashioning an ethics, theology needs to take God's Revelation and grace with full seriousness, regarding men as totally oriented to God and bound by his commands.

In short, man can come to know God in this world; created realities can bear the image of God for him. The possibility of knowing God does exist, both prior and subsequent to any *de facto* impossibility of natural knowledge of God.

Thus, despite Barth's strong objections to "natural theology" in Volume 6 of *Church Dogmatics*, we are not surprised that he stressed the possibility of knowing God in his own theological anthropology. For the latter deals with real men living under the real God of Jesus Christ; it is man's self-cognizance in the light of God's a *priori* Word. Theological anthropology starts with the revealed Word of God in scripture and then examines man's nature and his cognitive capabilities.

While the tension between the order of creation and the order of redemption (noted earlier) may be real, Barth did not want us to get caught up in the neo-Scholastic categories of *natural* and *supernatural*. In Barth's conception, there is no way of asking what man can know by nature, apart from Revelation; for Adam stands as close to the true God as Abraham and the Apostles. Within the context of man's real encounter with God, we can only point to the disposition of human nature which can be laid hold of by God's Word.

Barth now said things that directly contradicted his earlier polemic against Brunner:

Man is capable of perceiving the God who draws near and reveals himself. . . . In dealing with man, God presumes and appeals to this capability; if it were not present, summons and encounter would be impossible. If God has created man to live his Word and to participate in a Covenant, then he has created man as an intelligent being capable of response.[68]

Intelligent understanding is the central act of the spirit, the unsplintered act that makes thought and perception mutually operative on one another. Kantian dualism is *subsequent* to this basic act of the spirit. Because man is spirit, he can understand things; and the first thing he can understand is God, who is Another. Thus Barth can now talk eloquently about the indivisibility of body and soul. He stresses their mutual interaction upon one another and the integral body-soul act of understanding.

The central point is this: man, as a being with understanding, is essentially a being who can and does understand God. Man, of course, does grasp other things and other beings who are not God, but behind all his acts of understanding stands one central object, God. To put it another way, man is created and equipped to discover and encounter God in all things. That is man's real nature, and his common knowledge is meant to lead him to the special knowledge of God.

When a man abstracts himself from this special knowledge, when he tries to tackle the world apart from his relationship to God, then he falls into the vanity of which the bible speaks. His mind does not change, however. It remains oriented towards God and passes judgment on him. It is put on the wrong track, but it never loses its orientation. Man's reason can never be abstracted from God and remain true to itself, according to the bible: "The biblical man—the prophet and the Apostle—tells us what natural reason is."[69] It is an exterior thing primarily, because creation is not God but God-oriented; it is perception. It is also an interior thing, because it involves finding God through God; it is thought. This twofold face of reason fits in with the essence of creatureliness under God as viewed by theology.

The situation is analogous for the two moments in man's decision-making: desire and choosing. God presupposes these components, too, when he summons man. This decision-making is inextricably tied up with man's special knowledge of God; indeed it is part of his original image. Here again everything, including free choice, must be viewed as tied up with the original decision vis-à-vis God. To reject that protodecision is to get involved in the woeful abstraction of *liberum arbitrium*, a would-be neutral ground for man between God and the devil.

Now we can see why Barth seems able to grant and deny natural knowledge of God in the same breath. He denies it where man tries to achieve it without relying on the Word of God, where he remains trapped, disobediently, in the relative world of finiteness. He grants it where man's potential is tied up with the act of divine Revelation. The process of abstraction can betray us or lead us aright, depending on the absence or presence of this original link. Theological anthropology can and should involve a process of abstraction, so long as it starts from the ultimate concrete reality and ends up there.

One final question: What is the relationship between this original, basic "knowledge" and faith? While Barth's anthropology in Volume 6 does not touch on this question, the answer is obvious. They are one and the same. Obedient understanding and acceptance of God's Word is faith. Ultimately all nature rests upon the Revelation-happening, and the corresponding factor in creation is faith.

5. Sin

Having said all this, we need not linger long over the problem of sin. We can readily see why Barth started out by regarding it as the absolute contradiction in the very heart of nature, and we can also see why he eventually came to regard it as the "impossible possibility" of a nature not radically destroyed.

At the time he wrote *Romans*, Barth equated the contradiction of sin with the creature's distance from God. Since the act of creation and man's primeval union with God were subsumed under the notion of identity, sin could only be a meaningless contradiction and hence pure nothingness. To avoid this conclusion, Barth asserted that the contradiction of sin had been superceded by the reality of reconciliation. Dialectics then involved the victory of Christ over Adam.[70]

The consistency of Barth's thought is clearly seen in the fact that his early emphasis on Christ over Adam eventually led him to give up the old dialectics and to focus on Christ alone as the constant in created nature. In his early period, however, he concentrated mainly on the great transformation, barely managing to retain the perduring identity of the subject who underwent this transformation. Retain it he did, however: "It is not as if two worlds were involved here, or as if the old man and the new man were two men."[71]

In *Church Dogmatics*, this perduring identity is given great stress. There are two reasons for this. First of all, Barth now is prepared to see the basic goodness of creation as a reality distinct from God. Secondly, the goodness of creation, as a reality distinct from God, mirrors the distinction of persons within God, and this goodness finds its confirmation and its high point in the twofold nature of Christ, where the polarity between God and man is confirmed and carried to its ultimate dimensions. In Christ there is no longer any element of contradiction; there is only obedience to, and acceptance of, God's will. Christ establishes peace between God and man, even though man himself may contradict this fact.

The possibility of contradiction still exists for man, but now it is framed in the truth of the Redeemer. Now it is an impossible possibility: impossible in Christ, who has solved the contradiction; possible in man, who can say no to this fact even though he is a brother of Christ. When the sinner opposes God's summons, he contradicts himself and his own nature.

The sinner cannot annul his nature, but this does not mean that his sin is only a partial thing, that he cannot violate the goodness of his nature. When he sets himself in opposition to God and his own nature, he forces his nature to say no to God; he turns all its potential into an act against God. He gathers all his powers for good into one and hurls them out as a denial of faith, as a refusal to obey God. His *sensus fidei* is totally twisted.

Viewed in the abstract, his natural power of thinking and willing remains uncorrupted—and must remain so if the negation of sin is to be possible at all. Yet, however much this may be true, the core of this negation of God's Word makes him nothing less than a total sinner. In his negation, man cannot recognize God, even though his refusal derives from an encounter with God, from being blinded by the divine light that lies at the base of his own darkness.

If we follow up this distinction between creation's relationship in being to God (which cannot be destroyed) and its relationship to God in its actions (which can be perverted), we come back to Barth's distinction between ontic and noetic *ratio* in his book on Anselm.[72] Both the ontic and noetic *ratio* of creation are rooted in the uncreated *ratio veritatis*, which is identical with the Father's consubstantial divine Word. The *ratio veritatis* is the measure of ontic and noetic truth in creation, and the latter are what they are by virtue of their participation in the former. Creation's ontic truth participates more fully and continuously in the ratio veritatis, however, and man uses his noetic ratio properly only when he respects the object and its ontic ratio.

The relevance of this for our present question is clear. It is possible that the ontic ratio of things is not affected by sin, while man's pursuit of truth through his noetic ratio is damaged. Man could be blinded by sin, and his noetic ratio could fail to recognize God's revelations of the eternal ratio in the ontic ratio of creation. There is a strong temptation to interpret Romans 1:18 in this way.

There are inconsistencies in this interpretation, however, that suggest deep flaws in the whole doctrine of sin. To begin with, it would be wrong to place the mirroring by worldly, objective knowledge of the original model (i.e., in decision) in a line with the self-revelation of the divine in created things. For these do possess real truth content, even though it is created and relative; and this content is knowable, even though it is not known explicitly in God or God in it. Such knowability is guaranteed by the continuing veracity of created things.

In the temporal process of acquiring knowledge, the imagining quality of cognition possesses the same dignity as the object quality of the thing known—at least in principle. But the thrust of Barth's line of thought is only too clear: in subordinating the noetic ratio to the ontic ratio, there is an underlying tendency to deny to the former the same qualities as the latter.

Here noetic ratio seems to be reduced to almost pure hearing, but the cognitive process does in fact possess ontic dignity. There is no reason why it should not be a perduring image of the protosubject God, even as the ontic ratio images the protoobject God. This cognitive structure as such is not erased by sin; it remains intact, even when the cognitive act is corrupted.

Here clear expression is given to something that has

been obscured time and again in theological anthropology. The spontaneity of human knowledge is part and parcel of its nature, which is not corrupted even by sin. Thus the question of the basic a priori structure of cognition, so often discussed and debated by Catholic philosophy, cannot be simply passed by. In giving equal stature to the decision of the will, Barth clearly shows his unwillingness to deny this spontaneity. But he relates into silence when it comes to the a priori nature of the intellectus agens, for this is the danger zone which spawns the concept of being and the analogia entis.

One passage in Church Dogmatics may cast some light on this shadowy area. "Only through God can God be known," says Barth; not because a critical epistemology forces this conclusion on us, but because Revelation itself does.[73]

Theology is dependent on the Word of God, not on some epistemological theory. It is the Word of God that sheds light on the nature of man. True as that may be, however, the Covenant relationship between God and man is also a two-sided, reciprocal relationship. Barth did not fail to take note of this in Church Dogmatics (5, 6, 7). Whether the human side of this relationship is accorded autonomy and significance of its own will depend on the emphasis it is given. In any case, the difficulties of this vis-à-vis between the finite and the infinite are not resolved by denying autonomy to the finite.

The receptivity of reason in the act of faith lies above and beyond the natural tension between spontaneity (activeness) and receptivity (passiveness). Barth knew and admitted this.[74] Thus there can be no denying that spontaneity is present in both the act of accepting faith and the act of rejecting it. We cannot evade the problem of analogia entis, for it is a principle imbedded in the ontic-noetic nature of creation. It may be used well or badly, but it must be used. Used badly, it may well be the invention of the Antichrist, as Barth said, but it is offered to man as a good tool. Barth might have been able to accept this idea without feeling that he betrayed his basic outlook on the relationship between nature and its potentiality, on the one hand, and the concrete happening of God's Word on the other.

6. Analogia entis

We can now conclude our introductory exposition of Barth's thought with a brief look at his objections against the notion of analogia entis. They may be summarized under four headings, starting with the most important ones.

❰The notion of being is incapable of expressing the decisive element in the relationship between God and creation. In fact, it obscures this element, taking the relationship for granted from the start instead of bringing out the unexpected wonder of it all.

The notion of being turns things upside down, grounding our outlook on an element that is not the most basic and characteristic one. If we start at the core of both poles, we do not find similarity but radical difference. One pole exists a se; the other pole exists ab alio.[75]

❰However analogously we may apply it, the concept of being remains a concept, an organizing framework under which we lump both God and creature. We thus show disrespect for the creator and expropriate his prerogative of self-revelation. He alone has the capacity and the right to tell us who he is and what his nature is like.[76]

❰As the product of a finite, relative being, the concept of being itself can only be finite and relative. Its claim to absoluteness is a false claim. It is actually an attempt to turn our finite formula into an absolute, to project creatureliness onto the divinity. It is creation's attempt at self-apotheosis.[77]

⟮[In the hands of sinners, the concept of being becomes a tool for disobedience. It seeks to fashion something which can only be a gift from God. In this respect it is the clearest expression of disobedience; it secularizes and falsifies the real situation, it misuses grace.[78]

The *analogia entis* must be replaced by the *analogia fidei*, for the analogy of faith eliminates all these dangers and abuses. It makes clear that all knowledge of God derives from some foregoing Revelation by God, from his prior condescension. It makes clear that man derives knowledge form his Revelation only by freely submitting his own truth in an act of faith; in this act there is real analogy and a real acquisition of knowledge, but only insofar as created potency is immersed in the active happening of God's self-revelation. Finally, the analogy of faith clearly indicates that God's self-revelation is and must be grasped at its clear and unmistakable center, Jesus Christ, where it becomes a happening for the believer.

From the vantage point of this center, other things come back into the picture for our *fides quaerens intellectum*, and there seems to be room for the analogy of being after all. To begin with, there must be a periphery to this center. God's assumption of humanity in Christ presupposes the order of creation, and the two are not identical; and since the order of creation is oriented towards the Incarnation, it possesses images, analogies, and dispositions that truly are presuppositions for the Incarnation.

Interhuman relationships—the man–woman relationship, for example—is a real presupposition for our brotherhood with Jesus. Because he is a social, personal being, man is capable of entering into a covenant with God, and these intercontacts in the natural order are possible only because of the interpersonal relationships within the Trinity itself. Thus we can talk about *analogia relationis*,[79] *analogia proportionis*,[80] and *analogia operationis*,[81] even though Barth prefers to avoid these terms. And we can also talk about the highest form of analogy, the *analogia adorationis*, in which God gives his children power over his will and heart; it is a true image of the mutual interaction between the three divine persons within the godhead.

Barth had no difficulty in accepting and approving the analogy of being, in this form, within the context of an all-embracing analogy of faith.[82] He realized that it cannot be avoided in theology's treatment of God, even though it may be open to misuse,[83] and in many sections of *Church Dogmatics* we find Barth describing the God–creature relationship in classical analogical terms.[84]

Now we can explore Barth's concept of analogy still further by examining what he has to say about *obediential potency*. Barth started out with a strong antipathy to this concept, but his attitude slowly changed as Christ became the focal point of his theology. The creature's openness to Revelation was no longer a dangerous natural *a priori*, but a presupposition emanating from the Word of God itself. The whole creature, with its areas of light and shadow, now was seen as the occasion for the surpassing of nature in Christ's death and resurrection.[85] Creation truly was good.

On the basis of his own presuppositions, Barth had no difficulty in recognizing that the creature is clay in the hands of the creator, that he can heed the Word of God even though this obedience is not an immanent natural capacity. The bible clearly indicated that the creature had the capacity to obey God (obediential potency),[86] thanks to God's free gift. Of itself, nature can be ambiguous and two-faced, but in reality it is not, because God has so arranged it. God has made his creation in such a way that it can be used and incorporated into the lordship of Christ.[87]

Barth's acceptance of obediential potency shores up the validity of the analogy of being within the broader framework of the analogy of faith. Faith is an act that is offered by God as a gift and that fuses together all the elements of creatureliness. Obediently doing what he cannot do by himself, the creature transcends himself and thus fulfills the true meaning of created existence. "To that extent we can accept the oft misused phrase of Thomas Aquinas: *gratia non tollit (non destruit) sed (praesupponit et) perficit naturam*."[88]

PART THREE

A Closer Look at
the Framework

*In the previous section we attempted to spell out
Barth's thought on several key questions. We did
not try to present his whole theology but merely
to clairfy its thrust. Before we reflect critically on
his thought (Part Four), it would be wise to examine the form or shape of his whole theology,
so that we might get a deeper insight into it. This
will necessarily involve some personal judgments,
but their main purpose will be to clarify Barth's
thought.*

I · GOD'S ENTHUSIAST

The whole pageant of Barthian theology, from its earliest
days on, was dominated by the same single-minded pre-
occupation. Barth was consumed with a passion for God.
His outlook and terminology may change, but he resolutely
refused to move one inch away from the center where
Revelation, biblical man, and the upright believer reside.

Not for one moment did he forget that the purpose of creation is to give glory to God. His aim was to spell out this glory, to show his love for it, and to reveal its grandeur. Rarely in Christian circles has love for God echoed so forcefully through a man's lifetime work.

God stooped down to the world and became man, without detracting from his divinity. The Christian can imitate his example, becoming part of the worldly order without removing himself from the center of his faith and his witness. The Incarnation involves an "and," but it does not involve any compromise; the same possibility is open to the Christian in his temporal life. Barth's outlook, in the last analysis, resembled that of the Christian saints and martyrs. How else can we explain the consistency of his theme, the tireless variations around a central point of emphasis, the relentless subordination of everything to adoration and love of God?

It is not surprising that the young Barth, in his zeal for God, should adopt a framework that tended to relativize everything that was not divine. It is even less surprising when we realize that he was out to topple the false gods that upright men and even the Church had erected for themselves. In the attempt, our young Samson himself was almost caught in the falling debris.

In all his later writings, however, we find a trace of Old Testament pathos. Barth is Jeremiah, burning with zeal for God but surrounded by misunderstanding. Barth is Job, suffering the dialectical pangs of judgment and love. He is a sceptic for God's sake. The infinite difference between God and creation perdures to the end. In the last analysis, created reality is not God; it is created, and therefor relative. Created truth, goodness, and beauty are also relative. They come from God and go back to him; in themselves they have no consistency, no power, no meaning, no clarity.

Yet the truth of creation is no less true because of its limitations and its open-endedness. The mellower outlook on creation in Barth's later works was a reflection of God's own outlook, who has made men what they truly are and will make them what they truly should be. In the grace of his merciful judgment, God passes judgment on his creation: he brings it to his own truth, making it in eternity what it could not be in time.[1]

God becomes man, not to be backed into a corner but to establish his dominion over creation within the world itself. His passion, death, and resurrection will do precisely that. No worldly wisdom can compete with God's sovereign plan, and no foolishness on the part of creatures can frustrate it. On the contrary, the world's folly, sinfulness, and unbelief become the means by which God demonstrates his love. Schelling and Berdyaev are wrong when they picture creaturely freedom as an unfathomable obstacle to God's loving activity.

No one is more ready to accept human freedom and human sinfullness, but for Barth they are framed within the limits of finiteness, and God is above and beyond these limits. He proved his superiority by tackling the seeming tragedy of finiteness and overcoming it. God is infinitely free. Why should he not be free enough to establish genuine freedom within the confines he created? Those who truly believe in God should find no great problem in the cooperative interplay of these two freedoms.

The world of relative realities derives from the world of absolute reality. The cooperative work of created realities it guided and dominated by God's absolute activity. Creaturely activity is not closed in upon itself. It is grounded in God and, at every moment of its history, open to his activity. Through his activity, it is shaped to its true image and purpose. Even if there were an element of determinism within the created world, this would not close the world off from God and his activity. Because God is God, the relative world can rest securely in his absolute truth.

In *Romans*, the fire of God's absoluteness seemed to threaten creation. In *Church Dogmatics*, his awesome activity was depicted more and more as the fire of absolute love. Barth used the word *love* rather sparingly, in order to bring out the fact of divine love all the more clearly. For him, creation and Christianity were triumphant realities. God does not wrestle laboriously with his enemies. Instead, Christ brings hostility to an end on the cross (Eph. 2:16) and sits down at the right hand of God "to wait until his enemies should be made his foot stool" (Heb. 10:13).

The fire of God's victorious love encircles the creature on all sides. When Barth talked about what lies ahead for man, he stuck close to the biblical message. Ahead lies God, life with God, a bodily resurrection into his presence. The limits of finiteness are good because they are set by God. Death without God would be a descent into shadowy nothingness; for those who do not believe in him, it truly will be judgment and condemnation. But it will also prove that God is everlastingly right and just, and that his loving plan has succeeded.

God's love is the ultimate necessity, governing and controlling everything else. It is more powerful than any physical force in this world. Only one course of action lies open to us:

We have no choice but to heed and respond to the message of Revelation and the divine activity contained therein. We are compelled to take this course, not by force but by love. We can escape the constraints of force, but the power of love is unavoidable. Confronting God's self-revelation, we learn the truth of our existence: we are beings sought out by him— loved, redeemed, and called to faith. That is the whole story.[2]

Now love always involves a choice. It is directed toward a particular object, and hence it excludes other things. If God does not say "yes" to something, then he is saying "no" to it;[3] and his anger and wrath are expressions of his grace. He would rather express dissatisfaction with his creation than be the self-satisfied, contented God of a discontented creation. He chooses to enter the fray rather than to be a passive spectator. His love fights its own battles and, in so doing, it passes judgment and condemnation on everything it has not chosen.

But here we come to a crucial problem. If creation has come about through God's love, how could any part of it be rejected by this love? God does not hate anything he has created, and he would not allow anything he loves to be torn away from him. How do anger and condemnation, as elements of divine love, fit into the picture? We are face to face with the problem of predestination in Barthian theology.

Barth himself was astounded by his formulation of this doctrine. He realized that he was standing alone against the traditional doctrine, but he courageously faced that fact. It is time for us to look at his study of predestination, for it seems to hold the key to his whole theology.

II · PRAEDESTINATIO GEMINA

As early as the *Epistle to the Romans*, Barth's presentation of predestination diverged sharply from the view of Calvin.

As Barth saw it, the explanation offered by Augustine and the Reformation set arbitrary limits on God's activity and misconstrued this basic mystery.[1] Their presentation focused too quickly on the psychological reality of the individual and his fate, bypassing God's role in the ultimate decision.[2]

Barth's own doctrine of predestination took shape early. It can be found in the first edition of *Romans*, and the fourth section of *Church Dogmatics* is devoted exclusively to it. In six hundred pages, we find this closely worked doctrine presented with the utmost care. It is the heartbeat of Barth's theology, and no summary can match Barth's own presentation of it.

Here Barth's central thesis finds its ultimate triumph: he proves that man can understand the mystery of God only through God's self-revelation in Jesus Christ; that any attempt to resort to an *abstract* God would be disastrous for theology. The doctrine of election is the *summa evangelii*, the key to understanding God's whole Revelation in creation, reconciliation, and redemption.

God's Revelation gives us a glimpse into the innermost mystery of himself: his proto-choice and -decision, from which all his graces derive. The doctrine of election bears witness to the fact that

all his ways and works have their beginning in his grace. From the very start God, in his autonomy, is a God of grace . . . all created nature derives its being and existence from God's grace, and only through grace can it be recognized for what it truly is . . . even when it is a question of sin and death and divine displeasure.[3]

The doctrine of election tells us that God's grace lies at the source of all his plans and activities. As such, it is the "common denominator" that underlies every statement and can never be forgotten.[4]

The source and wellspring of election is Jesus Christ alone. In him God chooses himself, but in the form of a creature. On him, the merciful mediator and redeemer, all creation was established before the foundation of the world. This one person, and he alone, is the primeval object of the Father's election. In him the family of man is summoned to election; and through the latter, the individual is summoned to his private relationship with God. This primeval election is the foundation for the whole epic of divine providence, and the doctrine of divine providence must be regarded as part of the more comprehensive doctrine of election. To reverse the relationship between these two doctrines is to distort the true picture.[5]

Earlier presentations of the doctrine of election contained a serious flaw. They misconstrued the Christological base that is clearly brought out in the bible, regarding election as an individual happening between an abstract divine Absolute and a creation viewed atomistically. But it is the Son of God who is the object of God's election from all eternity. It is he who will bring the as yet uncreated world back to God. He will stand up for creation, take the burden of sinners' guilt upon himself, and thus become the object of divine rejection.

The one who offers himself to the Father in this way is himself God and therefore the subject of election. "This one person, Jesus Christ, was there with God in the beginning. Predestination is precisely this."[6] Here, at the start, everything is clarity, love, and grace. In God there is no shadow or darkness, and therefore the gospel is wholly a message of glad tidings. If there had been some shadow of hesitation, doubt, or reservation at the source, then the gospel could only bring partial good news, partial grace, and partial redemption; but that is not the case. If our theology and our Christian proclamation introduces shadows and ambiguities, if it sets limits on our faith, hope, and love, then it is not in tune with authentic Christian realities:

The history of the dogma of predestination is dominated by man's attempt to grapple with this assertion: that in the mystery of election we are dealing with light not darkness; that the God electing and the mankind elected are known quantities rather than unknown quantities. We cannot arrive at this assertion until we venture to take a big step, until we admit that the same person, Jesus Christ, stands on both sides of the equation describing divine predestination. One side of the equation (the subject or the object of predestination) is always lost in our musings and usually both are. But we cannot allow that to happen any longer.[7]

When God made his choice before the foundation of the world, he knew what the world and creation could be. The creator took a risk and assumed responsibility for it. To begin with, his decision to speak his Word, to send his Son, represented a decision about himself. No longer would God be alone with himself, for now this human being would be an integral part of His divine will. The danger that would confront the world would first be a danger for God himself. It would be the stimulus for the work he would undertake, the pledge of the grace he would bestow.

Already in Christ, election is "two-edged predestination." In choosing him, God destines man for election, blessedness, and life; but he also destines himself for rejection, condemnation, and death. He will have to reject sinners, and he will have to draw his sinless Son to himself, but he will do it in such a way that the Son of God takes on the burden of sin and experiences death and damnation while sinners, enmeshed totally in disobedience, are chosen to be set free for his Son's sake:[8]

This is the barter that took place once and for all on Golgotha. The Son of God suffered what the sons of men should have suffered, and the bargain is irrevocable. For this reason, there is nothing damnable in those who are in Jesus Christ. . . . No one who believes in Christ can believe in his own rejection. He could only do so if he focused on himself, or on a God who had not sacrificed his Son for the world. But if we have to come to know God's mercy and righteousness on the cross, we no longer have any grounds to fear that we have been rejected by God.[9]

God's election in Jesus Christ, our brother, is a two-edged situation from the start. This ought to be the basic theme and leitmotif of salvation history and the watermark of creation itself. Creation is the "election" of cosmic order and the "rejection" of chaos; and this two-edged process is carried on within creation by the division of light and darkness, day and night, earth and water. These latter divisions, however, take place *within the framework of election;* they mirror God's protodecision to choose *cosmos* and reject *chaos.*

This decision derives ultimately from Christ and the cross. Here God's will shows itself to be totally good and merciful, not at all two-edged. For the ultimate in divine rejection is the cross; the Christian is not permitted to probe any deeper than that. Only one person has been able to measure the full dregs of divine abandonment, the one who knew who God is and what an eternal life of love is. Only one person has drunk the dregs of suffering and descended into hell, the one who did everything for us and for all men.

Now we are not to descend into hell any more, nor should we even want to, in order to ask ourselves there why God has abandoned us. For we do not know what sin truly is. We can only ask its meaning from the one person who has experienced it in all its horror. Judgment took place on the cross and there alone. For those who cling to the cross in faith, judgment is already behind them. Christ also endured the eternal death we all deserved, and sin was buried in the sepulchre with him.

The two-edged nature of divine election is depicted even more clearly in salvation history than it is in creation. The choosing of one is always the nonchoosing of another. Yet, at the same time, the chosen one is chosen for the sake of the other and he vicariously experiences the latter's rejection. In a real sense, the one not chosen is the chosen, and the chosen is the rejected for the latter's sake. The dialectic of Jacob and Esau becomes the dialectic of Church and synagogue, pagan and Jew (see Rom. 9–11). "God has shut up all in unbelief, that he may have mercy upon all" (Rom. 11:32). Both are bound together in solidarity, thanks to Jesus Christ, who is the head of both the chosen and the rejected:

In bearing witness to the truth, the believer bears witness to what God *does will*. Likewise, in bearing witness to a lie, the nonbeliever bears witness just as forcefully to what God *does no will*. Thus both serve the revelation of God's will. . . . The believer is the chosen, bearing witness to the chosen man, Jesus Christ. The godless nonbeliever is the rejected one, bearing witness to the rejected Jesus Christ. Both bear witness to this one person, Jesus Christ, who is the chosen and the rejected one. Both represent him, even as he represented them.[10]

Barth never grew tired of presenting these paired images of rejection and election: Cain and Abel, Esau and Jacob, Saul and David, the two thieves on the cross, Judas and Paul. He tried to show how these images are explained in terms of the Mosaic Law and concludes with a discussion of the relationship between synagogue and Church. Here again we find a sharp contrast between the traditional doctrine of election and Barth's scriptural version.

Between the election of Jesus Christ and the election of the human individual, Barth interjected the election of the people of God (i.e., the Church). Christ is chosen (and rejected) for the sake of the Church, and so are the individual members of the Church. The essential aspect of community cannot be left out of a biblically oriented doctrine of election without destroying the whole edifice. Without the aspect of solidarity, we cannot plumb the nature and depth of Christian election, nor can we do it without the notion of vicarious representation. A religion of provisional solidarity and purely individual fate is not the Christian religion.

The insertion of the Church between Christ and the individual gives unmistakable solidity to the basic thesis of Barth's doctrine of election and makes it seem incontrovertible. It breaks up the narrowly individualistic cast of ecclesial salvation and opens the Church to the world:

The vocation of God's chosen one is precisely this: in his election and his mission, the process of divine reconciliation is integrated into the world and becomes a real happening there. The closed circle of election involving Christ and his community is opened out to the world.[11]

Grace must be understood as mission and apostolate, for that is exactly what it is.

For Barth, the Church is an open reality, a dynamic concept from the very start. For all its visibility, the Church on earth is merely the activity of God's kingdom in this world as part of an overall eschatological movement. Scripture speaks constantly of "the many" for whose benefit God deals with some individual. For as long as the Church is en route, the "many" is a dynamic and open-ended notion:

To speak of an open number of men here instead of all men is not to impute any impotence or limitation to God's salvific design. It is God's will to save all men, as 1 Timothy 2:4 and other scriptural passages clearly point out. . . . The open number of the elect should not be made a *closed* number, as the classical doctrine of predestination tends to do. . . .

On the other hand, it is apparent that we cannot expand the open number of elect in Jesus Christ to include *all* mankind. Why? Because we are dealing with God's personal and free will concerning the world and each human being. . . . God's intention remains his, and we are not permitted to restrict it or expand it as we please.[12]

What is left for us is the mission, the summons to go forth, in which we share the threefold office of Christ. The apostolate is "active participation" and "sharing" in Christ's own mission. Those who are sent must do what he did, because they themselves are prophets, priests, and kings. And because their grace is wholly invested in their mission, they have neither time nor opportunity to worry about their own election, to cut themselves off from those who presumably are not chosen or to formulate a static notion of election.

There is no subjective experience of one's own election, no subjective certainty of salvation; this aspect of Calvinist doctrine must be totally revised.[13] Our only assurance is the objective assurance grounded on faith in the redeemer and on personal witness to him; and the Christian's witness can be offered to himself as well as to others.

Christian existence can never be satisfied with some static conception of divine election and personal predestination. The Christian can only comprehend these realities by living his faith in obedient witness. In this way, he concretizes God's decision and God's judgment, showing them to be the irreversible transition from no to yes, the conquest of chaos by the power of light. Only in doing this will he find security and peace. Only in this way will he avoid the terrible fixation on God's judgment which brought ruin to Lot's wife.

God's decision has already been made in Revelation. To

pretend that it has not been made, to set oneself at the crossroads between bliss and eternal damnation, is to engage in pagan eschatology. We cannot conceive the fate of any individual or the fate of all individuals in that way.

Barth adopted certain useful notions from earlier theological concepts of predestination. He did not totally reject the supralapsarian or the infralapsarian view, although he leans more towards the former, but he does reject the pernicious presuppositions underlying both: (1) that predestination is a stable system; (2) that it involves this delicate balance between eternal bliss and eternal damnation; (3) that it can be regarded as something grounded on an absolute decree—even without Christ.

Barth forbade us to talk about God's free activity as if it were a natural process we could take for granted. We are not permitted to make an optimistic prediction about mankind's eventual restoration, because true Christian witness involves the profession of Christian hope. We cannot presume to stake out the boundaries of redemption or to talk about apocatastasis. Here, as elsewhere, Christian dogmatics must avoid drawing ultimate conclusions from its postulates.

Yet, it is clear from Barth's presentation of the doctrine of election that universal salvation is not only possible but inevitable. The only definitive reality is grace, and any condemnatory judgment has to be merely provisional. Even God's malediction is merely the reverse side of his blessing, and his punishment is ultimately a confirmation of His promise.[14] Even in the ultimate judgment of death, man remains a being created and redeemed in the grace of Christ. While Barth tries to avoid talking about universal redemption, it is clearly built into the very groundwork of his doctrine on creation.

Man exists only because he comes forth from Christ's grace and moves back towards it. His nature is preserved intact despite his sinning only because the grace of Christ preserves it from total wreckage. His sinning, indeed, is the impossible possibility of not believing in his redemption. The real pathos of Christianity is that we keep looking back at evil as if the cross had never happened, instead of looking forward towards eternal life. The Christian community has been doing this for centuries, betraying its faith and misguiding the world, failing to realize that audacious boldness is its normal state, its one possible line of thought.

Here we are at the cornerstone of Barth's whole theology. With it stands or falls the whole doctrine of God and the world, of creation and redemption, of man and divine providence. We must now direct ourselves to this cornerstone and, in so doing, we shall have to examine the whole framework or cast of Barth's thought. We shall see exactly how it differs from Catholic and other Protestant forms of thought.

III · THE OVERALL CAST OF BARTH'S THOUGHT

Barth frequently stressed the inevitable necessity of an overall framework: that is, of some philosophy or general outlook that serves as the basic scheme for one's thought. Even the man who rejects this notion cannot operate without it. Barth's own thought was delineated by a particular cast; it was dominated by a passion for reality and concrete realization. Theological anthropology, for example, must deal with man himself, his potentials, and his real life. It is there that we find out who and what man truly is.

But where is reality? It is there where we find concreteness in all its fullness. We can call it historicity or happening, if we want, or simply action. Being exists for the sake of action, and it is there we shall find an explanation for it. "Whatever man's nature may be, it is oriented around his activity in history; only there can we find an explanation for it."[1]

Here we have the most basic and fundamental difference between Barth and Scholastic thought. Barth looks at everything from the acme of concrete reality; everything else is the raw material for this ultimate stage. The whole realm of nature and its constituent elements, for example, are raw material in Barth's thought. He ponders and probes the meaning of everything from the viewpoint of ultimate act and supremely concrete activity.

Scholasticism seems to start from the same basic position, adopting the Aristotelian premise that act is prior to potency, but when it approaches the relationship between nature and historical realization, it does the exact opposite of what Barth does. It starts from natures and essences and then moves on to determine and describe their concrete activity: *operari sequitur esse*. Barth challenges this axiom and reverses it—*esse sequitur operari*,[2] but he does not mean to dissolve nature into a series of discontinuous happenings; his aim is to start from the high point of concrete realization in order to work back to the potentialities and capabilities disclosed therein.

There was no question in Barth's mind of isolating and abstracting from the reality of the happening itself. The happening itself is unique, and we must respect that fact; but its appearance does presuppose certain potentialities. Barth likes to use the terms "act" and "potency," but we must note what he means by them. For the theologian, the happening of Revelation is the most concrete reality for man; it is "act," and everything natural that precedes and participates in this happening is "potency." The summons of God's Word to man is the highest reality, and we must start out from there rather than from nature. To know the nature of man, we must find out what he looks like in God's eyes rather than trying to draw a line between the natural and the supernatural.

Barth has nothing but scorn for the definition of man as a rational animal. It is a definition that differentiates him from below, rather than telling us what Revelation has to say about man. It suggests that man can take a neutral stance, when in fact he has been enmeshed in the supreme reality of God's Revelation. That is the reality which theology must start with.

God, in the freedom of his love and in his personification as Father, Son, and Holy Spirit, is the supreme reality; and he opens up to us in his Revelation of creation, reconciliation, and redemption. His work, therefore, is absolute fullness embodied in a perfect and unique happening. In one Word we find all words, and in all the words of God we find the one Word. This one Word reveals the whole God, and it lays claim on the whole man. Contrary to what we may think, concrete reality is not our particular patch of time; it is the Word of God which reigns over us at every moment.

Since God's Word is reality at its most concrete, man lives in an atmosphere of perfect concreteness. God's Revelation cannot be subsumed under the general notion of revelation or religion. The faith is not some form (even the highest) of the general concept of belief in God, Israel is not one people among others, the Church is not one community among others, Christ is not the highest form of human religiosity. We can never reach the particular and the distinctive by starting out from the general. For we must start with the particular and try to evaluate everything else (i.e., the general) from there.

Christ proceeds from the Word of God. There he has

his roots and starting point. All the dictates of his nature flow from the freedom of grace. He lives from the fullness of grace, and his life is the concrete embodiment of it. His life is not a matter of whim or personal choice, it is a mission from God. Thus it has nothing to do with "fulfilling one's duty" or "practicing virtue." Christian obedience cannot be concerned with merits and rewards "because it flows from the noblest task allotted to man. It flows from his election and mission, from his participation in Jesus Christ, from the gifts and activity of the Holy Spirit. His reward is to be a Christian and to live accordingly."[3]

The prayer and supplication of the Christian is governed by this elevated position in which he finds himself. He prays that he may be allowed to participate in the conversation between the Father and the Son and in the Son's stance before the Father. Through the grace of Revelation, he has been initiated into the heart of the god-man's mystery:

He stands before God as one who possesses nothing and has no claim to anything, as one who has received everything from God himself. He trusts wholly in God, losing his life so that he might save it. As a beggar with nothing, he is heard by God. In the life of this man, who now voices but one plea, God's power and love wins the day.[4]

The supremely concrete reality of God is also the one unifying center that precedes the multiplicity of words, truths, and commandments. It is the source of man's oneness as well as the source of his fulfillment. The oneness of God, as it is communicated in Revelation, embraces and precedes all created oneness and multiplicity. God's uniqueness is not grasped in our abstract notion of monotheism. He stands above and beyond the antithesis between worldly unity and multiplicity, even as he stands above and beyond our notions of finiteness and infinity.

If we want to grasp the true nature of man, we must never forget that true humanity is allowed to live in the mysterious concreteness of God. It is here that his temporal life and his finiteness find their true features. Seen from below, from the confines of this world, they could be signs of the creature's frailty, abandonment, and separation from God. Seen from above, from the place where God lays hold of them in Jesus Christ, time becomes the medium for the revelation of eternity. The here and now of earthly time becomes the place where God's eternal time is made present and tangible. When the eternal Word becomes present in temporal time, our time is judged and saved, established and transformed. In Jesus Christ, God has time for man and man has time for God; in him, time is established and man is preserved.

Now time is a real participation in eternity, sporadic events are a real participation in the perduring existence of God, and finiteness and death express and allow creaturely surrender to God. In Christ, we can sing the praises of finiteness and find a sound rationale for death. To strip temporality, historicity, and finiteness of the reality which God has revealed, to reduce it to some abstract universal truth, would be to destroy it. We must examine vague universal truths in the light of this particular, concrete truth. To do otherwise is to go astray.

That is why Barth opposed neutrality in all its forms, particularly when it seeks to overlook the distinctive and distinguishing differences between concrete, particular realities. Only the concrete and the particular has color, shape, and substance; only it can give meaning to the general and the universal. We can only explore the universal if we are willing to start out from the particular and learn from it. Authentic existence is always colored in some way, either positively or negatively. To treat it in the abstract, to treat it neutrally, is to miss the mark.

Authentic existence is either exaltation and evaluation (i.e., more than itself), or guilt and lack of God (i.e., less than itself). The justification for existence can only come from God, who transcends and thereby justifies both aspects of the world in the death and resurrection of his Son. Nothing in the nature of Jesus Christ can be viewed neutrally; we cannot abstract from the fact that he is God and the Son of God. In Christ's free will there is no trace of neutrality between good and evil, in his intellect there is no hesitation between God and the world. Nothing in his nature is left untouched by his work; everything in his nature is made concrete through his work. "He is wholly the history of God's deliverance for each and every man. Mankind exists because this history actually takes place. He is this history."[5]

If we seek to understand mankind in terms of this history, we are operating from God's viewpoint. If we do not seek to understand him from there, we shall not grasp true mankind at all. Man is a hearer of the Word, or he is nothing. Man is history, or he is nothing. Man stands within the happening of God's Revelation, or he does not stand at all. In saying this, we do not describe the nature of man; we describe the free, gratuitous activity of God that established the whole realm of nature.[6]

All this is made frighteningly plain in the eschatology of the old Covenant; and it reaches its culmination and fulfillment in the new Covenant. Since the ground of man's nature and existence is a free grace, the thrust and goal of man's nature and existence must also lie outside man himself. It lies in the history that God has entered and oriented towards his own ends. "The ground of man's being is also the goal of his being. Man comes from God and goes into God, and therefore he is for God."[7]

Because Barth lays hold of man at his highest point, he refuses to disregard any part of man's nature or any speck of his temporal possibilities. He is as open to the world as any theologian could be. But he can never abstract from the relationship between God and man in Jesus Christ, as he goes about building his "intensive universalism."[8]

We might describe Barth's thought as an intellectual hourglass, where God and man meet in the center through Jesus Christ. There is no other point of encounter between the top and bottom portions of the glass. And even as the sand must run from top to bottom, so God's Revelation is necessarily the original impulse for the whole train of contact that ensues. In the last analysis, however, everything rests upon that critical point of contact in the center.

IV · THE INTELLECTUAL BACKGROUND

We gain further insight if we look for the roots of Barth's thought in German Idealism, which found its first transcendental form with Kant and its definitive form for Protestant theology with Schleiermacher. Mediating between the two was Fichte's philosophy of identity.

Barth learned much from Schleiermacher. In his formative period, he gained two things from him: (1) an armory of concepts; (2) a forceful intuition into the unity, grandeur, and totality of theology as a scholarly discipline. Schleiermacher was for Barth what Plato was for the thinkers of the Renaissance, what Spinoza was for Herder and Goethe, and what Schopenhauer was for Nietzsche.

Now, of course, this does not tell us anything about the theological merits of Karl Barth's work. Augustine was a Platonist, but so was Giordano Bruno. Nor does it tell us how Barth mixes his colors and fills up his canvas. This merely indicates the materials with which Barth set to work and separates us from those who would accuse him of Modernism (C. van Til) or philosophism (Gogarten, Rilliet, most early critics).

It became clear quite early that Schleiermacher would be the source of division between the dialectical theologians. When Brunner attacked Schleiermacher's mysticism in 1924,[1] his basis in eschatology stood in the foreground; but behind this lay his stress on religious personalism, which gave Brunner his major categories and served as the basis for his attack on the transcendental systematism of the great Idealists. Barth, on the contrary, eagerly laid hold of this systematism. In his eyes, Schleiermacher did something for theology that the great theologians before him (Augustine, Thomas, Melanchthon, Zwingli, Calvin) had not managed to do. He managed to provide "an *amazingly thorough overview* of the scattered limbs of the historical Christian faith."[2]

Later, to be sure, Barth would reject the possibility of strict systematization in theology and opt for open-endedness. But systematization is not the same as the thrust and orientation and style of one's thought, and Barth was "systematic" in the latter sense. His aim was to do correctly what Schleiermacher attempted for the first time in theology: to develop a comprehensive overview of theology. Barth took the only conceptual framework available, that of Schleiermacher, and tried to fill it with an authentic gospel content.

To be sure, Barth did not stay with Schleiermacher alone. He utilized the whole subsequent development of Protestant theology.[3] He showed particular interest in the ideas of Herrmann and followed the modern shift away from pseudodialectics to authentic existential dialectics and the principle of actuality. But the overall design of

Schleiermacher remained to set its mark on the contours of Barth's theology.

The relationship between Schleiermacher's transcendentalism and Barth's actualism may be summarized as follows:

⟨Everything depends upon one point of highest intensity. For Schleiermacher, it is the religious experience of "absolute dependence"; for Barth, it is man's encounter with the Word of God. This critical point is what sets the whole theological train of thought in motion.

⟨The supreme point involves two sides and, at the same time, the fusion of these two sides into oneness. Schleiermacher talks about "contemplation and feeling," which ultimately fuse into a unified awareness of God. Barth stresses the sharp difference between God's Revelation and man's faith, which are ultimately unified in man through the power of the Holy Spirit.

⟨The point of absolute intensity essentially lies beyond the knowledge of human reason, even though it is the ground of all reasoning. It is Kant's transcendental apperception. Fichte's protoground of the ego, Schleiermacher's primeval actuality of religiously toned feeling, Herrmann's personal decision of faith, and Barth's divine gift of faith to man. If our line of thought does not proceed from this absolute point and move back towards it, then it is a meaningless and empty reflection.

⟨Because the underlying reality is beyond the pale of human thought, our thought must necessarily be dialectical. On the one hand, our words and concepts mirror the gap that separates us from unity; this is static dialectics. On the other hand, our line of thought seeks to overcome this chasm and to recapture this unity; this is dynamic dialectics.

❲The point of unity, from which our thinking proceeds, is also the point from which we explain being and concrete objects. For Schleiermacher, the whole world is to be derived from the point of subject-object unity which is God. For Barth, everything is to be explained from the point where God and man unite in Jesus Christ. Both Schleiermacher and Barth regard the Church as the continuation of Christ's activity in the world.

Barth himself noted that there were other affinities between his thought and that of Schleiermacher. He insisted that theology was a helpmate of Christian proclamation and that its importance was only relative. Dogmatics was to be governed by the doctrine on Christ and to be developed as a middle-of-the-road policy between Modernism and Catholicism (as Schleiermacher sought a middle road between pietism and rationalism). Schleiermacher's principle of primeval peace and irenic reconciliation finds echoes in Barth's panegyric to creation, his discussions of the Sabbath as the contemplative moment in which the whole unfurls.

There is also the stress of the necessity of dialectics for expressing a unity that lies beyond human thought. Philosophy, of itself, cannot attain the transcendent point that is the ground of the world. The place of marriage in Barth's scheme and the role of man and woman in his *Dogmatics* echo the tone of Schleiermacher's thought. Barth picks up his concern for realism and stresses it even more, noting that the Church has a mission to the world and that "there should no longer be a distinction between the desert and Jerusalem."[4]

No one should get the wrong impression from these

affinities between Barth and Schleiermacher. It is the general thought framework that is similar, not the thought content. The content of Barth's thought is directly opposed to that of German idealism. Where the German Idealists posit identity at the source point, Barth posits an encounter between two radically opposed beings: the God of grace and sinful, self-centered man. There is no unity of feeling or experience to be found; unity comes only with the act of obedient faith, which itself is a gift from God. The vague pietism of Luther must give way to the pathos and reverence of Calvin.

Just as the source point involves an encounter between contradictory and opposite realities, grace and sin, so the tone of the ensuing dialectic echoes the harshness of this opposition. The soft Idealist pathos of concealed identity is replaced by a dialectic of scandal and of happening. The true is not some universal idea above and beyond history that is merely unfurled and embodied in history. On the contrary, historical reality—specifically, the protohistorical reality of God's Revelation to man in Jesus Christ— is the truth; the universal and the natural must be explained in terms of this historical reality.

At this point it would be well to see how Barth's ideas in this area took shape even before the first edition of *Romans*. An avid pupil of Harnack in his early student days, Barth found his real teacher, Wilhelm Herrmann, at Marburg in 1908. That same year, he was an editorial assistant on the periodical *Christliche Welt*. In 1909, he became an assistant minister in Geneva, serving there until he was named pastor of Safenwil in 1911. His publications during this period (up to 1916) indicate that he was in the mainstream of the prevailing liberal theology, yet hints and outlines of his later thought can also be seen. The conceptual framework was already there, but it was filled in with an altered content later on.

In 1909, Barth wrote an article on modern theology and the work of God's kingdom.[5] It drew some criticism, to which Barth gave a reply.[6] Two things stand out here as products of his recently completed studies: religion as an individual experience and history as a relative reality.

Religion is a strictly individual experience, notes Barth, so there is no universal salvation order or font of Revelation that one person could demonstrate to another. Hence there is no absolute reality in the realm of nature and the spirit. Religion knows only individual values, while history knows only universal facts. Applying historical relativism to theology, we see that our theology is one embodiment of the gospel alongside others. As Schleiermacher pointed out, our thoughts and words are changeable elements that cloak the unchanging reality that lies hidden behind them. The individual latches onto Life and the absolute norm by encountering Jesus in history, but only in this inner experience do we find the normative, the objective, the eternal.[7] In contrast to this experience, preaching and dogma always remain inadequate; they are never our source or our norm. In short, Barth's article seems to stress the nontangible, and nonobjective nature of religious reality.

In a subsequent discussion of history and the Christian faith,[8] Barth tried to inject all the strictness of the Reformation into Schleiermacher's methodology. Faith is the experiencing of God, direct awareness of a life force that lies beyond this world. The individual is elevated to this new life, which necessarily has a social side. It cannot arise or develop without history. And because faith is not bound up with the passing forms of time, past and future now become the perduring present.

The question then is in what way the historical person of Jesus is constitutive for the Christian faith. One line of thought points to a perduring, nonpersonal historical datum as the norm: the canon of scripture, the rule of faith (dogma) as its authentic embodiment, and the episcopal office. The Reformation broke with the last of these principles, but it elevated the first into a formal authority. In such a line of thought, rational assent must always take priority over trust in the act of faith. Now, however, scholarship has laid its hands on the realms of time and space. The process of relativizing historical data cannot be stopped, and we cannot abandon the new stress on the autonomy of consciousness. Critical rationalism is the only source of knowledge we possess.[9]

The other line of thought is that of Paul, which perdured in the authentic thrust of the Reformation and found new support in the Idealism of Schleiermacher. Over against the abstract epistemological considerations of poetic and philosophical idealism, Schleiermacher placed the thinking and acting subject, the living individual who is aware of both himself and God, the person who ties all the strands of reality together. Contemplating the activity of God in faith and obedience, we sense the work of justification and the fact of election that he has effected. But we do not sense it as some abstract or external possibility for man; we sense it as a real, concrete, individual happening of history.

Schleiermacher's "inner experience of pure surrender" now becomes our "experience of God through our relationship to Christ" in faith. Objectivity in religion is to be found only in this affective attachment to Christ, in this act of faith that brings justification; objectivity in theology is only to be found by projecting this attachment into thoughts and words. The circle is completed because "the Christ outside us is the Christ in us. Real, effective history is faith that has taken effect."[10]

To what extent is Christ the source and substance of

Christian faith? It is his person, not his external words or actions, that is the substance of the faith. While his words and deeds may help us to know him, it is his whole inner life that begets this most intimate historical "encounter." We leap from the relativity of history into the Absolute by a sort of Platonic vision of this life, which shines through the documents, and by the simple fact that this life proves to be efficacious. This life, which we view as objectively efficacious, becomes subjectively efficacious through the Christ that God brings about in us.

God does not stand apart from man, nor does he work with us or against us. Faith itself is the work of God; faith itself is justification. Faith, then, is the life of Christ in me: I *become* what he *is*. Setting aside biblicism and synergism, Barth finds the authentic theology of God-consciousness in the realm of the mystics and the pietists. Here all the proper equations fall into place. Here *fiducia cordis* equals *oboedientia spiritus*, here the Christ outside us equals the Christ within us, here history really does equal faith. It was Schleiermacher who used modern thought to give back to us this real heritage of the Reformation.

Finally, there is one more piece to the puzzle. The intermediary between the historical Christ and us is the *living* tradition of those who have truly been awakened to this new life and live it to the full. The divinity of the Holy Spirit, which has been imparted to scripture, must really be associated *with the biblical authors*. It is between them and us, not between their books and us, that a real rapport can take place and serve as the vehicle for coming to know Christ in our heart. And from this relationship, the Spirit spreads to all their descendants, both inside and outside the Church, whose deeds have served as a source of Revelation for their fellow men: not only Augustine,

Luther, and Schleiermacher, but also men like Francis of Assisi, Friedrich von Bodelschwing, and perhaps even Goethe.

In 1913, Barth gave a lecture on faith in a personal God.[11] Using the same categories derived from Schleiermacher, he attempted to tackle the problem of God's personality and to evaluate the opinions formulated in the history of theology.

The concept of personality lies on the border line between transcendentalism (logics, ethics, esthetics) and psychology. The former hints at the infinite aspect of personality, while the latter relates it to a concrete, historical ego; neither approach alone provides the whole picture. Viewed transcendentally, personality is an unending setting and resetting; it is mental and spiritual openness, endless potency, and activity pointed towards an eternal ideal. Viewed empirically, the finiteness of personality is a situation that is inseparable from personality.

Applying this to God, Barth warns us to proceed cautiously. God indeed is an infinite Spirit, but we would be foolish to think that we can divest personality of its finite connotations by a decree of human reason or use it to express a religious experience. We should avoid the forbidden bounds of pantheism and deism and not use the human cast of personhood as our starting point. The first hints of the analogy of faith break through Barth's suggested approach:

We cannot find in the human personality an analogy to the real content of religious faith in God. . . . A concept of God that results from projecting human self-awareness into the realm of the transcendent cannot latch on to the reality of God or describe it exhaustively. Religion's notion of God cannot be a projection from our side; it can only be the reflection of a fact that has been carried into us. This fact is the *life in God* which is granted to us through our *association with history*. This is the real religious experience; in it we possess God, and because of it we can speak of God.[12]

Moving on from this liberal foundation, Barth explores the nature of the religious experience more deeply. It is shot through with a basic antinomy between the infinite importance of the individual soul and the impersonality of the kingdom of God (for which the individual must offer up his whole life). This dualism, which is the essence of the gospel and of Christ's own life, is the core of religion and the authentic starting point for our concept of God. Both aspects must be preserved.

In these articles, which bear the outward trappings of liberal theology, we find all the basic contours of Barth's later thought.

⟨The starting point is immediacy to God, in which the divine displays no concrete objectivity.

⟨A certain point is designated as actual fact or event, hence historical reality, in contrast to the *a priori* categories of philosophy.

⟨This event is depicted as something effected by God, something which man cannot achieve or even understand. Anthropological structures are rejected.

⟨This event is depicted as reality, and all human realities are merely potential by comparison. They flow from this reality and tend back towards it; apart from this reality, they find no meaning or fulfillment.

⟨Barth attempts to fill the conceptual framework of idealistic philosophy with a content that is Pauline and evangelical.

⟨Barth draws a sharp line between his position and

Catholicism, which is clearly depicted as the opposing viewpoint.

❰[For the first time he sets the analogy of faith (or, the analogy of history) over against the analogy of being.

❰[The motif of religious socialism and comprehensive universalism is found here for the first time. It will crop up again in his *Epistle to the Romans* and find its ultimate formulation in *Church Dogmatics*.

Our examination of these essays seems to confirm and corroborate what we said earlier about the conceptual framework of *Romans* and *Church Dogmatics*. Barth's conscious linking of Paul, Luther, and Schleiermacher, which is evident in the earliest papers, suggests that the differences between the earlier works and the later ones are relatively minor. The stress may shift from one to another in various works, but he always tried to associate Pauline thought, Reformation thought, and the insights of Schleiermacher.

Even as Thomas Aquinas was accused of recasting Revelation in an Aristotelian mold, so Barth would be accused of recasting the biblical message in the mold of German Idealism. Barth himself accused Thomas of philosophism, but insisted that he himself was a theologian. Aware of the criticism leveled against him, Barth repeatedly pointed out that a theologian can only work with concepts and conceptual frameworks. They are only the helpmates of theology, they must be purified for theological work if need be, but they must be used.

We cannot object to the use of Idealistic categories on *a priori* grounds. Revelation was not predestined to one single conceptual framework, even though we may maintain that there is a "perennial philosophy." The Old Testament uses Babylonian and Iranian lines of thought; Paul and John use Hellenistic and Platonic concepts; and as J. Maréchal has shown, the basic intuitions of modern philosophy seem to agree with the Scholastic approach in pointing out the complementary nature of ontological and transcendental modes.

Our last task in exploring the framework of Barth's thought is to see how he uses the conceptual framework of idealistic philosophy in his own theological framework.

V · IDEALISM AND REVELATION

Barth repeatedly stressed that he was not trying to build any system at all, even a theological one; that he was simply trying to trace back everything to the mystery of the God-made-man. He insists on this over and over again,[1] particularly in his treatment of predestination where the danger of systematization was greatest. Let us start there, examining the thrust toward inner systematization in Barth's theology.

1. Systematization Versus Existential Emphasis

The critical point in Barth's thought was the doctrine of predestination. He himself was dazzled by the light that radiated from this doctrine and cast an illuminating glow on everything else. Did any man have the right to probe this protodecision in God's activity of self-revelation, to use it as the key to all God's ways and works? Was it a haughty step for man to take, or was it something permitted and even commanded by the gospel?

To Barth, the answer was clear. In his Revelation, God

is totally open and manifest to the eye of faith. To faith alone is the mystery revealed, and all the shadows are clarified in its light. Barth avoids the charge of gnosticism by clinging to faith and referring everything to it. There is no Revelation available to us outside the realm of faith, and faith is the great happening of encounter between God and man: "knowledge and comprehension of predestination is available only in the closed circuit which runs from the choosing God to chosen man and back to God again."[2]

Faith eliminated the possibility of neutrality, the possibility of contemplating the truth in an abstract, theoretical way. If a person does not stand in subjugation to God's judgment and grace (and only the believer does), he cannot have any knowledge of either or of the great mystery of predestination. The light that this truth disseminates is not a natural light; it is the divine light of Revelation. The existential character of Christian belief and Christian conduct serves as the counterweight to the Revelation of predestination, and it alone enables us to bear the dazzling splendor of this Revelation.

Only the person who truly lives the faith has a claim to this truth; and he has no time to distort it into some abstract, theoretical system. As a believer, he cannot for one moment forget the decisive and judicial character of divine truth. As a theologian, he cannot possibly overlook the existential character of faith and frame it in purely theoretical terms. And insofar as God's decisions are in time, giving time reality and full meaning, the believer cannot possibly abstract from time and regard these decisions in the abstract frame of eternity.

The deeply existential character of Barth's dogmatics is rooted in the supporting categories of actualism. It is actualism alone which justifies the boldness of the Barthian doctrine of predestination. They stand or fall together. If a theology attempted to minimize or eliminate the "happening" character of its topic in favor of an abstract treatment, it would have lost the right to enjoy the illumination of that central light.

In the last analysis, the doctrine of predestination is a *summons to the individual reader*. The promise of election is not a theory about some object; it is an appeal to each individual subject. It is doctrine, in the original sense of that word: instruction that calls for attention and faith on the part of the listener. The listener's reaction—acceptance or nonacceptance, faith or unbelief—determines in what way the truth is spoken to him. It is the truth in any case, telling him that he too is chosen by God. He must decide whether he will live this election as a chosen man or as a rejected man.[3]

Now we can see why ethics is an intrinsic part of dogmatics in Barth's theology. It is not a "practical corollary"; it is the decisive finale of our encounter with truth, and without it dogmatics would not be the full and complete presentation of Revelation. With ethics included, dogmatics moves out beyond the realm of theory; but it still remains nothing more and nothing less than a signpost and ordered pattern for the proclamation of God's Word, which must encounter the individual in the community. It cannot attempt to be a self-sufficient epistemological system on the one hand, nor can it say less than the Word of God says in reality.

The Word of God itself speaks "unsystematically" in this matter. It speaks in a two-sided way that does not close the chasm between the mystery that is revealed and the consequent judgment–happening character of the truth. If the theologian attempts to let one side disappear for the sake of the other, then he is making a decision that is not justified by the Word of God itself.

The theologian must also be aware of this fact when he is engaged in exegesis. If he chooses to shun Barth's decision about dogmatics, then he too has made a decision that will have serious repercussions on his interpretation of Revelation as a whole. He will have chosen a specific and limited conceptual framework and system. He will have chosen a different starting point than the one of scripture, so that the words of scripture will not be able to radiate their full inner light.

Barth realized that this is the very crux of theological exposition. How can theology speak truly of God's victory and lordship? It can do so by acknowledging the fact that "we manage to do this only by clearly depicting the necessarily broken and fractured nature of theological thought and life."[4] All theology is the theology of men "on the road," and it can never satisfy man's quest for completeness of expression. It can never be a perfect system, providing a full treatment of its object.

This is all the more true at the point where sin enters the picture, disrupting the relationship between God and man and thus precluding all possibility of perfect theological systematization. The continuity of God's truth, insofar as it is meant to make its way into the world, is broken up by sin. This moment of disruption must be reflected and depicted in our theology, *along with the whole history* of God's dealings with his creatures. Theology is a narrative account of this history.

Theology cannot abstract from history. It cannot promise any light save the light that Revelation lends from its perduring tieup with history. Theology must maintain the stress between the total reality of victory and the total gravity of the decision to be made, faithfully following what Revelation does. Insofar as it does this, it really can clarify and shed light on the two aspects of Revelation.

Maintaining this delicate balance between essentialism and existentialism, theology in its own way can depict the dimensions of God's Word faithfully.

Knowing that this was Barth's attitude, we will not be so quick to talk about "philosophical" a priorism in his theology. If there is an element of constraint about the point in question, this does not mean that it is not a genuine theological constraint. Since the freedom of the creature to choose and make a decision is not jeopardized, since the protodecision of God is a free one that is not essentially tied to his nature (though it tells us a lot about it), then there is no solid objection against the theological character of this constraint.

We might also note that Barth displayed a certain amount of courage here. He was willing to play his cards out in the open and to face all the difficulties as they arise. Many people, especially in the Lutheran camp, have criticized him for overstepping the limits of theology, but theology has no limits save those of Revelation itself.

2. Word and Faith

The charge of philosophism has also been leveled at another point that Barth borrowed from Schleiermacher. It is Schleiermacher's "feeling of absolute dependence," which Barth recast in terms of the encounter between God's Word and faith. The fact of borrowing can hardly be denied, but the real question is whether Barth was justified in recasting this concept.

In doing so, did he not restore and refurbish a key theme of the Reformation that had been secularized in pietism and philosophically systematized by Kant and Fichte? Can the core of Revelation be depicted as anything else but the interrelation of the spoken Word and the accepting faith?

And if this closed circuit is correct, do we not have a sound basis for criticizing Catholicism, which has interrupted the circuit with preambles and the analogy of being? Must not Catholicism acknowledge this basic fact of complete inter-relationship before proceeding to fashion its dogmatics?

We cannot accuse Barth of philosophism because he elevated this circuit into a basic truth and made it the starting point for any and all Christian dogmatics. The real question is whether he put the correct content into this frame of reference and described it properly.

Barth's circuit was not fashioned purely from transcendentalism or Idealism. Traces of both may well be found in his work, but his real intention is clear. He wanted to provide a concrete, objective doctrine of God. He did not want to reduce God merely to an extension of the subject (Idealism). He wanted to depict God as a real *Thou* over against the whole concrete world. That is why he turned to analogy, utilizing it to establish a sober relationship between God and creation, between the Absolute and the relative.

The primary circuit of Word and faith is inscribed in this sober relationship. In the first section of *Church Dogmatics*, he rejected and corrects his earlier view. The hearing human being is necessarily included in the notion of God's Word, but only *de facto* not *de jure*. Man is not necessarily included, as Schleiermacher's God is in the feeling of absolute dependence.[5]

With this *de facto*, Barth rules out all notions of making God immanent in human faith and of making human faith immanent in the free Revelation of God. The closed circle of Idealism has been surmounted. Self-introspection cannot be used to plumb the depths of God's will nor even to discover what man truly is.[6] At the innermost core of the *I* lies its relationship to a *Thou:* "the ego is not pure and absolute, not self-sufficient. But this means that it is not empty either. It is not an abyss."[7] The ego is ego in its interaction with another thou in this world; and this is what is presupposed in the fact that it finds life in an encounter with God.

Barth's doctrine of concursus resists all talk about God's power being infused into creatures, and it rejects the Idealist notion of the "moment as eternity." The basic relationship established by the Word of God is one of free interaction. That also happens to be the significance of the Sabbath. God steps back from his activity of creation; room is left for contemplation and freely chosen contact.[8] The basic phenomenon is not creation in and through the ego, as the Idealists would have it; it is the confrontation of two poles that strikes our consciousness through faith.

The most critical flaw in Schleiermacher's "feeling of absolute dependence" is that it is hopelessly abstract at the point where it should be most concrete. It depicts God as total power, and man as total dependence. At the core of this relationship, Christ is lacking. The same criticism can be made against Kant's categorical imperative. God's Word is indeed categorical, but its content is concreteness itself. The emptiness of Kant's categorical imperative proves that we are not dealing with the real God and real man. There can be no real vis-à-vis and no notion of real sin in the Kantian category, for the nature and being of the two partners has been forgotten.

Man's judgment by God is possible and meaningful only if we presuppose "that man is a member of God's household, a member of his people, a citizen of his kingdom."[9] Only in Jesus Christ is he that. It is of this relationship, and only this relationship, that theology speaks. It speaks from the relationship of faith, which, through the Incarnation of the Word of God, is simultaneously prayer, obedience, and grace. Schleiermacher merely offers us an intellectual framework to express this specific content.

3. Dialectics and Divine Judgment

In his *Epistle to the Romans*, Barth utilized the dialectics of German Idealist philosophy and managed to dissolve any authentic relationship between God and the creature. He resolved everything into God, providing an approach that was strongly actualistic and eschatological. The stress on philosophical dialectics as the exclusive method of theology was overcome when Barth turned to analogy. He found the compatibility of the divine and the human in Jesus Christ; and through him, he found this same compatibility in Christians, all human beings, and the whole of creation. The problem of dialectics in Barth's theology seemed to have been resolved.

It was not. When the problem of philosophical dialectics had disappeared, a purely theological dialectics cropped up at the very center of Barth's thought. It served to characterize the nature and operation of divine judgment and punishment, of God's yes and no.

To clearly distinguish the vast difference between philosophical dialectics and theological dialectics, we must recall what Barth had to say in his treatment of creation. The contrast in creation between light and shadow, power and weakness, perfection and imperfection, is not a dialectical one. It is altogether fitting and right. It may cast a shadow over the creature's existence, but it is not opposed to God's will in creating; on the contrary, it is the embodiment of His creative will. And the nasty thing about "vanity" (Barth's term for evil) is that it utilizes this goodly contrast in order to corrupt and defame creation.

We can indeed say that the creature, because of its

shadow side, has a certain affinity to vanity; it is open to temptation. We can even say that the creature, of itself, is no match for evil. God created the world by snatching it from chaos, but he did not erase all its affinities to chaos. Only the power of God can prevent chaos from breaking through. If the world moved away from God and relied solely on its own resources, it would open the door to chaos. And the intrusion of chaotic indifference into the world, as depicted in the bible, is the inevitable consequence of sin.[10]

For Barth, evil was not simply a consequence of creaturely contingency and finiteness. It was primarily that to which God, in his wisdom, has said "no" from all eternity. It is that which God has passed over and rejected and forbidden to his creatures, and this eternal divine no to vanity, which makes it what it is, confirms and corroborates his eternal yes. Through God's yes, the being and truth of creatures takes on substance and reality; in like manner, through God's no, the nonbeing and untruth of evil and vanity takes on substance and reality.

Let no one go off on the wrong track here. Barth is not talking about a philosophical antithesis between being and nothing. He is not presenting an Hegelian dialectics of negation nor a Kierkegaardian warning about the dangers of free will. Barth is talking about a situation that arises from the absolute reality and efficacity of God's free decision. Truth, in this view, is something brought about by God's yes, even as untruth is brought about by God's no. And both are related to one another through the *separation* which God's eternal judgment has effected.

There is no place, in the world or in God, where man can look at good and evil from a neutral standpoint. We cannot say that evil and untruth have a place within the total framework of truth. Evil has no real substance of its own it is the fleeting shadow of substantial truth. At the same time, evil is not nothing. It is something, but all its reality derives from God's no.

From what we have just said, it is obvious that we cannot accuse Barth of Manichaeism in any form. There are not two equally powerful principles at work against each other. There is only the eternal, creative power of God's yes, which also makes evil to be what it is. From God's standpoint, evil is that which should not be. When man opposed God's eternal decree, then he gives being to what should not be and makes the impossible possible.

Sin is the impossible possibility. From all eternity, God chose to be with man in Jesus Christ. Godlessness, therefore, is an ontological impossibility for human existence; yet man can be godless and sinful. Man in the concrete is called to membership in Christ, who is beyond all abstraction. Man in the abstract, apart from Christ, is necessarily a sinner.

The evident contradiction in Barth's definition of evil and sin ("the impossible possibility") must be traced back to God himself. God himself is the only one who can and does take responsibility for this contradiction. When his creation sins and is thereby enmeshed in contradiction, when his predestination casts its shadow over creation and salvation history, then that is something for God to handle and resolve. The resolution comes in Jesus Christ, who is chosen and rejected: chosen, that those enmeshed in vanity may not be cast off forever; rejected, that those enmeshed in vanity may be chosen in his place.

At the very heart of this theological dialectics, Barth uses the most expressive language possible to describe God's role. In the Incarnation, "God declared himself guilty of the contradiction in which man was enmeshed; and he made himself the object of wrathful judgment."[11] God took his creature's misfortune upon himself, so that the creature might be fashioned in his image. Our suffering and distress was his first. Before we experienced the darkness of his absence and the light of his presence, he knew both and separated them. Before death and life confronted us, he was the lord of life and death and bound them together.

He did not do this from a safe distance. In the full majesty of his godhead, he participated in these varied antitheses and experienced their interrelationship. In his eternal compassion, he plunged into these contradictions and became their point of origin. He himself was the first to experience the two sides of existence, and our anguished experience of them cannot compare with his. He went so far as to turn his Son into an object of divine rejection, and we live in the knowledge of that fact.

No philosophical considerations dictate Barth's treatment of evil. He tackles it on theological grounds and describes it in theological terms. He takes it more seriously than a purely human viewpoint could, but no more tragically than God himself does. Thus he arrives at the conclusion that evil is a force superior to man as creature, but inferior to God as creator and redeemer. It is reality, insofar as God's no is not on a par with his yes. For the same reason, the fallen angels cannot be put on a par with God's angels. The devils are "vanity" too; they are real only insofar as they embodiment of God's rejection.

Barth will have nothing to do with the philosophers of negation and nothingness. He expounds the reality of theological vanity and nothingness on an entirely different plane. For him, it is based on the creative power of God's yes and no, on the "dialectics" of divine judgment. Thus his theological concept of truth has nothing to do with the capabilities of a neutral human reason; it is related to man's capacity for divine truth, which can be called faith or prayer or obedience.

4. The Concrete and History

As we have seen, Barth's theological dialectics only begin where the dialectics of Idealistic philosophy leave off. In like manner, Barth's concept of the concrete is wholly different from that of Idealist philosophy. Hegel managed to demonstrate that the seemingly concrete world of history and sense experience was really abstract, while the seemingly abstract idea was the real concrete. Kierkegaard challenged this notion, championing the indissoluble concreteness of the ego in its relationship to God and the historically concrete Jesus Christ; but even Kierkegaard remained bound to Hegel's categories.

The dialectics of Idealist philosophy could only be surmounted by establishing that the indissoluble concrete of history is also the fullness of time: in other words, by establishing that the fullness presented by God in Jesus Christ is also the fullness of created time itself. It does not suffice to merely assert that this fullness is at hand in Jesus Christ and must be believed. Faith, in its quest for understanding, must start from there and develop the full implications of this principle.

This is the task of dogmatics. In carrying it out, dogmatics must show that Christ's fullness is not merely the inner fullness of God or the fullness of creation, but that it is rather the fullness of God revealed in a worldly cast and the fullness of creation within the framework of divine Revelation. It must also show that this fullness is the supremely concrete reality, which establishes the world for God and God for the world.

The concept of the concrete in theology, then, cannot rest on any philosophy of history or of the Idea. Still, we can hear altered echoes of Hegel in these words of Barth·

The truly individual and concrete is not our brief moment in time, as we might be inclined to imagine. Nor does the multiplicity and diversity of creation and its history account for authentic multiplicity. It is because the one unique God himself is multiple and diverse that we find authentic multiplicity in his creation. . . .

In like manner, it is not our human individuality in space and time that represents the original and authentic individuality. Our individuality is the created reflection of God's living individuality, personality, and freedom. His contingent activity and gratuitous grace would still be part of his eternal nature, even if we did not exist.[12]

This divine prototype of our concreteness and historicity becomes tangible and concrete only in the temporal historicity of Jesus Christ. Thus any philosophy that bypasses this event is bound to end up with a radically different concept of God. Moreover, our natural historicity somehow serves as a presupposition for the Incarnation of Christ. There is no reciprocal causality here, to be sure, no mutual interaction of the natural and supernatural, for the natural derives from, and tends back to, the concrete Christ. In him we can see everything that is to be seen.

Christ is the real ground of creation, insofar as he is prepared from all eternity to become man, to humble himself, to die on the cross, and to descend into hell. Even as he is the ground of being, so he is also the ground of moral law. Christ himself is the concrete law of God, and the imitation of Christ is the natural corollary of existence in Christ. Here we are not dealing with some abstract ethical dictate as yet unfulfilled. We are dealing with a reality already achieved in Jesus Christ. The law of God is a personal law, radically different from all other laws, urging obedience to this one person. It is concreteness personified.

Herein lies the radical difference between the old Covenant and the new. The former complains loudly about man's infidelity to God; the latter gently reminds man of the concrete ideal to be imitated. God's grace is now meant to insure that man's actions will allow God's activity to take effect. It is meant to protect and enhance our limited freedom, to remove fear and anxiety, to let us move under the assurance of Christ's accomplished fidelity.

Now we can understand and appreciate what Barth has to say about *Christian freedom*, for it is based on the example of Christ himself. Christ, as a man, is a man for the Father. In him, freedom is not so much an exercise of free choice as an act of humble resignation and obedience. The Son, as God, surrendered himself from all eternity; and therein lies the inception of all creaturely freedom. It is God's decision that accounts for the possibility and the reality of human choice.[13]

Freedom is a great paradox. God elects man, thereby making him a real entity *vis-à-vis* himself; man can then choose God and, as a chosen man, deserve God's protection and support. The act of willing implies obeying, but the act of obeying also implies willing and choosing. This willing, to be sure, must never be separated from the concrete reality of obedience; nor can the concrete reality of obedience ever be explained by a neutral act of choosing or not choosing. God's transcendent choice is reflected in human nature's *willing* choice to live as one man among other men, as an I among Thou. This willingness is the real mystery of human nature, and it derives its reality from the free will of God. Human freedom takes on reality from the free activity of God.

If we do not see God's activity as the ground of real human freedom, we cannot help but misconstrue the latter. To talk about the free will of sinful man is to go off on the wrong track entirely. Free will, as a real attribute of human nature, must be associated with the freedom of God the creator. If man can choose wrongly, we must call this "sin" not "freedom."[14]

Barth's notion of freedom is clearly Augustinian. True human freedom arises in the liberating spontaneity of divine grace. Human and divine freedom encounter each other in the supremely concrete reality of God's Word, Jesus Christ, and prayer is the only word to describe it. The prayer of Jesus Christ himself is the best description of this encounter. He, in his person and his saving deeds and his prayer, is the eternal will of the Father.[15] In the prayer of God's Word, we come to know God and his truth, we achieve freedom, and we get beyond the vague mysticism of Schleiermacher and the Idealists. Prayer is freedom in action, the real concrete encounter between God and man, and the source of all historicity.

It hardly seems necessary to point out that Barth does not hesitate to ascribe freedom to man and to human nature. We may even call it "freedom of choice" if we wish, so long as we remember that the freedom comes from God and that the choice is to be righteousness. Since such a possibility is real for man, we cannot say that man can lose this freedom through sin or that human nature as such is evil. Man can be evil only because his nature is good. In all his acts of willing, he uses his free will only when he wills the One. He can opt for his craving for God and against his godless cravings.

This is the possibility to which God appeals when he summons man and man has an "immanent, natural" freedom that is oriented towards this ultimate freedom. His immanent freedom is his ability to step back from himself and take a cold look at his desires and perceptions. As a soul-animated body, he can make himself an object of personal scrutiny. In the last analysis, however, this immanent freedom depends on man's freedom to hear and obey God.[16]

If we try to generalize Barth's position and to express it in more abstract terms, we can say a few things. There is such a thing as being, and such a thing as nature; but both become valid and authentic only at the point of supreme reality. At their core, being and nature are happenings in history, so they are not being and nature in the typical sense. Reality is more happening than being, and the being of God is one with his creative willing. In Barth's *Epistle to the Romans*, the notion of the eternal "image-concept" was so absolute that any and every real form inherent in being and nature was ruled out. Now, in *Church Dogmatics*, the notion of "concept" gives reality to being and nature and everything else; they are necessarily included within it, but in a very distinctive way. In Christ, who is the supreme happening, the being and nature and continuity of all creation finds its origin, support, and guarantee.

The concept of being has its place after all, because it reveals the acute preeminence of the concept of actuality. The notion of abstraction is also unavoidable, because it sheds light on the concrete. There must be a place where we can look out upon the singular concrete and that place can only be the realm of abstraction. We must talk about abstract potentials if we are to recognize concrete actualities.

Barth realized full well that intellectual activity involves abstraction. The notion of image is complemented by the notion of being, and the notion of action is complemented by the notion of contemplation. Barth's whole attempt to describe the concrete in *Church Dogmatics* indicates that he accords a positive role to the notion of abstraction.

VI · RESERVATIONS AND UNANSWERED QUESTIONS

Looking back, we can say that Barth's theology maintains its identity, even if it does use Idealist concepts and categories. These categories lend power and terseness to his treatment, but Barth realizes that no one style of thought can claim sole supremacy in theology. The extent to which it is used depends upon the needs of the theology itself, and Barth did not hesitate to utilize other conceptual categories as well.

The god-man relationship can be depicted in Platonic or Aristotelian terms. It is for a given theology to decide which is more useful, and how it shall be used. Use itself is not to be condemned; how it is used is the important thing. Theology cannot even pass direct judgment on the analogy; it can only decide whether this formula is capable of expressing a given datum of Revelation.

By the same token, we cannot pass direct judgment on the merits of transcendental philosophy. We can only evaluate Barth's attempt to express the data of Revelation with these Idealistic categories, to bring out the priority of Christ over creation and the fall of man. In both cases, we must ask whether Barth's philosopical schema is open-ended enough to preserve the full freedom of Revelation. Is the mystery preserved or is it "cleared up" in terms of human concepts? Is its full freedom and openness constricted into a system that precludes its full unfolding?

If a conceptual system produces constraints at one point, it will necessarily produce constraints at other points. If

Barth's doctrine of predestination is subject to constraints, this will have repercussions on his Christology and his ecclesiology. If we stipulate certain premises, we are left with certain conclusions. The question, then, is whether Barth's use of Idealist categories led him to present Revelation in a one-sided and dubious way. We would have three reservations to make about his treatment.

1. Despite Barth's open-ended use of transcendental categories, a tendency towards constraint and systematization is clearly evident. Indeed it is so closely tied up with the whole framework of *Church Dogmatics* that it affects every joint and limb in it. We are talking here about a nuance that colors the whole presentation rather than a basic flaw. In Catholic terms, we could call it an overstatement or an exaggeration.

A Christological emphasis is fully in accord with the biblical testimony. It is quite a big step, nonetheless, from such emphasis to Barth's wholly Christological orientation. Even if Christ comes first, this does not necessarily mean that the whole work of creation must be stuffed into a Christological mold. This straitened schematization becomes clear when we see that Barth has not left enough breathing room between creation and Covenant; the presupposed part of the equation, with its relative but real subsistence, does not get its due.

Christ may well provide the ultimate meaning of creation. It may well be true that we cannot say the last word about the creature until we have considered Christ, and this ultimate meaning may well be the ontological foundation for every provisional and preliminary meaning. But it is no less true that this very relationship obliges us to scrupulously preserve all the relative meanings and to avoid any appearance of *deducing* them from the ultimate meaning.

In his treatment of creation, Barth does take great pains to develop the distinctive traits of creation as a sphere of its own, but every time he tries to present the nature of some anthropological or cosmological function, he ends up by elucidating it from its Christological roots. Now one might object that Barth is presenting theology not philosophy, that he is trying to describe created nature from the viewpoint of Revelation. But Revelation itself does not presuppose creation in such a way that it equates creation with the act of Revelation. In giving its ultimate sense to creation, Revelation does not allow the original sense of creation to fade away. It does not put everything in such a tight, systematic, Christological frame that all other Christological explanations are excluded. It does not display the tight systematization of Barth's presentation.

Despite his open-ended tendencies, Barth seems to force his data into an *a priori framework*. The Catholic reader senses a trace of unsettling "Protestant" tendencies: anxiety to vindicate one's own position at any price; readiness to equate a human presentation with divine Revelation itself; presenting a partial, incomplete picture as the whole. Where such tendencies are at work, the relationship between philosophy and theology remains obscure in the last analysis.

While his position may allow for a discipline that studies nature itself, it leaves no room for this discipline to operate. It speaks of Christ as the authentic human being in such a way that all other human beings seem to be mere epiphenomena. Since the human race is not Christ, man and *his theology are incapable of measuring the distance between Christ and mankind;* he cannot measure the difference between Christ's "being for others" and mankind's "being with others." *To take this measurement, theology needs the direct or indirect help of philosophy.*

The same objection holds true for Barth's detailed description of human nature itself. His approach leaves us with a trace of uneasiness. It can easily turn down the wrong track, as some critics have pointed out and as he readily admitted.[1] The basic problem, then, is the legitimate independence of the natural order and its related philosophy.

2. Another feature of Barth's treatment is closely related to the one discussed above. We find a tendency (no more, no less) to overstep the legitimate limits and competence of theology, to give in to oversystematization. Here an inner affinity between Protestantism and metaphysics becomes clear. Barth's tight Christological mold is systematization because it closes the door on possibilities that are really open to God.

If Christ is the first in nature, then he is also the first in the realm of sin. His cross is not the result of sin, but of his own eternal decision to empty himself. All sin is framed within this decision of his, and it becomes impossible to pass an ultimate judgment on the sinner. God's grace works "absolutely and irresistibly,"[2] and the Christian is led joyfully towards the Last Judgment.

Is this what the bible tells us, or are we actually peeking *behind* the dark glass we are supposed to look through? Does this not clarify the mystery to such an extent that no mystery remains? Does it not turn the "merciful God" of the bible into the "innocuous father" of Harnack?

Admittedly it is extremely difficult to give theological expression to the bible's two-edged message of judgment and grace without doing injustice to one aspect or the other. Admittedly Barth takes great pains here not to reduce the mystery to metaphysics, but insofar as he constructs certain presuppositions on the basis of the reality of divine judgment and maintains them as the *necessary background* for all later comments on the god-man relationship,[3] he oversteps the limits and falls into metaphysical abstraction—the very accusation he brought against Thomas Aquinas and Schleiermacher.

Let us be very clear on this point. Our accusation here is much more reserved than that of Barth's early critics. We are expressing uneasiness about a *metaphysical tendency* or *thrust* in his work, not about a full-blown metaphysical structuring, nor would we say that this tendency represents Barth's innermost intention and purpose.

A concrete issue may clarify this point. Barth's portrait of the creature in *Church Dogmatics* retains some of the dialectical ambiguity that is found in his *Epistle to the Romans*. The creature is a reality grounded on God and safeguarded by him; of itself, it is not at all demonic nor chaotic nor oriented towards evil and darkness. Barth protested loudly against the detractors of creation. Yet, for all that, he could not help but depict creation, in its creatureliness, as subject to chaos. God alone is the master of chaos, and only he can save the creature from vanity and chaos.

Here we have an open concession to his earlier dialectic picture of the world. Why? Because Barth's ultimate aim was to depict the victory of God in his creation. He stressed the dark aspects in order to highlight this victory, and this same tendency is to be found elsewhere in his work.

3. The most serious doubts concern Barth's understanding of the Church as the realm in which God's all-supporting Word rings out. Our first question is simply this: Does this realm, as a concrete reality in the world, suffice to bear witness to the presence of Revelation and faith in it?

We have already seen how Barth opened this realm to the world. The presuppositions mentioned above were largely responsible for this step. If the essential substance of the

Church is, at the same time, the foundation of creation, then the Church must be a pretty temporary and provisional thing. She is openly what the world always is in a hidden way. Barth was forced to stress the relativity of the Church, up to the point where it would simply fade into the world itself; at the same time he proceeded cautiously on this score, lest the necessity of the Church no longer be apparent.

As we have seen, Barth had great difficulty in demonstrating how it is possible for man not to have faith. Man can say "no" to God, but his no can never be strong enough to challenge or abolish God's yes to man. Christ has triumphed for all and over all, and men are what they are through him. Faith is the ultimate ground of man's reason and will and of his whole nature. Through Christ, every man is a hearer of the Word,[4] so the unbelief of the sinner can be nothing but a vain, already quashed rebellion against the truth of God within him.

If this be true, what are we to say about Barth's assertion that only in the realm of the Church "is God known and accepted in faith"?[5] Is it a counterassertion made purely for the sake of dialectical balance? On the basis of Barth's doctrine of predestination alone, it seems to be a very questionable statement, and when he labels man's religion and mysticism as atheism, his position seems quite forced.

On the other hand, we also run into problems if we stress the other side of his dialectical coin. If we emphasize the intangibility of faith (though it really is there), then its concrete side and that of the visible Church become nothing more than a purely superficial representation. Here we see Barth's universalist and anti-institutional tendency at work. Here is the root of his antipathy to National Socialism and to the Catholic Church. Barth must say "no" to both because both, on different levels, make absolute, perduring, *institutional* claims on man's mind and spirit; only in the name of Christ himself can such claims be made.

Barth's theology poses these problematical questions for Catholicism. Is the *tendency* noted in points 1 and 2 merely that, and therefore correctable, so that point 3 is not a necessary conclusion? Or are we dealing with metaphysical categories in points 1 and 2 that lead to the conclusion of point 3? Put even more pointedly: Are the first two points formulated for the sake of the third, that is, for the sake of polemics against Roman Catholicism? Or does the Christological emphasis represent the real core of this theology, thus ruling out metaphysical systematization and providing a sound basis for interdenominational dialogue and agreement?

Before we try to answer these questions, we ought to see what is the thrust and shape of Catholic thought on the same basic issues. Is it one unified line of thought? Is there such a thing as a Catholic conceptual framework?

PART FOUR

Catholic Perspectives

I · THE VARIETIES OF CATHOLIC THOUGHT

Karl Barth once noted that there can be no such thing as the "essence" of Christianity or of Catholicism. God's Revelation is as mysterious and inexhaustible as God himself. If man wants to comprehend it and put it into some order, his understanding will be taxed to the limit. It is something he must do, however, and therefore it is something he can do.

Revelation also taxes the noblest fruit of man's understanding, philosophy. It forces philosophy to place its conclusions in the service of this process of understanding. This task, too, is feasible, and it is carried out by the Church from age to age. Insofar as the concept of reason rules out relativism in the matter of truth, insofar as truth must always remain true, there must be some such thing as a "perennial philosophy." This form of human truth, growing and developing through time, would be capable of serving as a vehicle for Revelation.

Truth is too profuse, however, to be wholly contained

within any finite concept, and mankind includes a wide variety of individuals, cultures, and historical epochs. Like beauty, truth can be expressed in a wide variety of forms and styles. The interesting thing is that the most individualistic and personal styles are also the most felicitous and universally valid ways of expressing truth and beauty. Through the encounter of differing individual styles, new aspects of truth and beauty come to light. The Roman architectural style, for all its distinctiveness, is inconceivable apart from the Greek. Romanesque presupposes both, and the Gothic style presupposes all three.

The same holds true in the realm of philosophy and thought. What would Aristotle be without Plato? What would the Stoics be without both? Thought systems are open to each other. It is not a matter of piling one atop the other, but of correlating the valid elements of other systems into one's own ordered framework, into a new philosophical form.

Thomas Aquinas constructed a form of thought that was capable of leaving room for past and future thought. It would be strong enough to incorporate new ideas, fertile enough to be transformed into something new. Now if a sound philosophical system should be capable of preserving the individuality of various thought styles and utilizing them in its own framework, without sacrificing the truth, then we have a right to expect the same thing of theologians.

The object of theology surpasses the limits of any individual thought style, but it needs all these styles to express its full richness. It is not that the content of Revelation is irrational or that it can only be viewed as a series of disparate and conflicting doctrines, but insofar as it is the divine Logos himself, it needs all the varied *logoi* of men to give expression to its inexhaustible content. It needs the abstract and general approach, even as it needs the concrete, individual approach. Theology must work from below, where all human truths are taken in and used by the Church, and from above, where God's Logos encounters human words in this world and brings them back to the Father. For this reason, Catholic theology cannot be confined to one single thought framework. In claiming to preserve the totality of Revelation as the deposit of faith, the Catholic Church can never commit herself to a single, definitive system.[1]

Barth once accused Catholic theology of being dialectical to the core,[2] but his accusation could just as well be a compliment. Catholic theology is dialectical, because human words and concepts can never fully echo God's inexhaustible Word and Wisdom. Heretical thought has a tendency to exclude things, to overlook certain aspects, and to end up as a definitive, apodictic system. Catholic thought remains open, and it tends to keep opening up even more. To those who like finished systems, it is quite likely to appear unsatisfying and formless. Its apparent evanescence and elasticity may seem to contradict the clear definitiveness of dogmatic definitions.

There is no contradiction in this. While a dogmatic definition is definitive and irrevocable, its object remains Revelation rather than the philosophical system from which it borrows terms and concepts. The doctrine of transsubstantiation does not define Aristotle's philosophy of nature, nor does the doctrine of two natures in Christ provide the definitive word on the relationship between nature and person. We must remember that when the Church is engaged in apologetics, she often must immerse herself in the terminology and thought patterns of a given era to make her own position clear. Later generations must know the terminology of that era to understand and evaluate the position taken by the Church. However much Catholic theology may try to bring order and precision into her exposition of Revelation, one cannot attribute something like a philosophical system to her presentation, or talk about the underlying principle of the system. It is not correct to say that the analogy of being is "the ground scheme of Catholic thought and doctrine."[3]

Realizing all this, we can see clearly that it is not a matter of setting Barth's thought framework over against a "Catholic" thought framework. For one thing, Barth himself is a single Protestant theologian; and his view of the dividing line between Protestantism and Catholicism is not shared by other Protestant theologians (e.g., Emil Brunner or Rudolf Bultmann). Barth's assertion that the analogy of being is the crux of Catholic thought represents his own private opinion. It is not shared by Catholic theology nor by his own Protestant colleagues.

Moreover, the dialogue partner of an individual theologian is not a whole Church but another individual theologian, unless that Church feels compelled to pass an official judgment on his teaching. The Church as such cannot possess a hidebound metaphysics. Obedient to Jesus Christ, she tries to be what he wants her to be: the steward of his grace and the proclaimer of his words and works. To carry out this mission, she must preach, teach, and sanctify. On occasion she may have to take a stand on certain ideas and lines of thought, especially if they set limits on her proclamation or block her progress. Every theologian must think with the Church and serve her interests if he wants to join her in the task of giving adequate expression to the message of Revelation.

So now we come to the use of philosophical categories within Catholic theology. Here we find an evident and age-old tension between two types of theology: a more concrete and positive theology focusing on the historical facts of Revelation and its "happening" character versus a more speculative theology that steps back from this happening to survey its rational aspects and the relationship between the individual truths. Patristic thought leans more toward the first type of theology, Scholasticism leans more toward the second type. Yet we find both kinds of thought in every period of Church history. Thomas Aquinas himself operated from the concept of act in both his epistemology and his ontology.

We must also remember that Dante stood alongside Aquinas in the medieval period and that Calderon inhabited the baroque period with Suarez. Both poet-theologians gave supreme and theologically relevant expression to the actualistic and dramatic side of Catholic thought. There is no question of an either-or here. Both types of theology condition each other and overlap to some extent. This follows naturally from the very nature of worldly being and thought. Even more basically, it is tied up with Revelation itself and its two-edged aspects: action and contemplation, faith as action and faith as a viewpoint, obedience, and prayer.

We cannot slough off the second part of each pair as worthless abstraction. For it is an intrinsic dimension of the Revelation event itself, giving it room and distance in which to operate. A theology of actualism cannot do without the contemplative aspect, as we saw in the case of Barth's own theology, nor can a contemplative theology lose sight of the Revelation happening that is its true object.

Here Catholic theology and Protestant theology find themselves enmeshed in the same tension. They are caught between focusing directly on the central happening and meditating on it from a contemplative distance. Indeed, they both must face another question here that is even more basic: Where is the real happening to be found? If it is to be found in the historical realm, then timeless speculation must ever shift to a theology of the kingdom of

God, such as we find in Augustine, in the early Middle Ages, and in the theologians of the eighteenth and early nineteenth century. If, on the other hand, the real happening is to be found outside of concrete events, in contemplative and mystical exploration, then the seemingly abstract musings of the Scholastics and mystics are a more effective way to reach the core of the Revelation happening.

To be sure, Catholic theology has also been accused of being philosophy in disguise. It is a charge often leveled by Protestantism. As early as the days of the Church Fathers, it is claimed, Greek concepts and categories were adopted in such a way that the message of Revelation was falsified. The process reached its culmination when Thomas Aquinas took over Aristotle and removed himself completely from the thought and outlook of the bible itself.

As we have seen, Barth refused to go along with this flat accusation. He maintained that every theology needs philosophical forms, he undertook the same experiment that the Scholastics had, and he saw much merit in the use of certain Greek concepts (e.g., secondary causes, *fusis*). Indeed, there is a certain similarity between Catholic theology and Barthian theology, insofar as the former couched Revelation in the framework of neo-Platonic Hellenism and the latter couched it in the framework of German Idealism. In both, we find a general schema of egress and regress, initiated by Origen, continued by Thomas Aquinas, and echoed in the German Idealists.

This schema of egress and regress dominates Barth's doctrine of predestination, where he tends to go behind the veil and read the creator's hand, but it can also be found at the very beginnings of Catholic theology, when the Alexandrian school set the style and thought patterns for the next thousand years. It is there in the Church Fathers and in Duns Scotus and even in Thomas Aquinas, who had such a high regard for the works of Pseudo-Dionysius.

So the real question for both Protestant and Catholic theology concerns the validity of the egress–regress schema. Is it general enough and empty enough to embrace the Revelation happening without damaging it? Could it perhaps be so suitable that it would clarify the most hidden and mysterious corners of Revelation, the "background" of which Barth speaks?

If the answer is yes, then the general schema of egress and regress would find its *authentic* validity and truth in the particular confines of Christian Revelation. It would not bear witness to a universal natural presentiment of the human race at all. It would indicate that this seemingly natural presentiment actually derives from some proto-Revelation or from the glow of God's Revelation in history. The latter facet is what must be stressed, for the Revelation happening represents God's challenge and summons to the world. Christian theology will avoid the danger of empty categorization and excessive systematization only if it keeps God and his judgment in the foreground of its thought.

II · BARTHIAN THEOLOGY AND THOMISM

At this point, we cannot fail to see a curious and somewhat paradoxical kinship between Thomas Aquinas and Barth. It is most evident in the fact that the doctrines of Trinity and Church do not play a central role in the shaping of their theologies. Both theologians choose to stress the tracts on the one God, creation and elevation, divine conservation and providence, and perhaps ethics and eschatology. At the center is the overall relationship between God and the world, God and man, nature and the supernatural, or creation and Covenant. They both focus on a cosmos that comes from God and points back towards him and on a (Pauline or Johannine) Christ who stands in relationship with this cosmos.

The tracts on the Church and the sacraments are still included, to be sure, because redemption makes them meaningful (more so in Barth than in Thomas), but the main interest of both theologians is in the doctrines mentioned above. They both hope to gain a broad overview of the world and of God's relationship to creation; and their use of different categories cannot obscure this kinship. Some have tried to push their affinity further, seeing a common base in neo-Platonism and a compulsive thrust towards "identity" in both.[1] But the same thrust could be found in any philosopher's presentation, if one were looking for it.

Thomas managed to withstand the temptation to which Origen succumbed: he did not reduce the notion of divine judgment to a shallow schema of *apokatastasis*. This alone demonstrates that every schema is simply an ordering principle for him and Catholic theology; no scheme represents an autonomous, all-pervasive thought framework. We must also remember that Catholic theology had found its essential form long before the problems of "natural" theology became an acute issue (in late Scholasticism). So this particular question, like the analogy of being, could not possibly have provided Catholic theology with its basic structural form. The whole Patristic tradition, right up to the high Middle Ages and St. Thomas himself, conceives the issues within the framework of the one and only *real and supernatural order*: that is, within the framework of the *analogy of faith*. Greek concepts and categories were used merely to express and make explicit this conception.

The issue becomes a bit more complicated when we move from the overall history of Catholic theology to the ordering framework of Aquinas himself and his heirs in neo-Thomism. Here we do find some real contrasts between his thought framework and that of Karl Barth, and this is hardly surprising. If we are engaging in dialogue, we must remember that Thomas Aquinas is not the only Catholic philosopher. The Church's preference for his work is not a canonization of his system, nor does it mean that it is the only valid one in every detail. Our failure to relate various thought systems to each other has often prevented us from understanding past and present ideas.

The most characteristic feature of Thomism is probably its strong emphasis on philosophy as something to be employed *before and within* theology. The indivisibility of this *before* and *within* probably testifies to the historical position of Thomas Aquinas better than anything else could. Behind him lay the world of the Church Fathers —the one, concrete supernatural order where philosophy stood within theology. Ahead of him lay the twofold order (natural *versus* supernatural) of modern times, which found its ultimate formulation in Vatican I (DZ 1799).

Aquinas is the most important representative of a transitional phase in Church thought. Profane philosophy was beginning to break into the Christian empire. Strains of the old unified order (*ordo supernaturalis*) remained, but the profane sciences had begun their victorious march toward autonomy. If we do not realize that Thomas Aquinas was open to this past heritage and this future thrust, we cannot properly appreciate his rightful position in the history of human thought. His stress on *pretheological* philosophy and his clarification of the concepts to be used in theology (see the first questions in the *Summa*) point to the incipient thrust of the natural and philosophical sciences towards autonomy. Eventually they would find their own principles and methodology, and Vatican I would approve this step.

Two points are worth noting about the historical position of Aquinas. First of all, it is a *transitional* position, and it cannot be tied up or explained wholly in terms of what preceded or what would follow. As such, his position serves as a *model* for Catholic theology in general, as we shall see in the next section. Secondly, the position of Aquinas must also be evaluated in terms of the historically irreversible *line of march* into which it fits. It comes from a world view of undifferentiated unity and points towards a world view where differentiation and diversity will dominate; and it is to be explained more in terms of the future thrust than the past framework. The notion that each discipline has its own principles and methodology is part of the authentic spirit of Thomism.

The spirit of Aquinas would lead people to accept the new situation and, in *ever increasing measure*, to safeguard the proper methodology of each discipline. This does not mean that there would be increasing equality and interchangeability between philosophical and theological methodology, but it does mean that the proper task of each would be given increasing respect, thus permitting a more fruitful interaction between them.

What would this mean for theology? It would mean that theology would take greater pains to distinguish between the pretheological (i.e., philosophical) use of concepts and conceptual frameworks and their use within theology itself. The two uses should not be equated. Moreover, there should be no philosophical predetermination that would set a priori limits and strictures on theological inquiry. Theologians would owe a debt of thanks to philosophers for their sober preparation of useful concepts, but they would be free to use them as they saw fit within theology.

What interested Aquinas most was the consideration of the various *tractati*. Yet the three central *tractati* of theology—*de Deo trino, de Christo, de Ecclesia*—would not hold a central structuring place in his theology, even though they structure and dominate all theological thinking. Why?

In accordance with the Aristotelian approach, Thomistic thought operated emphatically from below up. From the world of sense perception and concrete experience it moves, through abstraction, to universal concepts and a demonstration of the principles contained therein. Here again we have a methodology that is predominantly philosophical; its use in theology is limited. Theology concentrates on God, the supremely concrete reality, in whom nothing can be abstracted, and insofar as theology examines the Revelation of this God in the world, its object is historical, concrete, and particular. Aquinas readily admitted this, but he went on to point out that particular realities *"non pertinent ad perfectionem intelligibilium."*[2]

In short, Thomas was not inclined to allow these concrete events to stand as the chief objects of theology.[3] In his *Summa*, they are presented as examples of God's eternal, supratemporal wisdom, examples granted to man by God, and sacred scripture treats primarily of this wisdom. Aquinas dealt mainly with the general, suprahistorical essence (*quidditas*) of things and the formal structure of the universe; the historical and temporal and actualist dimensions recede into the background.

Aquinas's style of thought, with its predilection for induction (from below to above) is clearly in sharp contrast to the exclusively theological approach of Karl Barth. However much Barth felt at home with the *theological* rationality of Anselm, he could not feel at ease with the *philosophical* rationality of Aquinas. We must realize, however, that the antagonism is only relative. Insofar as the Thomistic synthesis pointed toward Vatican I, it could not avoid an encounter with modern Protestant theology. Insofar as it was a transitional system, that encounter is already at hand. We shall explore this point in the next section.

We do well to remember how dearly Catholic theology must pay for schisms and heresies. When Protestantism upheld and propounded the principle of "scripture alone," the Catholic Church was forced to stress the rights of tradition and human reason. She had to defend the other side of the scale and stress the philosophical aspects. When modern agnosticism and fideism denigrated the natural aspects of God's creature, the Catholic Church had to come out vigorously for nature, reason, and the work of creation.

To be sure, the opposition between the two sides never became absolute. If it had, Protestantism would have chosen the better part (scriptural revelation), and Catholicism would not even have preserved the full meaning of creation. In reality, Vatican I presented a total picture of two complementary orders. Yet we still can ask whether the theological stress in Catholicism over the past few hundred years has allowed for a truly fruitful defense of sound methodology and sound theological principles.

The direction of concern here is not the opposition between rational theology (Aquinas) and mystical theology (Bonaventure), between philosophical realism and nominalism, or between ontology and actualism. As we saw in the work of Barth himself, this opposition is not as real and absolute as it might have seemed. The real concern here is the object which Barth hoped to provide through his approach: a theological science of concrete singulars and the absolute Concrete, where happening and doctrine are embodied in the person and activity of Christ.

It may well be that historical nominalism sought this

very goal but failed because it remained on the philosophical plane, thus paving the way for Luther. Today we cannot perpetuate this mistake. Our philosophy must preserve and justify the rights of ontological inquiry, in order to preserve the basic foundation and conceptual panoply of the theological data. Barth's dogmatic work could possibly contribute a great deal to this renewal in Catholic theology, even if his conclusions were not adopted.

III · THE CONCEPT OF NATURE IN CATHOLIC THEOLOGY

1. Transition and Historical Development

Nothing more clearly indicates the transitional place of Thomas Aquinas than his concept of nature. The two-sided character of this concept enables us to grasp the two-sided character of his whole theological synthesis. While this two-sidedness is now outdated to some extent, because it is tied up with a specific point in history, it still has something fundamental to offer us in our dialogue with Barth.

As we saw earlier, Barth gradually moved from a dialectical and unserviceable concept of nature towards an undialectical, exclusively theological concept of nature. Perhaps, in our present discussion of nature within Catholic theology, we can move from a single, undifferentiated concept of nature towards a middle meeting ground, where the concept of nature is differentiated. If we can do this, we shall have created a platform where mutual understanding and agreement may be possible.

The transitional place of Thomas Aquinas is clearly evident in the fact that he attributes only one end, a supernatural one, to the created spirit. Like the Church Fathers, he sees only one indivisible world order in which nature and grace form one unity. Man, as a created being of nature, has but one goal, the supernatural vision of God;[1] and Thomas does not regard this end as a hypothetical one. To be sure, he recognizes a natural end for man, one that would correspond to the immanent structures of man's capabilities, but it is merely the shadow side of the coin within the one supernatural order. It cannot be separated, even *hypothetically*, from the supernatural vision of God.

Theology was not forced to posit such a hypothetical order, to maintain the *possibility* of a natural created order without grace, until Baius tried to make a *de jure* right out of the *de facto* tieup between the natural order and the supernatural order. The Church rejected this position in order to preserve the mystery of grace. Grace is free *vis-à-vis* the natural order, and God does not have to grant it to created nature. Therefor there can be a natural order without grace, so the concept is meaningful.

This conclusion gave birth to "natural theology" in the modern sense of the term, i.e., a theology of nature in the pure state (*natura pura*). A theology of the natural order within the concrete world order, however, is as old as theology itself. The new theology of a hypothetically possible nature was intended to preserve the *supernatural character* of grace and God's freedom in dealing with mankind. The new hypotheses, spawned as a reply to Baius, soon managed to develop into a full system detached from their theological presuppositions.

We cannot form an unfavorable judgment on the meaning and value of these new notions by pointing to their hypothetical character and their late appearance in the history of theology. Any attempt to evaluate them must consider the transitional role of Thomas Aquinas and the ambiguity that has surrounded the concept of nature itself. It has had various meanings in the history of theology, and we must appreciate this before we try to understand the Thomistic concept of nature.[2]

As we all know, the most crucial theses of Baius, Jansen, and Quesnel can be found, almost word for word, in the works of Augustine and the canons of the Council of Orange. The Church was not contradicting herself, however, no more than she did at the Council of Chalcedon when she rejected the notion of "one nature" in Christ which she had approved at Ephesus. For the "one nature" (mia fusis) of Chalcedon did not mean the same thing as the "one nature" of Ephesus.

At Ephesus, one nature in Christ meant that he was one single being, in which God and man were not only morally but physically united. When Eutyches tried to eliminate two natures in Christ by appealing to this unity, the Council of Chalcedon was forced to refine the conceptual material and to distinguish between nature and person in Christ. It proposed that Christ had two natures but was one person, to preserve his reality as God-made-man and to prevent him from being turned into some tertium quid that was neither God nor man.

A similar development took place in the history of dogma between the era of Augustine and the era of Baius. Here the concern was to refine the concept of nature so that one could preserve the reality of a charismatic union between God and man in Adam and every redeemed human being. To appreciate the union brought about by grace, God and creation would have to be kept completely separate in the concept of nature.

Augustine and all the Church Fathers stressed the de facto physical unity of man. Adam was grounded in this unity of being and grace from the first moment of his existence, and this was Adam's "nature" for Augustine. But he and all the Church Fathers realized that this was a de facto synthesis, not a necessary one. Created beings, of their very nature, are real creatures; but they are not, of their very nature, endowed with divine grace and elevated to a higher order.

The Protestant reformers, followed later by Baius and Jansen, fell into the same temptation as the Monophysites had. They tried to see this de facto synthesis as a necessary one. For Baius, it is part of man's essence and nature; he must naturally participate in grace to be an integral man (DZ 1021). Only in the man endowed with grace do we discover what it fully means to be a human being. Only in grace are man's intellect and will capable of performing their proper, natural functions. The lack of grace (either in the hypothetical state of pure nature or through a sinful fall from God) does not simply weaken human nature; it essentially destroys it. Sin ruins human nature, robbing it of its total meaning. Man is a person only through grace. This view, intent upon preserving the deepest intimacy between God and man and man's orientation towards God, transformed grace into an essential ingredient of nature.

In the hands of Protestant thinkers, therefore, the concept of nature is used dialectically. For Calvin, nature can mean the pristine creation or human nature as it really is. "Here the ambiguity of the concept of nature reaches its high point. It can be something positive or something negative. Calvin can say that sin is unnatural or that it is the epitome of human nature."[3]

If we are to have a solid concept here, we cannot allow this ambiguity to persist. The concept of nature cannot include grace at one point and exclude it at another point. When Catholic theology fashioned a theological concept of nature that did not include grace as an integral part of human nature, she was reacting against the attempt to naturalize grace; her sole purpose was to preserve the purity of the concept of grace. Faithful to the spirit of Augustine and the Church Fathers, she brought more precision into their terminology.

As the Council of Chalcedon showed, the ultimate union between God and man could only be preserved by establishing a sober conceptual separation between God and creation. Just as Chalcedon definitively clarified the whole Patristic debate over Christology, so the period from Trent to Vatican I developed definitive safeguards for the entire order of grace. The twofold order proclaimed by Vatican I culminates a process that began with the defense of nature against Baius. In this respect, it is identical with the "two natures" (*duo fuseis*) of Chalcedon. Both decisions are irreversible, and no longer problematical.

2. Analogous Use in Philosophy and Theology

There are other problems, however, that were not resolved nor considered by Vatican I. It is clear that if a person is using a concept to express the nature of created reality, it makes a difference whether he is using it philosophically or theologically. Theology can utilize the philosophical concept of nature for her purposes, of course, but she will certainly see things from a different angle than philosophy when she tries to pinpoint the nature of created reality. If this were not true, then there would be some *neutral* conceptual zone between philosophy and theology, a standpoint that overlapped both disciplines; but this is ruled out by the very nature of theology.

The only choice open to us is to recognize a definite element of analogy in our use of the concept of nature. This element represents a middle ground between two possible extremes: (1) a necessarily pantheistic metaphysics that makes no distinction between philosophy and theology; (2) a radically Protestant dialectics in which the concept of nature would actually be split into two different concepts. At Chalcedon, the concept of *fusis* was an analogous concept, embracing both divine and human nature. So too is the concept of nature developed between Trent and Vatican I, embracing as it does both human thought and divine Revelation. It is used *both* as a philosophical concept *and* as a theological concept; in short, it is used *analogously.*

Let us explore this point more thoroughly. The *philosophical concept of nature* was established by Aristotle and worked up by the Stoics and Scholastics. It is both a static and a dynamic-teleological concept, explaining the nature of a being not only in terms of its essence and potentialities but also in terms of its immanent activities and the related environment.[4] The nature of a bird, for example, includes not only the abstract ability to fly but also flying (and air as a presupposition), not only the desire for nourishment and the ability to digest it but also the actual finding and digesting of food (and hence the existence of such food), not only the capacity to procreate but also *de facto* procreation.

Now this does not mean that every single potentiality and tendency must be concretely realized in each individual of the species,[5] but it does mean that the teleological and dynamic scheme of a being, i.e., his nature, is conceivable only in a set of interrelationships with the world that are viewed as *real.* This dynamic-teleological scheme is the authentic core of a being's *nature,* so much so that its nature cannot be grasped apart from this scheme.

In determining the nature of a being, the realm of finality is just as basic an element as the active potentialities that come to realization in that realm. In a full logical construction of a being's nature, we must also include everything that this nature essentially *requires* for its existence. Thus we cannot picture, *even in the realm of logic alone,* a moment when nature could exist as a purely static thing. The traditional Latin textbooks provide us with an accurate philosophical formulation of the Aristotelian concept of nature when they tell us that it includes whatever belongs to it *constitutive, aut consecutive, aut exigitive.*

Baius took off from this starting point, applying this concept to the dynamic unity of Adam's being. The finality of his nature resided in its vocation to be a child of God and to enjoy direct contemplation of him. Therefore this finality included, *consecutive* and *exigitive,* all the ways and means to attain this goal: an intellect and will enlightened by God's grace, the theological virtues of faith, hope, and love; a clear complex of commands and prohibitions; and the like. Should not Adam, of all beings, be the exemplar and prototype of a dynamic-teleological nature?

From the viewpoint of philosophy alone (insofar as it knows nothing about divine Revelation), there seems to be no reason to challenge this viewpoint. Greek philosophy before Chalcedon never thought to distinguish between *fusis* and *hupostasis,* and later philosophy would never have thought to delimit the concept of nature as Catholic *theology* has done since Baius. The new distinctions required could only stem from new theological insight.

The new insight cut across the definitions of philosophy, and it was based on faith. It involved the realization that the creature's vocation to the beatific vision, and everything oriented to this goal or existing solely for its sake, could never be explained or interpreted from a purely philosophical, secular viewpoint. They could only be explained on the basis of an insight available to theology: that the vocation to the beatific vision, God's decision to give creatures an intrinsic participation in his own divine life, could in no way be regarded as deducible from the essence or being of a creature. If it could be deduced from the essence of a creature, if we could conceive of a creation to which God *had to* give grace, then it essentially would not be simply a creation.[6] If the beatific vision is made the goal of a creature and his whole nature is ordered towards this goal, we can use the Aristotelian concept of nature to express this fact; but we must never forget that this use can only be analogous.

Most Catholic manuals of dogmatic theology start out from a philosophical concept of nature: "*Naturale est quidquid pertinet ad naturam aut constitutive, aut consecutive, aut exigitive.*"[7] Now aside from the fact that it begs the question, this approach is unsatisfactory here because we are seeking a theological counterpart to the philosophical concept of nature, and no matter how we try, we cannot derive a sound theological concept of nature from this philosophical starting point. Lacking this theological concept of nature, we cannot set off grace and the supernatural order clearly from nature so understood.

At this point some manuals try to formulate a truly theological concept of nature by working from the definition of grace. But because their definition of grace and the supernatural is a negative one, set up in opposition to a *philosophical* concept of nature, their "supernatural realm" contains much that might well belong in a *theological* concept of nature.[8] Even the appeal to "what man has no rightful claim to" does not provide a definition of grace. For in reality only God can claim anything on the basis of creation, and the creature's claims are tied up with God's creative action.[9] It is really God who has a claim on the creature.

The positive definition of grace can only be given through grace itself. God himself must reveal what he is within himself. The creature cannot delimit himself clearly over against this unknown quantity nor can he know exactly what distinguishes grace from himself. Only Revelation can clarify the distinction for us. So we must formulate our theological concept of nature by working darkly from grace: "Nature is that aggregate of things which is *set off from* grace and the supernatural order."[10] Anything that is not truly supernatural is natural.

Now, within theology, the recurring logical defectiveness has lost its dubious character; indeed it clearly reveals the nature of theological concern. "Set off" tells us that, in the real world order, "nature" must be drawn off *a posteriori*, through a process of *subtraction*, from a totality that we are given at the start. We cannot determine *a priori* from below what belongs to the nature of Adam insofar as he is oriented towards the beatific vision.

The philosopher does not know what nature theologically, and his concept of nature certainly is not nature in the theological sense. God's real world order is the *de facto* union of two distinguishable and distinct orders that are not separable in reality. Insofar as the philosopher knows nothing of Revelation and looks out upon a cosmos that is noetically and ontically impregnated with supernatural aspects, he will always be a cryptotheologian in his work as well. This mental outlook will not be the outlook of pure reason but of a mind immersed in the teleology of belief or unbelief.

By contrast, the theologian will study nature as something distinct from grace. He will try to discover those traits in man's concrete being which belong to him by virtue of creation alone. Thus only the theologian can scrutinize and examine the object of a pure philosophy—which does not mean, however, that he can spell it out concretely. In short, reason alone will always be theological thinking to some extent, while faith can do a bit of pure philosophizing.[11]

As *fides quaerens intellectum*, faith can distinguish between the two realms and probe the structure of this complex concrete reality. It will use philosophical concepts in this probe, to be sure, but in a critically altered way. Its use of these concepts is not arbitrary, because its object is creation, whose immanent laws reason seeks to express. Between the philosophical and theological use of the same concepts, we do not find pure disparity but analogy. We encounter a noetic analogy imbedded in the unceasing suspension of nature between its concrete and abstract sense.

Now the created order as a whole cannot be deduced from the order of Revelation, no more than it can be deduced from grace. Grace is something for a nature and in a nature. Thus it presupposes a nature, logically if not chronologically. Human nature exists concretely as an elevated nature imbued with grace, but it is still a human nature. It exists aliter (in another way), but it has not become alter (something else). Herein lies the ontological fundamentum in re for the noetic analogy in the concept of nature.

The two analogies here—in being and in concept—do not coincide neatly with one another. The analogy in our concept cannot be covered adequately by the analogy in its object, otherwise there would be no analogy. The analogy in our concept does express a certain objective happening in its object (i.e., grace perfects nature), but it also tells us that no human concept can depict this happening clearly and univocally as God sees it. The mystery remains, because the standpoint of faith does not allow itself to be covered adequately by the standpoint of human reason.

Seen in this light, the typical textbook definition of the supernatural—what does not belong to nature constitutive, consecutive, or exigitive—is itself analogous. "No rightful claim" here is used analogously with reference to God and creatures. As one man has no rightful claim to the full self-disclosure of another man, so analogously creatures have no right to God's self-disclosure in Revelation. Here we have a real analogy, because a real analogy exists between the divine and human subject. It is only an analogy, however, because the divine subject is both nearer to, and farther from, the human subject than any other human thou is.

When we appreciate this fact, we can begin to understand the seemingly paradoxical cast of all the theological texts that predate Baius. On the one hand, they depict a much tighter relationship between human nature and the supernatural than we would dare to do today, i.e., man has a natural desire for the beatific vision. When it comes to talking about the attainment of this goal, on the other hand, they seem to be totally antirationalist. They stress the need for God's free self-disclosure—as ontic grace and noetic Revelation within history. Time and again we can find this paradoxical presentation in the works of Thomas Aquinas.[12]

3. Nature as a Theological Concept

The theological concept of nature is primarily a negative concept that attempts to establish a boundary line. It can only be gained through a process of subtraction, because God's original creation was already supernatural and remained so after the fall of Adam. Even as an abstract structural principle invisibly pervades a concrete building, so the theological concept of nature pervades the concrete world structure without ever being tangible.

Common sense claims to know what created nature is. Yet the more it tries to spell out this nature, the more difficult it becomes to separate it from the realm of grace. Any question we ask about pure created nature turns out to be unanswerable. Some theologians do not hesitate to give answers, but their constructed image of pure nature turns out to be a pale shadow of the real, existing world order, a satirical double image.[13]

In short, the content of the concept *pure nature* cannot be given exact elucidation. Anyone who proposes to present a fully developed picture of *purely natural* traits and relationships from his scrutiny of existing world structures is open to question. For by what right does he dare to view these concrete worldly structures as if they were separated from the transcendent world? The only ultimate end we know is a supernatural one, and we cannot presume that the world would have a definite, self-sufficient ground of fulfillment apart from this end. The freedom of grace *vis-a-vis* nature does not justify this presumption.

The proper approach for theological thought is a different one. It must operate within the complex overall structure and orientation of the real world, which is the *only legitimate object* of theological thought. Recognizing the summons to grace and the reality of grace as a gift already made, theological thought must step back reverently and acknowledge that this grace is totally undeserved, that creation is wholly unworthy to receive it. Theological thought must acknowledge the servant status surrounding creation's relationship to God.

Without going on to describe this servant status of creation, we can say that it basically represents nature as opposed to grace. Nature is represented in that *minimum* which must be evident and present in every possible situation where God might choose to reveal himself to creation; that minimum can be called the *analogy of being*. If there is to be Revelation, it must move from God to a creation, to a creation that does not include the notion of Revelation in and of itself. The nature which is presupposed by grace is *createdness as such*.

This concept of nature may be called the *formal* concept of nature. The minimum is presupposed by grace because the necessity of its presence must take priority over the fact of any and all Revelation. Insofar as Revelation does take place, it sets nature off from itself as the antechamber that is not, of itself, the grace of participation. Insofar as the incomprehensibly free happening of grace does take place, it becomes clear that it is truly gratuitous and does not have to be.

The necessity that we mentioned above is not an absolute one, independent of God's divine decision, for the necessity of nature's presence, like the freedom of grace, depends on God's free decision as to whether there is to be a world or not. If he does decide that there is to be a world, however, this decision must take the form of the analogy of being, which is grounded in the essence of God himself. Created being as such must be nondivine, relative, and dependent, but it also cannot be wholly dissimilar to its creator. If it is a spiritual-intellectual being, both its ontic and its noetic structures must bear some relation to its creator. Its thinking process must be affected somehow by the fact that it was thought up by the creator.

This also tells us that the philosophical necessity, upon which the theological "contingency" rests, is not a ground into which the latter can ultimately be dissolved. Theology is not a superstructure built atop philosophy. The relativity of the philosophical necessity is made clear in the fact that it only becomes fully evident when it is set off (dividitur) from the theological contingency.

Philosophy focuses on this temporal world, which was created for the sake of Revelation. Thus the necessity of the God–creature relationship is supported and caught up in the fact of Revelation, without ever becoming identical with it. The relationship between philosophy and theology is such that we cannot move in either direction (from below to above in philosophy, from above to below in theology) to form a "totally philosophical metaphysics" or a "total theology." The two movements point towards each other, but they can never meet in a total, unifying embrace. This very fact is proof of the difference between them.

Looking at what we have just said, someone might be tempted to explain the analogy of being and the formal concept of nature in an erroneous way. They might be tempted to present nature simply as the point of dissimilarity between God and man, and grace simply as the point of similarity (participation). That would be a dangerous oversimplification, leading us right back to Baius. Creation, by virtue of its nature as creation, is not dissimilar to God; it is, rather, similar to the God who is ever dissimilar.

It is quite right to say, as Barth does, that being *God* and being *creature* are totally dissimilar as such. Insofar as we are focusing on this aspect of the relationship in our formal concept of nature, then the stress is on the dissimilarity. Even here we are already talking about *being* God and *being* creature, however, so we are also talking about the similarity between God and creature. This point becomes plain in theology when we ground the possibility of distance between the creature and God in the distance between the divine persons within the Trinity itself.

Grace, to be sure, does stress the similarity (stemming from a participation in the divine nature). But what it does is allow man to come to know the unknown God; and it operates concretely, not by tearing man from this world and bringing him to God, but by having God descend to this world in a creaturely shape ("the servant of Yahweh") and even in the *forma peccati*, which is radically dissimilar to God.

The theological analogy does not abolish the philosophical analogy, nor does it fulfill it in such a way that it is not a real analogy on the purely philosophical level. In reality, the theological analogy sheds definitive light on what the philosophical analogy is as such: it shows us what similarity can mean (i.e., participation and sonship) and how far the dissimilarity can go (i.e., to God's abandonment of himself).

Yet we are quite right in saying that nature *stresses* the distance between God and man, while grace *stresses* their communion. For grace remains "only" grace and does not turn into nature; this is effected by nature itself (as creature). Nature is also responsible for the fact that the good news of grace appears not only as *love* (what it is in God) but also as law and commandment and fear of the Lord. Fear is not eliminated nor is the distance removed, but now this fear shows up in its authentic form (e.g., in Gethsemane and on the cross) and becomes holy fear.

The theologian will not fail to point out the theological foundation of the distance embodied in the formal concept of nature. All creation is grounded in the Logos, more precisely, in Jesus Christ. The possibility of creation being distant from God derives ultimately from the Son's readiness to empty himself, to stand over against his father in a relationship of obedience and service. The relationship between the necessity of nature's presence and the contingent fact of Revelation becomes plain when we realize that the distance of formal nature is a *real presupposition* for the descent of the Logos to humanity; that, at the same time, on a *higher* plane, the formal concept of nature presupposes the Son's willingness to make this descent.

The formal concept of nature, as we noted, embodies the absolute minimum of content; and it can be summed up in the analogy of being. In using it, the theologian cannot strip it of the ambiguity and two-sidedness it contains, insofar as it has both a philosophical and theological side. If this is true of the theological concept of nature when it has minimal content, it will be even more true when we try to inject content into this concept. In other words, the more we try to inject real elements into this concept, the more we shall seize on elements in the real world that have been affected by the *de facto* ordering of nature towards a supernatural end.

The formal concept of nature tells us that everything touched by grace retains its natural side: grace is always *in* a nature and *for* a nature. At the same time, however, grace is such a radical transformation of nature that no aspect or corner of nature can escape its impact. The realm of sin, which would seem to be the area farthest removed from God, was chosen as *the* site for God's Revelation of grace in Jesus Christ.

What does this mean? It means that nature *de facto* has only one end, a supernatural one. It means that not only its acts but the very seat of these acts (i.e., nature itself) must in fact, be radically transformed and realigned. There is, in fact, no slice of "pure nature" in this world. While the sinner may be denied the life of grace, even his nature is no longer pure nature. A negative relationship to the God of grace is still a real relationship with him.

Adam's loss of grace does not mean that he lost the order of grace (i.e., the supernatural vocation to grace) when he lost possession of grace; that a pure nature endowed with purely natural capabilities returned, to be restored to the supernatural order only later within the economy of redemption (when? with Christ or Moses or Abraham or Noah or the promise made to Adam?). In solidarity with Adam, all human beings share Adam's hope and its fulfillment in Christ. All, in their own way, share humanity's supernatural goal; hence all somehow share in the supernatural means to attain it. Through Christ, who died for all, and through the Church, outside of which there is no salvation, all men somehow participate in the grace of the divine-Christological-ecclesial order, whether they lived before Christ or after him.

We only introduce confusion when we try to equate fallen human nature with some "pure nature" that stands outside the order of grace. This is quite apart from the fact that this hypothetical concept of pure nature cannot be given any contentual structure, so that it is not a usable model of a truly existent condition of nature.

In the realm of Catholic theology, of course, there are several ways in which we can explain the *de facto* union of the natural and supernatural order and its orientation towards one supernatural goal. At one extreme is Ripalda's presentation, where every natural act is caught up in the vise of grace no matter how remote it is from our supernatural goal. In the middle are various presentations, where a nature that functions purely naturally at first is "intercepted" by grace at some point and oriented towards our supernatural goal. And at the other extreme is a view that still finds adherents. It leaves room for a full blown, purely natural finality within the existing world order (e.g., Billot).

In all these systems that have been constructed since the Counter-Reformation, we find a distinct tendency to protect the concept of nature from Protestant subversion. The tendency goes so far, however, that they not only try to set off nature from sin and grace, but also feel obliged to prove that the sphere of nature can be isolated and depicted *in se* within the real world order. This is probably the price that had to be paid to rationalism:[14] theologians did not realize clearly enough that the analogy in the concept of nature and the concomitant formal character of the theological concept of nature did not permit such a procedure.

The pure nature theologians presumed to have set off from grace was really the concrete nature that is enmeshed in the order of grace, only raised to some cruder level of abstraction. As a result, when they tried to put some content into their talk about nature, they were actually talking about the tension between creation and Covenant that Karl Barth stressed; they were talking about the older patristic and scholastic tension between nature and grace, which was theologically adequate to depict creation's distance from the gift of grace it received. When they tried for more than this, they necessarily came up empty-handed. The older, transitional concept of nature had decided advantages over their new conceptions; it underlined the ambiguity and two-sidedness of the concept of nature, the two possible meanings that can be conceptually depicted but never mastered or resolved.

This does not mean that the theologian cannot concern himself with the phenomenology of nature, of human nature in particular, but he must never forget that an irresolvable chasm remains between the concrete nature of salvation history and the abstract concept of nature and that both concepts are to be viewed in proper perspective. The concrete concept is the essential and dominant one; the abstract concept, which cannot be filled out contentually, does serve to protect the concept of grace and has its proper place.[15] All too often, however, theologians have projected aspects of the concrete concept into the abstract concept or tried to construct the concrete concept from their abstract model.

The process of subtraction, which we mentioned earlier, cannot be conducted along the lines of a mathematical formula or a scientific experiment. Many attempts to analyze the act of faith have only led to deeper obfuscation. People have tried to separate neatly the traits of reason from the traits of grace, in order to delimit the role of free will from the role of grace. We find this same tendency in the "philosophy of religion," when it tries to pinpoint the supernatural factor in the pagan's noncclesial, non-Christian knowledge of God. We find it in ethics, when it tries to distinguish between the natural and supernatural motivation behind the ethical act. We find it in mysticism, when it pretends to unravel the purely natural and truly supernatural strands of the mystical phenomenon.

The thing we must do here, and it is the only thing we can do, is to investigate the whole matter reverently and gropingly with the eyes of faith. Only this can keep us from posing questions and pursuing answers that are ultimately out of order in the study of grace. Because of the ambiguity and two-sidedness involved, the realm of nature will always remain a loose area that cannot be given full and sharp definition. Its lower limit will be the formal concept of nature mentioned above. Nature fundamentally is creation as such; in terms of the hearer of Revelation (angel or men), it is the conscious, free subject.

As far as man in particular is concerned, this reality of being a subject can be analyzed in terms of a body–soul unity, with all that each term implies singly and in association with the other term. From there we can move on to develop an analogous notion of subhuman nature and some vague idea about a created nature that is pure spirit. In this process of conceptual formulation, God will enter as the source and end of the world, and thus it will be possible to develop an ethics approproate to created being as such. For man, this ethical natural law will devolve from his dependence on the creator and his specifically human nature—a social, sexual composite of body and soul.

The more we try to move from the abstract to the concrete, however, the more distant the experimental material will become from the "purely natural." It will become clearer to us that all our fundamental concepts—nature, spirit, subject, reason, freedom, religion, morality, and such—are already enmeshed in the concrete analogy. The more concrete our philosophy becomes, the less it will be pure philosophy.

The formal concept of nature provides us with the bare minimum of content, *but there is no upper limit to the concrete content that can be injected into this concept.* In the last analysis, philosophy remains *open-ended.* It is, after all, the thought of a creature; and no creature can set arbitrary limits to what God does or could say to us. This is all the more true because the concrete object of philosophy is not purely philosophical, because it transcends the boundaries of philosophy.

Philosophy does have a *formal* object, i.e., the nature of the created world as such. It does not have a *material* object that can be neatly isolated, however, because the created world is tied up positively (by grace) or negatively (by sin) with the Word of divine Revelation. Because he is meant to hear this Word, man is by nature a subject. We must never forget, however, that grace not only presupposed man as subject; but also elevates and completes man in a radical way; it is *in the summons* of grace that man is enabled to become God's partner and elevated to a hearer of God's Word.

Let us repeat once again. The distance between the two subjects here is not created by grace. It is a distance that belongs to nature itehlf, but it has its deepest roots in the distance that prevails between the divine persons in the Trinity, and it is grace which makes this interdivine distance visible to us and makes possible a fruitful interchange between Word and faith in the distance that separates God and creature. Since participation in the Trinitarian persons is the purpose for which creaturely personhood and subjectness was provided, it is also the thing that grounds and makes possible this natural substrate.

At this point we can only speak in dialectical terms.

The more intimate the union between God and man becomes, the more clearly we see the difference between them, the sharper becomes the subjectivity and the personal character. Ultimately, as Paul tells us (1 Cor. 2: 9–16), it is the mystery of the Holy Spirit that is at work.

4. Further Insights

In more recent discussions of this problem, three contributions deserve special attention. The first contribution was the ground-breaking work of **Joseph Maréchal** in France,[16] who sought to establish a positive relationship between German Idealist methodology (Kant, Fichte, Hegel) and the structures of Thomistic philosophy.

In his attempt, Maréchal moved towards the systematic focal point that we find in Schleiermacher and Barth. Two characteristics typify Maréchal's approach: (1) he fashions his picture of finite spirit from the identity of the divine archetypal intellect, and thus sees finite spirit oriented and impelled toward the absolute, transcendent, direct vision of God; (2) by the very nature of his concerns, he is divided from the very start between the realm of mysticism and the realm of metaphysics.

An early work on the feeling of *presence*[17] provides the key to his work as a whole. The feeling of presence is an experience of reality that forms the basis for all our conceptualizing. In the higher stages of mysticism, it develops as an intuition of being that prolongs the initial movement of our intelligence even though it is inaccessible to the unaided effort of our intelligence. The identity point, where God is immediately present to the spirit, is only given to us by grace, but it is the authentic object of both mysticism and metaphysics. Why? Because it represents the why and wherefore of the whole spirit complex even in its most concrete and worldly activity.[18]

Metaphysics is the science of absolutes, which can only be God, the existing Absolute. All abstraction proceeds from the absolute concrete, and no absolute can maintain itself apart from God. Thus an inductive, semiempirical metaphysics, which purports to move from the sensible world to the spirit world, and from there to God by logical deductions, is an intrinsic impossibility. We must start our thinking from the Absolute point.[19]

We do not seize the Absolute, it lays hold of us. Metaphysics is the human science of the Absolute, in which we bear witness to the fact that our intelligence has been laid hold of by the Absolute. This seizure is not a yoke of slavery, but a life-giving principle. And so, starting from this absolute point (the vision of God), Maréchal explains all spirit in terms of its orientation towards this ultimate end.[20] The absolute end of the thinking subject is a constitutive element of his every judgment.

The human spirit, then, must be construed outside the framework of abstraction on the one hand and intuition on the other. For Maréchal, reason and will unite to form a capacity (spirit) that strives towards an intuition that lies outside its own power. As nature, the human spirit possesses a relative, or inchoative, or tendential intuition of the absolute being.[21]

Maréchal did not manage to find the unifying point of mysticism and metaphysics. His work tended to split into two separate parts, as he labored to protect metaphysics from the threat of ontologism. He resorted to neo-Thomistic principles to explain that the natural vision of God remains an ineffectual and conditional desire in pure nature—a pure velleity.[22] We must never forget that a great *reversal of perspective* lies at the core of his thinking. We must turn back from the dynamic thrust toward the necessary being that it presupposes.[23]

The main issue here, however, is Maréchal's focal point,

which unifies mystics and metaphysics. If this is the real unifying point of his philosophy, if discursive reasoning and willing must be traced back to an Absolute, then his philosophy is actually a cryptotheology. He is a philosopher trying to find in man's nature the possibility of the *visio dei* as man's ultimate goal. So the question is: Is not the object of Maréchal's investigation, human nature, already a *theological* object?[24]

Theology would soon confront the problem raised by Maréchal's philosophy. The second important contribution, therefore, would be the historical and systematic inquiry of **Henri de Lubac.**[25] He pointed out that the whole problem of man's natural longing for the vision of God finds its roots and justification within the concrete concept of nature that was held by the Church Fathers and the medieval scholastics. It really operates within a framework that presupposes Revelation and grace, and the shift to a hypothetical "pure nature" at the end of the sixteenth century produced an historical absurdity.

De Lubac also turned a powerful spotlight on the latent *theological a priori* in Maréchal's system. In our *concrete* creation, the "identity point" of which Maréchal spoke is not a purely *philosophical* one at all. It is actually a *theological* one: namely, the one and only goal which God has set for human nature, the beatific vision. Since this is our one and only goal, says De Lubac, it is a waste of time to talk about some other world order where man might possibly have some other "purely natural" goal.

If we adopt this theological *a priori* as our starting point, then God's self-revelation (culminating in Jesus Christ) becomes the cornerstone and focal point of all our thinking. All talk about a "pure velleity" or an "ineffectual desire" can be dropped entirely. Man's natural spirit is a paradoxical creation which rests on the borderline between natural and supernatural and which belongs to both orders in the concrete creation we know.

Now this does not mean that we are intermingling the two orders that Catholic theology has sought to keep distinct. On its own level, creation is fully a grace; but its elevation to divine Sonship is a second and loftier work that *should not be explained in terms of the first but in terms of its own intrinsic character.* The goal of man's natural desire and the gratuity of grace do not rule each other out, and the supernatural need not be defined in terms of the infrastructure it supports.

De Lubac's approach involves an even more radical reversal of perspective than did Maréchal's. He not only starts from perfect act to move to potency; he also starts from the real world of history to move to nature and its qualities. We must first focus on the goal, for it is the goal that provides the ontological ground of a being and its characteristics. Catholic philosophy and theology must change its approach to these questions; it must stop moving from nature to its goal.[26]

We can make two observations about De Lubac's overall conception. First of all, it is a daring line of thought that stresses the importance of the divine and moves from there to examine lower realities. Divine realities are to be judged from their own inner nature, not from their relationship to created realities. Respect for the holy and its radically different nature shine through De Lubac's presentation. Secondly, the transition from Maréchal to De Lubac seems to mirror the transition from Schleiermacher to Barth. Once again we have moved from a philosophical concern with nature to a theological concern with real history, from "natural" desire to man's response to grace. At this point a dialogue between both parties is clearly feasible, because neither side has to surrender its own convictions or its basic position.

De Lubac's presentation was certainly Catholic in intention. The question was whether this train of thought would hold up when it was developed to its logical conclusion. Most Catholic theologians misconstrued De Lubac's thought and criticized it accordingly, but a few reacted approvingly.[27] **Karl Rahner** was one of the few theologians to subject De Lubac's presentation to a careful, informed critique.[28]

Rahner begins by agreeing with most of De Lubac's basic positions. Yes, we must reject the older "extrinsic" interpretation of grace; grace is not some accidental appendage to a nature already fully constituted *in se*. Yes, it is foolish and dangerous to think that we can neatly separate the sphere of nature from the sphere of grace in the concrete world order. If God gives man a supernatural goal to attain, then that is something that goes to the intimate core of man's nature. Man and the world are wholly different from what they were before they had this goal, and grace must be viewed in terms of its own nature.

Rahner is anxious, however, to avoid the ultimate conclusions that flow from De Lubac's premises. He does not want to get rid of the concept of pure nature entirely and poses this question: "Is man's inner orientation to grace so constitutive of his nature that the latter cannot be conceived apart from grace, i.e., as pure nature? If we answer "yes," then Rahner feels that we have somehow made grace a requirement of human nature and leveled the two orders involved. Why? Because God could not put an unconditional dynamism in human nature and leave it unfulfilled.

Rahner proposes that we make a distinction here. Yes, man's spirit-nature is such that it is open to the possibility of a supernatural existence, but it is also such that of itself it does not have an unconditional claim to this existence. In other words, we must distinguish (*in abstracto*) two

dynamisms in the human spirit: the first makes our spirit-
nature what it is; but we cannot simply equate it with the
second dynamism that we experience in our concrete spiritual existence within the one real world order.

To preserve the concept of grace in all its purity, Rahner
proposes a difficult experiment in conceptual distinctions.
Yes, the supernatural, existential openness to grace is man's
most real and intimate aspect; it is the source and center
of what man really is. But if we are to maintain the concept of nature as a counterpoint to the concept of grace,
we must disregard this center. Nature, then, as a theological concept, is a *residual concept*: it is what is left when
we remove the center element from the complex of man's
concrete being. What is left over is "pure nature" which, of
course, *cannot be specified concretely*. It is something we
must postulate and retain, on the presupposition that God
could refuse the supernatural to human nature.

Here a few comments on Rahner's position are in order.
The notion of pure nature as a "residual concept" is certainly feasible in theology. Indeed it is unavoidable if we
want to establish a real correlative counterpoint to grace.
We attempted to do the same thing earlier by working up
a formal concept of nature through a process of subtraction.

The very presuppositions which De Lubac offers, and
which Rahner accepts, show us the limits of this exercise.
If we admit that the ultimate meaning of creation and
human nature resides in the fact that God willed to grant
the gift of grace, what right do we have to "abstract" from
this ultimate center? What purpose or value could such a
procedure have? How can we do it?

A second question is this: Do we have to identify the
residual concept with man's spirit nature as such? Rahner
quite rightly wants to preserve the relative significance and
meaning of nature as such, but this does not have to be

the absolute significance of a "pure nature." Statements about possible worlds may be tolerated at the frontiers of theological thought, but only if they serve to clear up certain aspects of the one and only reality we have. The relative significance of nature itself is protected well enough if it is viewed as a particular and relatively consistent sphere of meaning within creation as a whole, e.g., the sphere of culture, or I-thou, or man-woman. It can be viewed as a sphere of provisional meaning that is not directly derivable from grace but rather serves as a presupposition for grace. We need not assert categorically that the significance of this sphere is so great and so absolute that it calls out to God for existence.

Rahner felt he had to complement the notion of "gratuity from above" with the notion of "gratuity from below," to undergird the former with the latter. From the standpoint of man, who receives grace as a totally gratuitous gift from God, there is good reason to underline the gratuitousness involved. A "creaturely theology" justifiably seeks to maintain the formal concept of pure nature in order to stress man's servant relationship to God, but what happens when we look at it from God's standpoint?

From all eternity God willed one and only one thing: to reveal his love to mankind. For that reason he created the world. From God's standpoint, therefore, it is idle to ask whether there could have been a world without this grace. And if something has no weight in God's eyes, then it should not have any weight for man in his lowly condition. But insofar as man cannot work out a divine theology, insofar as he must give human expression to the Revelation of grace, he is caught in the tension between "necessity without reality" and "reality without necessity."[29] In short, he is caught between the tension of a pure nature, which is a necessary precondition for the gratuity of grace but has no reality, and of the de facto supernatural world order, which is the only reality but evinces the gratuity of both creation and grace.

Obviously we are at one of the outer limits of human thought. Here differing denominational approaches are unable to speak adequately and to come to grips with one another. It is the point where Brunner and Barth must let their differences be cleared up, where Catholic-Protestant differences on this question offset each other. Put simply, the question is: How much in concrete human nature do we ascribe to grace, and how much do we ascribe to man's capacity for God?

Philosophy, even Christian philosophy, will have a tendency to extend man's natural capabilities as far as the vision of God. Theology, on the other hand, will tend to see the latent presupposition of grace in the strivings of nature and to reduce nature's portion to a passively structured, obediential potency. Since the theological a priori in nature can never be excised, however, the battle can never be settled one way or the other. We are confronted by a nature which of itself has no opening to the realm of grace, but which derives its ultimate reality and meaning from grace.

Barth himself could not get around this paradox. Indeed it stands out clearly in his work. On the one hand, he locked nature up in itself, to the point where it becomes impossible to derive a truly transcendent concept from it. On the other hand, he opened it wide to grace, to the point where he almost deduced a natural capability from the Revelation happening and the act of faith (Church Dogmatics, 6).

Each tendency is offset by the other in his work and reduced towards some middle ground. Barth did not ascribe the immanent restrictedness of nature to nature as such; he ascribed it to the contingent sinfulness of nature, without carrying this line of thought through to the end. Neither did he go so far as to deduce a natural capacity from the Revelation happening; he was content to provide a phenomenology of "concrete" nature based on the light of Revelation. Even Barth could not do without philosophy.

The important thing is that at this point any and all polemic against natural theology and the analogy of being becomes superfluous. If both sides agree that the grace order takes absolute priority over the natural order in the order of intention and that the created order takes relative priority over the grace order in the order of execution, then we can and must permit a glance from Adam to Christ, and from creaturely reason to Covenant faith, within the prevailing priority of Revelation and faith. This is valid, even if the acceptance of God's Word is the highest capability of human reason and even if created nature is hardly "pure nature." For his part, Barth chose to speak from within the interplay of natural and divine freedom. He left obscure the noetic side of the problem: that is, the interplay of natural knowledge and supernatural faith.

Insofar as natural reason is concerned, we may interject a few reflections on the teachings of Vatican I. Its assertions dealt with the noetic side of this question, but it did not tackle the whole question of nature which we are considering here.[30] Its primary concern was to deal with the extremes of rationalism and fideism.

Vatican I proclaims that God, the origin and end of all things, can be known *with certainty* from the natural light of human reason and from created realities (DZ 1785). In short, it proclaims natural knowledge of God as a *possibility* for man, but it does not say that such purely natural knowledge is a concrete fact within the existing world order. Indeed, it also proclaims that Revelation is a moral necessity if man is to achieve knowledge of God with firm *certitude* and no admixture of error (DZ 1786).

Vatican I, then, does not say anything against the

analogy in our concept of nature. Instead, its assertions move within the framework of such an analogy, and the two assertions mentioned above (DZ 1785, 1786) represent an almost dialectical formulation of the issue. The possibility of man's natural knowledge of God is the *de jure side* of the coin; the necessity of Revelation for firm certitude is the *de facto* side. There is nothing to stop a theologian from saying that all natural knowledge of God operates *de facto* within the positive and negative conditions of the supernatural order.[31] There is nothing to stop him from saying that man's whole intellectual and cognitive life is enmeshed in a supernatural reality. Vatican I merely reminds us that, within this concrete situation, man's nature is not destroyed and his natural capacity to know God remains functional.

Barth's approach is not ruled out by Vatican I. There is no reason why he cannot start with the concrete and the historical to elucidate the possibilities open to man; nor does Vatican I preclude his anthropological assertions about human reason's capacity to know God within the concrete order of Revelation; nor can we build up any real opposition between his focus on Christ as the ground of creation and Vatican I's concern to assert one specific truth over against two possible extremes.

Where Barth places faith as an *a priori* for all human knowledge, there Vatican I places the natural and supernatural contact of the created spirit with the true God. In both cases, the sinner rejects something that he really perceives in an all-inclusive way and that he could reason to in a discursive way. The God with whom man has to deal in this world is *de facto* the God of retribution and grace, even as man is a being pointed away from God by sin or pointed towards God by grace.

If man has only one goal, a supernatural one, under which any natural goal is necessarily subsumed[32] and if the natural order has no autonomous significance,[33] then this must also hold true in the noetic order. The whole order of reason is theologically imbedded in the order of grace, even as the created order is. To encounter the God of this creation in a personal relationship of intellect and will is to encounter the God of Jesus Christ and none other.

IV · CHRIST AT THE CENTER

In the last section, we attempted to present one possible Catholic interpretation of the relationship between nature and grace. In our opinion, it is the best possible interpretation because it takes all the pertinent data into account. At any rate, we can now turn to a relatively easier task: by citing a sufficient number of qualified witnesses, we hope to show that our interpretation is a real one supported by Catholic scholars. We also hope to show that the viewpoints which Barth regarded as the pillars of his dogmatics are not exclusively Protestant or Calvinist, that they are in fact supported and maintained by prominent Catholic scholars.

This effort may give us an opportunity to break down the drift towards tight systematization that we find at many points in Barth's work. It may also enable us to cast his overall conception in a framework that would be acceptable to Catholic dogma. No one can say that the Catholic viewpoints expressed here are tied just as closely as Barth's theology to Idealist philosophy, for these authors, like Maréchal, merely want to introduce modern insights into the Scholastic approach.

Adopting themes from Barth's dogmatics, we shall first

consider Christ as the ground of creation. Then we shall move on to examine the relationships between nature and history, nature and grace, and judgment and redemption.

1. The Ground of Creation

The theology of an older day tended to make this question (Christ as the ground of creation) dependent on another question. Was sin the underlying reason for Christ's Incarnation (yes, said the Thomists), or would God have become man even if Adam had not fallen (yes, said the Scotists)?

Thomas Aquinas himself was very circumspect in tackling this issue. On the one hand, he noted that God's will in the supernatural order can only be known from scriptural Revelation and that this seems to associate the Incarnation with man's fall.[1] On the other hand, he felt the unity of the whole creation plan was so strong that Adam, without anticipating his sin, already possessed an explicit faith in Christ's Incarnation before the fall and that he also sensed the great mystery of Christ and his Church in his own relationship to his wife.[2] In this context, he cites the words of *Acts:* "For there is not other name under heaven given to men by which we must be saved" (4:12).

The real difference between Aquinas and Scotus, then, is simply this: Thomas focuses on God's one concrete plan for the world; it foreordained the Incarnation from all eternity but also foresaw man's sinful fall, and thus it foreordained the Incarnation as redemption.[3] Scotus, on the other hand, stressed the grounding of creation in Christ, the God-made-man. Suarez combined both views, according to the Incarnation two motives: an absolute motive (the Scotist one), and a relative motive (the Thomistic one).[4]

We can follow in Suarez' footsteps; but we shall shift the emphasis a bit, subordinating the relative, logical motive to the absolute one, and stressing the unity of the concrete, historical world and the divine plan underlying it. **Emile Mersch** puts it this way:

The creation decision was one stage of the unique decree that willed the Incarnation. The god-man . . . was willed and foreordained in all and through all, and we, together with this all, were elected and blessed in him. . . . The Incarnation, then, is essentially a means of salvation against sin. Nothing tells us that it would have taken place without sin, for in that case there would not have been so much reason to display God's mercy as to celebrate his love. But, at the same time, the Incarnation was willed for its own sake. For a redemptive Incarnation is but the ultimate form of Incarnation itself: the Incarnation itself is the act in which God gives himself unstintingly.[5]

The work of **Erich Przywara** is framed in this same perspective, beyond the Thomist-Scotist opposition and beyond any theology of possibles. In striving to uncover the necessity in the de facto world order, Przywara adopts a thoroughly Christocentric approach. The following words clearly reveal this thrust:

The way to God and the image of God is only a shadowy hint of something which is brightly revealed by Christ alone; he is the unique exegesis that maked God visible to us. By his own decision, God is revealed to us nowhere else but in Christ. . . . All the flourishes that present God to the creature are flashed out and explained in Christ. They are features of the one and only real God, who is Father, Son and Holy Spirit. There is no other God beside him, and any other general features of God are merely the foreglow or afterglow of Father, Son and Holy Spirit.[6]

It is in this radically Christocentric framework that Przywara develops his presentation of the analogy of being.

Philosophy is not a purely formal framework into which we inject the content of theology. Every concrete philosophy must be measured in terms of its yes or no to the supernatural order of Revelation and to the one God in Christ. This Christocentric outlook of Przywara must be taken into account before one tries to contrast his themes with those of Barth.[7] In his main work,[8] Przywara relentlessly seeks to reduce every aspect to the one central aspect: God in the crucified Christ and his crucified Church. All logic (and hence ontology too) is judged by this Christological, historical, actualist measuring rod.

The flaming expressionistic style of Przywara finds its counterpoint in the measured style of **Romano Guardini**, but the message is the same. Guardini early adopted a Christocentric emphasis, and it continued to dominate his work. There is no abstract "essence" of Christianity because the historical person, Jesus Christ, is this essence. All universal and abstract categories of nature and creatureliness find in him their measuring rod. Christ is not in the world, the world is in him; existence in Christ is the decisive category.[9]

Christ is the way, the truth, and the life. All finite things find room in him:

Paul teaches that Christ truly is the framework and the force that takes in and transforms the believer and existence as a whole. We can actually experience this. . . .

At first man lives with his thoughts in the world. He measures them by his experience of reality and by the general rules of logic, and thus he forms judgments on what is and what can be, but as soon as he comes up against Christ, he must make a decision: Will he form a judgment on Christ on the same basis? He tries to at first, but he soon notices that he is dealing with something special here. He must now reverse the process, and take Christ as his starting point. . . . Christ must be the measure of what is real and what is possible. . . .[10]

In his treatment of dogmatic theology,[11] **Michael Schmaus** offers a very similar formulation. For him, too, Jesus Christ is the essence of Christianity, the ultimate meaning of all that happens in nature and history. From the very beginning, God did in fact ordain creation to participate in his Trinitarian bliss, not to dwell outside it. Whether the Son of God would have become man only in a fallen world or not, the Incarnation was actually willed from all eternity, and it is God's crowning work. All the earlier Words of God, uttered in natural or supernatural Revelation, are tied together and explained in Christ. Indeed, the Father would not have spoken them at all if he had not determined to speak the final Word, Christ. All things, including man, have their existence in Christ. In the last analysis, the world has no fully autonomous order of its own. It is, in fact, subsumed into the order that is grounded in Christ.

All the problems of theodicy are to be resolved in terms of this framework. We can say that God permits evil only because he foresaw that he could free humanity from its bonds, only because he willed the Incarnation of the Logos. We can refer to the whole salvation economy as the coming of the kingdom of God, but Christ is the real content and substance of it.

Because Christ is the ground of existence in the supernatural world order, creation looks forward to its promised divine Sonship in Christ from the very start. In God's creation plan, a supernaturally elevated nature was the first thing he willed; nature in itself was only willed secondarily. The world was created for Christ; Christ's human nature was not created for the world. The risen and glorified Christ is the ultimate goal of all God's activity and the prototype of the ultimate shape of man and the world; for this reason, the "new heaven" and "new earth," whose center is the glorified Christ, was the first-willed element of God's creation plan. God created nature as a vessel into which he could pour his divine life.[12]

In a very special way, Christ is the ground and measure of human existence. It is he alone who tells us what man really is. As the ground of creation, Christ typifies what the union of the natural and supernatural really is. The synthesis of divine and human nature in Christ is the measuring rod for all Christian syntheses of these two natures. There is no need to reconcile Christ with the world or to mediate between them; Christ himself is this reconciliation. As soon as we set nature off as an autonomous entity, we run the risk of giving it predominance over the order of grace. There is a danger of placing philosophy over faith, dialectics over Revelation, Aristotle over Paul, philology over theology, secular history over Church history, and official functions over true piety.

The crucified Christ is a standing judgment on nature. He reminds the world that nature is something that must die and rise in him to attain the true purpose of its existence. When we say that grace perfects nature, we must realize exactly what we mean. We can only be talking about a nature that is perfectly submissive to God. Such a nature has not existed since Adam's fall, so all human life and culture stands under the judgment and blessing of Christ's cross.[13]

The notion of Christ as the ground of creation finds its logical fulfillment in the Patristic and early Scholastic notion of the whole Christ as the central object of theology. This viewpoint found a vigorous modern proponent in Emile Mersch.[14] Every scholarly science, he notes, tends towards unity because it seeks knowledge. In theology, men have often tried to introduce unifying forms and principles from the outside, e.g., from philosophy. But since these forms are external to the content of revelation, they cannot provide an internal understanding of revelation and its content.

The true inner unity of theology can only be the whole Christ. Theology is truly theocentric only when it is Christocentric. Echoing the outlook of the Tübingen theologians, Mersch goes even further and calls for a theology that would unfold and develop the self-awareness of Christ in the Holy Spirit as it is disclosed to his members in faith. This disclosure takes place only in and through the Church, his body and bride, which watches over his truth and makes it explicit for his members: "Christians as such are members of Christ; they can only be defined through Christ, who in turn can only be defined through the total authentic content of Christian doctrine."[15]

Christian self-awareness, then, coincides with the total authentic content of Christian doctrine. It is unfolded as the oneness of Christ by the Spirit of the Church, in the living relationship between the head and his members. This view of theology completes the Christocentric outlook of the authors cited earlier in a methodical way, and, as Mersch demonstrates, it is in accord with the best Catholic tradition.

2. Nature and History

Our considerations here are but a further development of what was said above. We are not engaging in a philosophical attempt to show that the nature of man and the world is temporal and historical. We are trying to show that if the historical fact of God's Incarnation in Christ is the meaning and goal of history, nature, and creation, then the necessity of temporal history and nature rests upon a decision that cannot be reduced to any sort of general or universal norm of legitimacy.

Robert Grosche[16] points out that it is the radical, supernatural historicity of the Christian happening which has made it a scandal for everyone. It leads non-Christian thinkers to reduce Christ to an unhistorical myth, and it leads Christian thinkers and theologians to go off on a tangent also. "It is worth noting how ready the Catholic Christian is to talk about universal truths instead of concrete, historical reality, and religion instead of Christianity. Christianity is often viewed as one instance of religion."[17]

In modern Catholic theology we do find an earnest attempt to explore the depths of historicity and its meaning. The original impulse came from the Tübingen theologians in Germany, from Blondel and Laberthonnière in France, and from Newman and the Oxford School in England. It has been picked up by many important Catholic thinkers[18] and is closely tied up with the work of many leading Protestant theologians, although there is no causal relationship involved.

For both Christian confessions, this work on the theology of history represents an attempt to overcome the historicism of the nineteenth century and the existentialism of the twentieth. Both latter movements stimulated Christian thinkers to tackle questions from a truly theological approach and to use an exclusively theological methodology.

It was a stroke of bad luck that the Reformation thinkers chose to construct their theology on the basis of philosophical nominalism. Indeed, the nominalist reaction against Aquinas in the realm of philosophy was itself an unfortunate detour. If theology is to be an authentic science of *singularia* that is universally normative, then it needs a philosophy that safeguards the essential and realist aspects (e.g., that of Thomas Aquinas): the incarnate Logos is the norm and fulfillment of all authentic *logoi* in nature and history.

For theologians, the immanent historicity of man cannot be separated from the transcendent historicity of God's Revelation in the world. It is not just that philosophy became fully cognizant of immanent historicity only in the light of this transcendent historicity; even more importantly, the immanent finality of history and individual existence must henceforth be regarded as dependent on their transcendent finality. Individual human beings and the whole human race have but one supernatural goal that is both immanent and transcendent.

"Natural" and supernatural historicity stand or fall together, even if we grant that man's immanent history has some inner laws of its own. In the last analysis, it rests on the historicity of Christ: the analogy of divine and human history unites in his two natures, and there the knot of protohistoricity between God and the world is tied securely. Why? Because Christ is a free, divine person, hence Lord and shaper of the Revelation happening, of his own human history in the world, and of all world history. As Schmaus puts it:

In Christianity there are eternal, immutable, universally valid truths; but they rest upon historical events. The events reported in scripture are not catechetical or pedagogical vehicles for conveying some loftier, eternal truth. They themselves are the way God speaks to man and deals with him.[19]

Romano Guardini focuses persistently on this historical aspect.[20] He does not neglect or deny the aspect of nature but, like Karl Barth, he rests everything on the real happenings of history. Man is an historical being by nature, to be sure, but in the last analysis he is an historical being because God engages him in a supernatural history. Man is the being whom God created for an encounter in the Revelation happening; he gave man an immanent historicity so that man would be capable of this encounter.[21]

In an earlier day it was **Laberthonnière** who forcefully underlined this theme.[22] He pointed out that in Christianity history itself is the system. We cannot abstract from real events, we can only interpret them, and our interpretation must derive from an involvement in the happenings themselves. In the Christian context, the social aspect is immediately present with the historical aspect. Now when we immerse the Absolute in history, our notion of act changes. God is no longer simply pure act vis-à-vis the potency of the world and its history. He is now Act as action, power, and love; he is absolute happening within the world and its history. The element of happening in God's Revelation is also the element of grace, and the corresponding act of concrete human reason is faith. If a philosophy does not open up to the act of faith, then it will remain hopelessly empty and isolated. In trying to be self-sufficient, it will slip away from the ground of being.

Maurice Blondel found the same line of thought at an even earlier date.[23] He, too, sought to base nature on history and the happening character of being. His aim was certainly not to turn Revelation into an immanent reality that could be construed from an analysis of human consciousness. On the contrary, his aim was to leap beyond the whole realm of nature into the sphere of Revelation— an already accomplished Revelation that served as the real foundation for the whole natural realm.

It is Blondel who comes closest to Karl Barth. His "philosophy" moves from the abstract to ever more concrete realities, and the ultimate in concreteness is the act in which man comes to rest on God in Christ and makes the decision of faith. In the divine happening, man is subsumed into the fullness of being in Christ, or else he rejects it and lives in the void of hell.

Both Blondel and Barth can easily be misunderstood. Failing to grasp their real intention, a person might readily convert the necessity of divine Revelation into a natural, immanent necessity. But they are aiming in the opposite direction: they want to pioneer the concrete, historical element in ontology, not from a philosophical viewpoint but from a theological viewpoint. In short, they want to relate temporal being with the concrete, personal, incarnate Logos.

Subsequent Catholic philosophy would focus on the happening character of worldly being as such, but the point that interests us here is that the whole effort arose from a problem that was posed in purely theological terms. We are dealing here with the Catholic response to Barth's image of the hourglass. Guardini expresses it this way: "The basic point of Revelation is that God not only exists but also acts, not only rules but also involves himself, not only fulfills but also comes; he is a person, and he freely chooses to fulfill history and accept its workings. . . . The world arose from action, not from nature, and through action it will reach its goal."[24]

The happening character of being does not exclude the element of nature in it; on the contrary, it includes the aspect of nature as the precondition which makes happening possible. Hermann Schell, whose line of thought was close to that of Blondel, expresses it well: "Spirit is activity, actuality and subjectivity. But it is an activity that goes out to others and relates them to oneself. . . . It involves a living relationship with the object grasped. The aspect of actuality includes the aspect of substantiality . . . and the subjectivity includes objective being. . . ."[25] For Schell, therefore, the chasm between heaven and hell becomes clearer as we gain deeper insight into Revelation. Only in the light do we see the darkness of its shadow side.

Today dogmatic theology tends to view God not only as pure act but also as pure action, without in any way denying his divine nature. Being and action coincide in God, who is ever in the act of doing, but man's encounter with him in grace is something far more than a physical reality. It is a new personal relationship to Christ and the Trinity, which the creaturely spirit freely chooses.[26]

All this means that we must alter our traditional conception of *physical versus moral*. In the past we tended to equate physical with *real*, and moral with *purely notional*. This view is incorrect. The realm of spirit is just as truly being as the physical and material realm is. Indeed it is more so, because it is not subject to dissolution. Thus it cannot be equated simply with something subjectively thought or some objective truth *in se*. Both are aspects of a spirit realm that is truly being, that becomes operational in a subjective way but has an objective character as well.[27]

3. Nature and Grace

Here again we should like to show how approvingly Catholic theology looks upon this concrete historical focus, and how advantageous the focus is. The main advantage is that it allows both philosophy and theology to stick close to the real world instead of ruminating about other possible worlds. The only thing to be avoided is apodictic comment on what God could or could not have done. We should not say, for example, that God could not have created a spiritual being without ordering him towards the beatific vision. We must hold to Aquinas's comments on the open-ended nature of man.

Romano Guardini vividly portrays the paradox that is man. As proclaimed by Paul and explained by Augustine, grace is not something added to the nature of man; it is the definitive form of man as such. It is, paradoxically, a pure gift and yet something that is intimately a part of the one who receives it:

The world does not take the shape of nature; it takes the shape of a history carried through by God. Man does not take the shape of a subject closed in upon himself; he is what he is insofar as God sends out a summons to him. Every aspect of real existence proceeds from grace. Our distinction between nature and history is situated within the all-embracing and freely initiated history that God set in motion. Our distinction between nature and grace is situated within God's all-embracing decision to grant grace. All existence flows from this divine decision.[28]

Guardini has no intention of turning grace into an intrinsic element of human nature. He insists that grace is supernatural, totally beyond any natural claim of man, but he also insists that man is a creature created by God and through grace. There is no such thing as "natural" man, however much we may try to construct him.[29]

Daniel Feuling goes so far as to use the word *contradiction* for the paradox of human nature. Of its very nature, created spirit is such that its awareness of God somehow points beyond itself toward the fullness of God's hidden divinity. At the same time, man knows that he cannot pursue this line of direction in which his nature is pointing. His life will remain unfulfilled if he has to rely on his natural powers alone. What are we to make of this puzzling aspect of created spirit? Why does God create a spirit that cannot find fulfillment on its own? Must we not conclude that created spirit would be a contradiction if this impotence were the last word we could say about it, if God were incapable of guaranteeing its fulfillment by elevating it to the immediate vision of God?[30]

All the theological analysis of **Oskar Bauhofer** rests on the same paradoxical foundation: the pure otherness of grace and the unfulfilled nature of creation and history without it.[31] By the very nature of his spirit, man is created and ordered for a supratemporal and supernatural goal. The natural personhood of man establishes a real relationship with the supernatural:

By virtue of his natural makeup, man is not locked up in the natural world. Man, as set up by God, *is given* a supernatural goal. This does not mean that man can achieve his supernatural goal by his own natural powers . . . but the supernatural destination of man is part of his full metaphysical definition. . . .[32]

Bauhofer's statements might appear questionable, if it were not for the fact that they are grounded on Patristic tradition and a whole series of Thomistic texts. On the basis of his clearcut premises, Bauhofer proceeds to analyze the status of nature. It is either locked up hopelessly in itself or reconciled with God in Christ; it exists concretely with the dying and rising Christ. Mankind may choose between myth and faith, between hopeless fate and redemption. Those are the only two forms of existence open to him, and they both "come under a general presupposition that is situated on the borderline between history and the suprahistorical. It is not a logical premise but an action, a happening, which belongs to history and yet forms the axis of all human history."[33]

Josef Pieper complements all this by treating the noetic side of the picture. All real philosophizing, he notes, necessarily goes beyond the borderline of purely philosophical considerations. It makes some statements that are not the product of purely human epistemology, that come to us from outside. A truly authentic philosophical inquiry into the nature of things oversteps the boundary between philosophy and theology (or faith, or Revelation). If we choose to remain "purely philosophical" in our philosophizing, then we are not truly philosophizing at all. We are not following in the footsteps of Plato and Aristotle.

This is particularly true in any attempt to explain history. The beginning and end of history are either revealed to us or not known at all, even though we must try to think our way through them. When man comes to theology in his scrutiny of history and its meaning, he encounters a theological statement about man's salvation. In theology, we catch sight of a goal shaped by God's wisdom, and this goal serves as a constant stimulus and guideline for our philosophical inquiry in this world.[34]

In the spirit of Patristic thought, **Eucharius Berbuir** provides a forcefully argued clarification of this whole idea.[35] He points out that the notion of pure nature was a theological tool developed to meet a particular situation but that it now has become a powerful reality in the consciousness of the Church. Its real weakness shows up precisely where it is supposed to be useful, however: in our discussions with the unbeliever and with the atheistic anthropology of Marxism.

In the latter encounter, two dissimilar quantities confront each other. Marxism offers us a perversion of reality, and we offer it an abstraction. Marxism says "no" to the concrete meaning and purpose of man; we exclude this concrete meaning at the start and try to talk about some neutral presupposition. The dialogue is bound to be unfruitful.

Berbuir objects to the Catholic approach that proposes to isolate human nature and natural law from its concrete historical condition. He grants the permissibility of this approach for apologetic purposes (even that is open to question!), but he points out that the same approach is often carried over to other areas. Berbuir himself, on the other hand, presents man's concrete nature as enmeshed in the grace of the real historical order which has Christ at its center.

The theological anthropology of **Michael Schmaus** stands

or falls with this same conception.[36] Real man, as willed by God, was meant to live in an elevated, supernatural state. So we can say that supernatural elevation was natural for the first human beings. To say that man is a rational animal is merely to provide a preliminary and provisional definition. A definitive definition of man's nature must also take into account his enduring relationship to God. In this sense, we can say that man is an *animal orans*.

Creation finds its fulfillment in the divine self-communication that took place in Christ. It is in Christ that creation exists. This fulfillment, however, does not proceed from nature; there is no ready passage from a purely natural to a supernatural type of existence. There is a way, however, from God's inner life to the natural world, and it takes the form of a gratuitous self-emptying on God's part.

Alluding to the work of de Lubac, Schmaus contrasts the two complementary lines of thought on grace: the Patristic and early Scholastic notion *vis-à-vis the* modern notion. In their extreme versions, the former tends to erase the boundaries between nature and grace while the latter tends to make pure nature autonomous. Yet, as Schmaus sees it, the dangers of the modern notion are incomparably greater than those of the older notion.

Nature cannot reach its fulfillment outside the realm of divine lordship and love. It can only find it within the realm of divine, Trinitarian life. If it misses its goal, it loses everything for which it was created, and that is what hell is. There is no third alternative.

Man, the king of creation, is the most insecure being in the world because his only refuge is God. He is set on the verge of nothingness and death so that he will find no other refuge but God. As this being, who is singled out through the Incarnation of God, he is the center of the world. For this reason, Schmaus rejects the traditional Neoplatonic and Scholastic hierarchy of created being that ascends from lower matter to pure spirit. To him it is theologically off the mark.

It was in human nature that God definitively revealed himself, and the dignity of a creature ultimately resides in his attachment to Christ. The body, as the corporal embodiment of spirit, takes on a wholly new significance through Christ. Here Schmaus echoes one of Barth's fundamental lines of thought. But the most intrinsic aspect of man remains the fact that he is opened to God through divine grace; he is, as it were, a supplication in fleshly form. He is what he is only through Christ, the head of mankind, the great pleader who stands before his Father and receives everything from him.

From there Schmaus goes on to show that natural reason is also enmeshed de facto in the one, concrete, supernatural order, without ever losing its own autonomy. The reason is not the weakness of natural reason, as the fideists and traditionalists would claim, but the de facto oneness of the concrete world order. Schmaus, like the other authors cited here, agrees with the view of Ripalda: every act which relates to the supernatural end of man is borne up by grace and enmeshed in the divinely willed order. Here again we hear echoes of a Barthian line of thought.

If someone asks whether mankind has ever lived in a condition that was totally devoid of grace, Schmaus would say that our only answer can be no. Even God's malediction is framed in the promise of the Redeemer. His wrath on man is meant to save and sanctify him. The world, in which the Incarnation of God's Son was part of the original plan, had a spot from which an all-encompassing blessing went forth; it was never totally surrendered to sin. Mankind has never experienced the heavy condition of pure, unadulterated sin. Our Father in heaven enveloped even this sin-filled world with his love, for he saw his Son living and dying in it.

The man redeemed by Christ is tied to him forever. No matter how hard he tries to break free from Christ, his relationship to Christ remains the hallmark of his existence. Even in his no to God, a faint glimmer of yes may still remain. We cannot plumb every nook and corner of our being.

Many Catholic religious philosophers have tackled the noetic side of this problem, even more so than the theologians.[37] Whatever name they may give to man's basic personal attitude (e.g., Marcel's *hope*), they all operate within the realm of concrete, grace-filled human nature. Thus their philosophy is clearly animated by the theological *a priori* that Guardini and Barth point out.

Speaking as philosophers and phenomenologists of this *a priori*, they focus cleanly on the basic existential condition of man's concrete spirit that Barth too vaguely designates as *faith*. It is not to be equated with explicit faith in Revelation; it is simply the realization that our thinking and being is grounded in the fact that we were thought and brought into existence. In the concrete supernatural order, all this happens in and through Christ.

Christ is there as a presupposition before creation. But there is a corresponding presupposition in the creature, and it is this that these religious philosophers seize upon. There is no question of irrationalism or relativism here, and no danger that reason will be lost or mixed up with faith. The priority of reason to faith (as a logical presupposition) and the truth of the preambles to faith remain intact. The order of creation does precede the order of redemption, and the first Adam does precede the second Adam, but, on a deeper level, the first Adam is mysteriously grounded on the second Adam. He is created for the sake of the second

Adam, and he cannot deny the traces of this relationship. Thus Schmaus, in his own way, can say what Barth said:

Because of his absolute power, God's being is the surest safe-guard of our own existence. We feel the threat of nothingness, and we quake before the chasm of emptiness. Creatureliness means being bound in by nothingness. At the same time, however, creaturely existence is a participation in divine being. It is grounded in God's being and bespeaks a relationship with him. The person who *believes in God* experiences this security in God more than he experiences the threat of nothingness. *In God's impregnable reality we find the ultimate assurance of our own reality.* . . .[38]

We cannot conclude this section without considering the ideas of Josef Bernhart. In *Chaos und Dämonie,*[39] he presents a view of the real world order that is closely akin to that of Barth. The tone of the two authors, to be sure, is radically different. Barth is highly optimistic, while Bernhart is melancholy and pessimistic. Moreover, Bernhart constructs his picture of man on the daimon of free will that Barth so savagely denigrates. The effect of Bernhart's presentation is to raise questions about Barth's optimistic outlook on the end result.

Bernhart begins by noting that the present world situation forces us to reexamine the relationship between reason and Revelation. We thus confront human nature *as it really is*—demonically ambiguous and undecided between good and evil, God and Satan.

Man and nature did not become what they now are after the fall. It is of their very essence to be that way. The possibility of sinning belonged to the elevated, grace-endowed nature of the first man. Aware of the dialectics in the concept of nature, Bernhart still chooses to work from a position stressed in Catholic theology: that nature is substantially the same in all its states. Thus he selects fallen human nature as the master image of human nature in

general. For Bernhart, this concept of nature is not a residual one that we arrive at by considering the gratuitousness of grace. Rather, it is something we find by looking
into the depths of concrete history (Bernhart's whole line
of thought follows the realistic thread that runs from
Irenaeus to Gregory of Nyssa).[40]

This nature has been drawn out of chaos, and it bears
the scars of its origin. In itself it is subject to chaos, but
chaos and evil are not to be equated. Indeed, the choosing
of evil represents a separation from chaos, albeit a perverse
choice. But precisely because man as pure nature is deliv-
ered up to chaos—and here Bernhart's affinity to Barth is
most evident—creation points back to an earlier, deeper
point. Created freedom and its frailties betoken our dependence on God's mercy and love. We can plead for this
mercy, but we have no right to it; for God's freedom vis-
à-vis man can be no less than man's freedom vis-à-vis God.
Totally insecure, we wait in hope for God the savior.

From the very beginning, it is Christ, the slain lamb,
who is this savior. It is he who shows us the meaning of
creation and the possibility of chaos. His work of reconciliation is the a priori of the created world, the explanation
of everything. For Bernhart, this view of redemption has
far greater religious depth than the prevailing juridical version. Primeval man was created in the image of the divine
Logos, who is himself true man and bears the burden of
humanity from all eternity.[41]

For all his subjection to chaos, man does have an inner
point that raises him above the stormy seas of his being.
There is a point where we can stand above the storm and
survey the drama of chaos below. So says Bernhart.

Now Karl Barth eventually arrived at the opinion that
human nature was good in itself because God chose to
separate it from chaos but that it was also subject to chaos
and in need of God's grace. His reluctance to talk about

the "dämonie" of creaturely freedom and his attempt to posit a second kind of real creaturely freedom at this point seems to fit in with his general Protestant reluctance to call man's creaturely situation and responsibility by its right name. In the last analysis, the difference between Bernhart and Barth seems to be one of nuances. We may say with Barth that in creation God rejected chaos, but it still threatens us from without; or we may say with Bernhart that God has placed man in a chaos-ridden situation.

Insofar as the question of nature and grace is concerned, we have shed some light on the question posed to Catholic dogmatic theology by Barth's theology. Man should be content to deal with the real world of experience: to confront nature as it is in reality and to accept the undeservedness of grace vis-à-vis this real world. He should not set himself up as the judge of what is possible and what is not. Only God knows what is really possible in the order of existence. When man presumes to know the whole picture here, he is a victim of rationalism.

Knowing that grace is a free gift, we can say that God *did not have to grant it*. Even this judgment, however, which is a human one, should submit itself obediently to God's perspective. In the last analysis, we should view things from the perspective of God and divine Revelation —totally free, yes, but also the one thing necessary.

4. At the Inexpressible Limits

When we come to the question of judgment and redemption, we are at the inexpressible limits. The priority of Christ over creation and sin brings us to the rim of an eschatological mystery that we cannot talk about directly, as Barth rightly noted. Our eyes and mouths are closed by the flood of light and grace which greets us here.

Yet we must not hesitate to say everything that can be said. To be groping about in Plato's cave with a dim background light is one thing; to turn around and stare into the full light is quite another thing.

To be sure, we cannot set down one particular norm as the only valid one for theological pronouncements on this question. Scriptural Revelation itself provides a whole range of varied expressions that are dialectical and indirect. To be true to this Revelation, we must respect all these varied pronouncements and not make an arbitrary selection between them. Arbitrary selection is the path of the heretic. By the same token, direct or oversystematized pronouncements are also ruled out. Barth himself was fully aware of these facts, but it seems to me that he stepped a bit too close to the light and tended towards oversystematization.

What can we say about those Catholic thinkers who start from the Christocentric focal point described earlier? They, too, often find themselves driven towards the same eschatological perspectives. In many cases, we will not appreciate the real import of their words if we do not keep their unexpressed but real focal point in mind. Other thinkers move towards the Christ a priori, rather than starting from it. The recourse of many to pre-Augustinian Patristics and, even more, the recent stress on the social element in our supernatural life seems to go out of the way to stress the Johannine theology of judgment.

All these thinkers realize nonetheless that they ultimately come up against something that is inexpressible. They face a mystery, and every statement about it must be qualified immediately. It is framed in the total context of the Church's proclamation, and it can only be contemplated in faith, hope, and love. These virtues are something more than human knowledge, but they are something less than a transcendent vision.

Our statements and conceptions fluctuate between two *tendencies*: systematization (e.g., Barth and Przywara) as the upper limit, and a mere ethos (e.g., Guardini) as the lower limit. All our statements are feeble attempts to give ample room to the mystery in Christian consciousness. The difficulty in this exercise is clear to anyone who has tried it. The statements range from a dialectics that rejects the possibility of unity to a dialectics that attempts to reduce everything to unity; and the same dilemma confronts both Catholic and Protestant theology. Both must confront the veiled speech of scriptural Revelation, both must try to reconcile its doctrine of divine judgment with its doctrine of redemption.

In this context we must not overlook the most noteworthy model of modern Catholicism, Thérèse of Lisieux. Her mission, as she saw it, was to teach that God's righteousness is not in opposition to His love, that it is identical with His love. Looking forward to the Last Judgment, she proclaimed that love casts out fear and that she was the real trailblazer for all little souls.

Hopefully our presentation has shown that a Christocentric emphasis is not an exclusively Protestant approach. We have cited major Catholic authors to prove the point. To regard them as outsiders or exceptions would be incorrect and unfair. The least common denominator is not the real measure of Catholic nor of Protestant thought.

Barth's opinions represent one view among many—perhaps a well-founded view. The Catholic authors cited above propose one view among many possible ones—a view that I regard as well founded. In its basic outlines, it is the view of Patristic and classic Scholastic theology. It is not in conflict with Przywara's version of the analogy of being, because his version is merely a provisional, abstract formulation of the ultimate Christological truth.

Hopefully, the Catholic perspectives cited above have also shown that we can be as radically Christocentric as Barth without falling into the narrow corner that he seems to have got caught in. At every point we have left spaces and breathing room. A real priority of nature and reason is presupposed if there is to be a real Incarnation, and this in turn requires a relatively solid range of meaningfulness that is not totally devoid of meaning when we abstract from our ultimate supernatural goal.

The first act of reason is not faith, for then faith would not be possible at all. We must posit some distance here, for the sake of grace and Revelation and faith. Moreover, out of respect for human nature, human freedom, and human decision-making (a respect that God clearly shows), the eschatological climax must be open-ended. The necessity of God's freely proffered love can in no way be turned into a necessity of nature itself.

It is not a game between an Absolute party and a relative party where the former is the winner from the start. God takes man so seriously that he subjects himself to the abasement of human nature so that man can be a worthy partner in the game. There are more nuances and transitions here than are evident in Barth's theology. There are transitions between faith and unbelief, initiatives of nature (under the influence of grace), progress and setbacks, countless forms of resistance, and also of *appropriation* and *cooperation*.

The notions of appropriation and cooperation crop up at the border of Barth's theology, particularly in *Church Dogmatics, 7*. They lead us into a final question concerning the relationship between Barth's thought and Catholicism.

V · GRACE AND SIN

When we talk about appropriating grace and cooperating with it, we are face to face with a deeper question. We must consider the ontology of grace and the concomitant doctrine of sin.

According to Catholic theology, grace is the divine self-disclosure and self-communication in which God pours out his own inner life on the world and gives the creature a participation in it. Now because God is both absolute spirit and absolute being, this participation must be something involving both consciousness and being or (closely allied to this) both happening and being. If it merely involved consciousness, that is, if it were solely of the cognitive order and involved merely the revelation of some truth about God that we had to believe, the benefit to us would be illusory. In reality, it would mean that we were shown a world that we could not and should not enter. A purely cognitive revelation of this sort is self-contradictory and impossible. God's truth is one with his being (i.e., God is love), so God could not communicate his truth without offering us access to his being.

The correlation between happening and being should be just as clear. God's Revelation is a happening only if something really takes place. There must be a real change in the ontological order: a real communication of divine being, and a real creaturely participation in it. If nothing of an ontological nature happens between God and man, then nothing happens at all. God remains in his heaven, man remains in this world, and our talk about *happening* is illusory. If that were the case, then we would be dealing with a hoped-for transformation (in spe) not a real one (in re); we would be dealing with a purely eschatological transformation and a purely forensic justification that was wholly in the cognitive order and did not really touch the creature's being and nature.

Interestingly enough, the ontic categories of Catholic dogma which seems to obscure the happening character of the grace event actually do most to bring it out into the light. If men are not "partakers of the divine nature" (2 Pet. 1:4), if they are not ontologically incorporated into Christ as members of his body, then the Revelation happening does not reach them at all. Dietrich Bonhoeffer realized this back in 1931. In Akt und Sein, he sought to combine an actualist theology with an ecclesial ontology (being in Christ), and Barth himself should not have closed his eyes to this fact, if he took seriously his shift to the analogy of faith.

Barth started out by focusing on the absolute character of divine act. This necessarily led to a theopanism in which created being was totally disintegrated. Crossing over into God's world meant the destruction of the creaturely world. Since creatures still existed, however, the crossover had to be viewed eschatologically and projected into a distant future when created being would no longer exist.

The schema proved to be unacceptable. It did not fit in with the data of Christian Revelation, and it did not preserve the real analogy between God and his creature. Once we believe that the Revelation happening enables the creature to participate in God's inner reality without losing its own nature, then we cannot be satisfied with an exclusively eschatological framework.

If something is going to happen to the creature in an age to come, why can't it take place, in some form, here and now? If the real analogy between God and man will

prevent the creature from being destroyed when he enters
God's future world, why should it not give him entrance to
God's world here and now? And if it does give him such
access now, why should the creature's present sanctification
be a purely forensic one? Why must real ontic sanctification be postponed for the future world?

Catholic dogma took these questions seriously and tried
to draw the ultimate conclusions. If creaturely being is
something willed and protected by God, then it is so
because God willed to enter a real history with it; and
history means an encounter and exchange between what
is truly proper to each partner. If it is a real history, then
real ontological elements are involved. There is a real participation and a perduring ontological effect (qualitas
inhaerens). What is more, within the absolute predicates
involved, there is room for degrees and variety, for more
and less, for drawing closer and moving farther away, for
increase and decrease.

Moreover, because we are dealing with God's Revelation
and his initiative here, the real ontological aspect takes
unconditional priority over the purely cognitive aspect. The
fact that man is laid hold of by God takes priority over
man's realization of this fact. It is a priority of order, not
necessarily of time. Note well: we are not simply talking
about the priority of opus operatum over opus operantis
in the sacramental economy. We are talking about the
overall priority of God's activity in man. God's activity
touches man's being and transforms it, so that it then can
reach his consciousness and summon him to faith.

All this is true, and it does not prejudice the chronological order of the de facto justification process. The
Catholic distinction between actual grace and habitual
grace is secondary to this basic law. There is only one grace
and one nature of grace, even though it may take countless
forms in coming to man. No one should know this better

than Barth, who strongly opposed any taint of synergism and every attempt to put man's response on the same level as God and his Word.

The theology of the Reformation overemphasized the pretemporal reality of God, as their doctrine of predestination indicates. The theology of the eighteenth and nineteenth centuries stressed the supratemporal reality of God. Early twentieth-century theology overemphasized the posttemporal reality of God.[1] Barth himself fell in line with this latter tendency, but he came to realize that it was wrong. As he himself puts it: "We were inclined to reduce the eternity of God to a purely posttemporal reality. . . . We had not grasped the full biblical picture of God's eternity."[2] When he did grasp the complete picture, he was forced to rework many notions and to tackle ethics anew.

When he tackled Christology in *Church Dogmatics*,[3] Barth tries to effect a reconciliation between Luther and the extra-Calvinist notions. He also makes energetic use of the concept of being and rejects the "horror of *phusis*" shared by actualists and eschatologists. In discussing the history that God's Word creates in the world, he wants to make it something more than a protohistory. He describes it as a real, temporal history that can and must be explained in terms of analogy. History has its own natural course and meaning. God's Revelation enters this history and, insofar as it becomes a real, worldly history, it becomes the measure of all temporal history.

Complementing this new line of thought is a theological consideration of time and its analogy. Like Barth, we may choose to strip away all the purely philosophical features of time because concrete time is subjugated to sin, but if God has truly come into the world in Christ, then his presence in the world signifies that there is also a present for man and time. God's presence in the world is, as Barth puts it, "a piece of what we call world history."[4] It does not remain transcendent to our time; it actually enters our time and creates it anew. Just as humanity is created anew because the eternal Word becomes flesh, so our time is created anew insofar as it becomes the time of Jesus Christ.[5]

So we confront the pendulous two-sidedness of the analogy of time. God's time becomes our time so that our time, without ceasing to be ours, may participate in God's time. And if we are willing to admit that God's time does not destroy our time (as Barth does), then we can draw out the full implications of the transformation involved. Once again the whole problem of nature and grace allows room for development and elucidation.

The analogy of time (i.e., God's descent into our time and its consequent elevation) tells us that the two times (as forms of being) do more than touch each other tangentially. They encounter each other and interact. Thus something really happens to man and the world when God communicates his grace, and, by the same token, the relative factor (i.e., the creature) plays a part in the process. God's self-communication to man means that man's being and actions, with all their relativity and provisionality, are relevant for God in this history.

It is at this point that we encounter the whole question of man the sinner and his justification through grace. Since the Reformation and the Council of Trent, it is here that the denominational differences come to a head. Luther's formulation, *simul justus et peccator* (man is simultaneously sinner and saved), was an ambiguous one. It can mean exactly the opposite of the Catholic doctrine, but, as Robert Grosche has shown,[6] it can also be given an orthodox Catholic interpretation.

In general, we can say that the formula is right enough for what Luther was talking about specifically. On the one hand, he was considering the state of *homo viator*, where man is not yet fully justified before God, where he is involved in a real history and a daily conversion from the old man to the new man. On the other hand, Luther was stressing the fact that man's justification, from beginning to end, is something bestowed upon him as a gift from above. The formula becomes unacceptable for Catholic theology only when it becomes one-sided: when the first consideration is turned into pure eschatology, and man's justification is made a future hope, not a present reality; or when the second consideration is turned into a juridical nominalism, so that justification never becomes a real, intrinsic part of man.

The formula could represent a pure contradiction in terms. It could mean that the sinner, precisely as sinner, is justified; or that the sinner, still totally a sinner in himself, is nevertheless regarded as justified by God because of Christ's merits. Karl Barth has repeatedly stressed that these two possible interpretations do not come into play here at all. For him, the formula sums up the real happening and history that takes place between God and the sinner, and it must be interpreted as Luther himself meant it. The two terms, sinner and just man, are not equally valid, simultaneous, and interchangeable descriptions of our existence. The only equation here is between our past and our future, and it is the latter that dominates the former:

Our sin has taken place, our justification is coming. . . . That and that alone is the real Christian concept of time. In Jesus Christ, man's existence is moving from the first realm (sin) to the second realm (justification). To live in time, in the Christian sense, means to live in this process of conversion from one realm to the other.[7]

Yet we must still ask whether Barth's explanation provides for a real happening and a real history in this area. He is reluctant to use ontic categories when he talks about grace and justification. He relegates the effects of the sacraments to the cognitive order exclusively and refuses to accept the Catholic and Lutheran doctrine of a causative process. He transfers both time periods back into a pretemporal eternity, where sin is ever the past and justification is ever the future. He avoids all talk of growth and progress and all talk of relapses into sin and loss of faith. In short, he avoids all talk about those things that would provide for a real ongoing history between man and God in the sphere of the temporal and the relative. Thus we cannot help but feel that nothing really happens in his theology of history, because everything has already taken place in eternity.

If it is true that in the eternity of Jesus Christ sin is already the past, how can sin and unbelief ever become the present in time? Are they not illusory phantasms without any reality at all? And if this be true, does not the cross of Christ (in which sin and sinner are rejected) become God's monologue with himself?

How can we give a truly Catholic interpretation to Luther's formula, an interpretation that combines a truly Christocentric viewpoint with a truly temporal history? To do this, we must distinguish various layers of this whole question and scrupulously separate them from one another. In the multilevel depths of this question lie the real mysteries of Christian existence, and they are just as mysterious as the inner mysteries of God himself. Viewed in the light of these mysterious depths, Luther's formula appears to be an oversimplification. It points towards the mystery, but it does not allow us to grasp it adequately.

1. We can start by agreeing with Barth's description of temporal existence. Man's temporal existence in faith is a moving process (1 Cor. 9:24). He is engaged in the process of turning from his past towards a new future (Phil. 3:13), of dying to his outer man and renewing his inner man (2 Cor. 4:16). Our definitive redemption is eschatological (*in spe*), and here and now in this world we are sinners among sinners. Daily we must beat our breast and confess our sinfulness.

Admitting all this, the Catholic must go even further than Luther and Barth in stressing the paradox here. For this eschatological perspective must be combined with another perspective that is presented just as clearly in scripture: in this present age the Christian, now freed from sin, participates in the divine life through grace and is under no compulsion to sin further.

The *in spe* of the first perspective does not eliminate the *in re* of the second perspective. However much the statements of scripture may seem to clash with one another, the Catholic will not allow either perspective to erase the other. Nor will he regard their encounter as a purely dialectical contradiction.

His emphasis on the happening in process (man's *becoming* justified) will always be tempered and guided by his ontological understanding of grace. Grace is a real participation in the divine life here and now, in which man *is* justified.

2. The righteousness of the Christian is a gift granted to him by virtue of Christ's merits. It comes to him as a grace from outside, unmerited on his part. Prior to all man's personal cooperation in the process of justification lies this gratuitous gift of grace from God, who loved us while we were still sinners. All our subsequent cooperation

does not obliterate the gratuitous character of our new life.

Here again, however, the Catholic feels obliged to combine the gratuitous character of grace and justification with the notion of real sanctification. The latter notion was not totally neglected by the Reformers, but it was greatly underplayed by them. There is a real sanctification, a real participation in Christ's merits and the divine life he opens up. It is not merely a passive receiving; it involved an obligation to cooperate with Christ and to become a light in turn. The gift of grace is meant to become an intimate part of our own inner self, so much so that its fruit will be our own.

3. This plunges us into a deeper and even more paradoxical level of the mystery. The more the believer tries to live a life of faith, the more he will come to realize how grace transforms his own deeds. He will come to see his paltry human deeds in the light of God's grace and love. Here the noetic side of the grace process will come to complement its ontological reality.

The tension pervades both relationships: the relationship between the sinner and Christ's grace and the more general relationship between creation and God. In the latter case, too, the relative, timebound deeds and activities of creation must be "transformed" if they are to have validity and durability in the realm of God. Adam himself needed grace to become the partner of God. Even he could not ascribe his good works to his own capabilities; even he experienced the chasm between the Lord and his servant.

In the order of sin, man's awareness of this chasm becomes even more acute. When he encounters the gift of grace, he draws back in shame from the knowledge of his own sinfulness: "Depart from me, for I am a sinful man." And the more worthy he becomes to share in the grace activity of the Lord, the more he becomes aware of his own unworthiness and his true self. The saints bear witness to this.

4. This brings us to another level. It is the man justified by grace and living by faith, and only he, who comprehends what scripture means by "the world." The world is not individual, personal sin that can be neatly demarcated. It is the whole realm over which sin (hamartia) holds sway, even where it is not imputed (Rom. 5:13). It is the realm of desire and "lust" (1 Jn. 2:16), the root from which sin breaks forth as the typical and normal fruit. It is not so much a passive potency as an active potency, a pregnant womb ever ready to procreate (see James 1:14–15).

The dividing line between this active potency and actual sin is a real one, to be sure, but just as real are the manifold connections and crossing points between them. So long as the root has not been torn out of a man—and this happens only at death in the case of most people—new sins continue to blossom and all our good deeds are tainted with its influence. What good deed of ours does not have some ignoble motive behind it somewhere?

The working out of this whole process in our present life cannot be projected onto a purely psychological plane. Between our present activity and the intangible world of faith stretches an intermediate zone where purely psychological factors are transcended. Why? Because faith can be incarnated in our experience without ever ceasing to be faith. This is the zone where we talk about "the discernment of spirits," where faith moves out in its quest for understanding and meaning, and where we see concretely what world means.

Our primary insight in this zone is that there is some radical lack of order in man and human realities. Just as the scientist sees all sorts of impurities under the microscope, so the man of faith discovers all sorts of impurities in the spiritual atmosphere he lives in. Experiencing this, the saints are driven to the point of despair over themselves, and they long to live wholly in God. Once again, however, the full paradox of this whole situation can only be experienced in a Catholic context, that is, a context that recognizes and professes a real, inner process of sanctification in whose light we glimpse the real nature of "the world."

5. The paradox deepens as we gain deeper insight in our experience of "the world." The distinction between my sin and your sin disappears, and we confront the mystery of man's solidarity in sin. Every personal sin is also community sin, and it is produced, to some extent, by the sins of the community. This does not diminish personal guilt. On the contrary, it complicates personal sin and heightens our responsibility as sinners; and since the effects of evil committed and good deeds left undone multiply relentlessly, our debt is not paid off when our personal guilt is forgiven.

Writers like Dostoyevsky and Claudel, and the saints in general, were deeply aware of the social aspect of sinful guilt. And Catholic doctrine goes far beyond any Protestant explanation in heightening the paradox here. It stresses that the more the just man partakes of the redeemer's holiness, the more he assumes responsibility for the guilt of others. He no longer can say whether he is suffering for his own guilt or for the guilt of others.

Christ himself, hanging on the cross, no longer chooses to make this distinction. He endure's God's malediction, suffering vicariously for all men. He chooses not to be the exception to the rule, but to be the rule, and, because of Christ, the sinner who shares his passion can no longer make this distinction either. His suffering is heightened by the knowledge that he is bound in solidarity to all sinners, who are jointly responsible for the cross of Christ.

6. The human experience described above finds full expression in the whole matter of *temptation*. Temptation mercilessly reveals the chasm between what is and what should be. It reveals it from the viewpoint of God's righteousness and divine judgment, which is a true viewpoint even if it hides the radiating light of God's transforming love and grace.

In the perspective of temptation, we come to glimpse a persisting chasm and incapacity. All our good works are hopelessly off base, and all human realities are lost before God, if we leave the gift of grace out of account. No one who has found himself in the coils of real temptation has been able to salvage even one of his good deeds from the fire of divine judgment. No one in such a situation could lay claim to any reward.

In temptation, we glimpse the very *real possibility* that God could have operated out of pure justice. This is not a delusion or an illusion; it is a real insight into what would have been *if* God *had not*. . . . In temptation, we come to appreciate that sin provides no exit. It is a hopeless blind alley. All the acts of the sinner are off base, if grace does not come (gratuitously) to transform them. And while the saints are the ones who look most closely on this naked truth, it is an insight available to every Christian conscience.

7. Now we can formulate the objective dogmatic counterpart of the Christian experience we have been describing: the redemption of the world occurs at the prescise moment when sin reaches its unsurpassable acme, in the death of God on Golgotha, where every sinner participates actively. There, where human beings and the whole human race

are at their sinful worst, they are objectively redeemed and made righteous. The whole process described above echoes, on the personal level, the objective law of redemption itself: God's grace takes the form of a judgment on sinners, who are embodied *in toto* by their representative on the cross.

Christ on the cross is the *simul justus et peccator*, the sinless one who was made sin for us (2 Cor. 5:21) and turned into a curse (Gal. 3:13), so that we might be redeemed from sin and God's curse. The Son of God did not become man solely to embody the definitive analogy between God and the creature. His mission was to portray and embody the concrete analogy between the God of wrath and grace and his damned and redeemed creation. On the cross, we see what sin is, and at Easter we find out what grace can do; only God himself could show us this.[8]

This happening alone tells us what temptation, suffering, and death mean in the old and new Covenants. This happening alone tells us what grace can achieve. We cannot find the true meaning of *simul justus et peccator* in ourselves; we must look to Christ for it.

That does not mean that Christ's form is directly our form as well. We are the sinners, while he is the just one. In being made sin for us, he does not cease to be the just one; while we, in being justified, do cease to be sinners in a very real sense. In taking on the form of sin, Christ experiences the full reality of the contradiction between God and sin and overcomes it. Only he does it, so he is the definitive form of the *simul justus et peccator*.

Here again we encounter the priority of redemption. It does not mean that sin is possible only because there is a redemption, but it does mean that all concrete sin is subsumed within the spotless, freely chosen form of Christ. We remain separated from this form because we really are sinners, and as sinners we really do stand in contradiction to God. But God's decision and judgment is more powerful than that of sinners. Where sin abounded, grace did more abound. Here, too, the last word is Christ's.

Let us sum up briefly. God's grace is a participation in his inner divine life; it elevates the creature above and beyond any claims and longings he might have. This participation is not purely forensic or purely eschatological; it is real, internal, and present. It is the happening that lays hold of created being and transforms it.

Because it is a real happening of this sort, it leaves room for all the phases and stages that go to make up man's journey to God. It leaves room for conversion, progress, backsliding, cooperative effort, and obstacles. Redemption does not turn all our frail human realities into meaningless elements of a bygone past. It leaves room for us to change as we follow the footsteps of the Lord. Our own faltering steps have real meaning and weight. Our frail decisions are taken seriously by God, who works them into his overall design.

Epilogue

I · A LOOK BACK

We have examined Barth's outlook on nature and grace and then offered a Catholic Christocentric viewpoint on the same topic. In so doing, we observed a gradual rapprochement taking place. This does not mean that both sides are in full agreement, nor need they be. Between Barth and his Catholic partners in dialogue there always remained some points of disagreement, but if we perceive the deep underlying layer of agreement and leave aside purely terminological differences, we will realize that these differences are certainly no greater than those between Barth and other Protestant theologians (e.g., Brunner) or those between Catholic theologians on many issues.

My book, then, has achieved its purpose. It has shown that the problems and approaches of Barth are not such that they justify or necessitate a split in the Church. Here, of course, I am only talking about the problems raised in the tracts on God as creator, sanctifier, and redeemer (*de Deo creante, elevante, redimente*), not about the tracts on the Church and the sacraments. My point is that Barth's basic ideas in the first tracts are not such that they *necessarily* require a split among the Churches when we come to the later tracts. Within the later tracts themselves, to be sure, we may find sound reasons that call for such a split; but they would not be the necessary corollaries of the ideas presented in the earlier tracts.

In order to justify itself, the Reformation focused forcefully on the tracts on the Church and the sacraments. It sought to present the reasons which justified a split on the basis of these doctrines. My purpose here has been to show that there is no necessary logical tieup between the dogmatic problems of the first tracts and the schism-producing conclusions of the later tracts.

This may not seem to be much of an accomplishment, but, in fact, we have untied a knot that Barth himself chose to tie. Barth chose to have his ecclesial and sacramental theology (the later tracts) flow logically from his theology of God (the early tracts). All the basic decisions are set forth in the early tracts, and they form the framework for the decisions reached in the later tracts. Barth's theology was presented as a unified whole.

The Reformation theologians started from the other end. They moved from the abuses in ecclesial and sacramental practice to ecclesial and sacramental theology; then they went back to modify the teachings of the tract on God, creation, and redemption. Barth, the theologian, chose to move from the other direction; but this approach proved incapable of justifying the split. In order to justify the Reformation's charge against Catholicism, Barth was forced to ground Catholic theology on a mistaken notion of the analogy of being and then develop a proper counter-notion.

We have tried to show that the supposed opposition is an illusory one. The Protestant–Catholic conflict is not a battle of formulas. It simply concerns two different ways of understanding God's one Revelation in Christ. If we choose to sum up the approaches in formulas, then we can put it this way. Barth's way of understanding God's Revelation in Christ (the analogy of faith) includes within itself the analogy of being; in the Catholic Christocentric approach presented here, the analogy of being becomes concrete and real only within the more all-embracing analogy of faith. The Catholic Christocentric theology presented here allows us to combine the inalienable tenets of the Catholic Church with the insights of Barth.

What tenets must be respected here? First of all, one must acknowledge that there is a real natural and rational order that is relatively independent of the order of grace and that it has a real, albeit relative priority over it. This tenet is fully respected and upheld by those Catholic authors who see grace as the ground and goal of creation. One can maintain that the why and wherefore of nature is grace and, at the same time, that nature does have a real priority over grace. One can maintain that the wherefore of reason is grace (and ultimately, the beatific vision) and, at the same time, that reason has its own proper structure and legitimacy.

Nature and reason have a meaning; grace and faith are the ultimate meaning of this meaning. The first Adam had a specific nature; the second Adam is the ground and goal of that nature. Thus the Catholic preambles to faith are real, and we can insist upon them. Framed in the ultimate and definitive priority of grace and faith, nature and reason do have a relatively priority. It involves an openness, an obediential potency that enables man, once the order of grace is opened up, to explore the inner meaning and content of Revelation (*fides quaerens intellectum*) and to comprehend the meaning of nature and reason insofar as it is tied up with faith and grace (*intellectus quaerens fidem*).

That this process of moving from reason to faith is possible only within the revealed order of grace does not contradict what we have just said. The right conclusions to be drawn are different, as we have tried to show. We must conclude that reason has been created for the sake of faith, that it finds its ultimate meaning in faith, and that it can only proceed to the act of faith through grace. We must conclude that reason is truly itself only through faith and that it can come to know itself only through a real faith in God and Revelation.

The order of grace and the process of justification are particularly open, dynamic, and progressive. They leave room for an ongoing process, such as that described by Trent (DZ 798). It is a process that is initiated within the framework of grace (*excitati divina gratia*) and that does not tone down the fact that man is justified through grace without any merit on his part (DZ 801).

We cannot simplify our explanation beyond referring to this twofold perspective; the absolute priority of grace and divine Revelation, the relative priority of nature and its potentialities. Only within such a perspective could Barth talk about the external ground and the internal ground. A Christologically framed analogy of being is merely Catholic theology's attempt to take this twofold (but unequal) grounding seriously.

What insights of Karl Barth deserve serious consideration from Catholic theology? The primary ones are those involving a Christocentric framework, the historicity of nature, the created character of worldly truth, and the tieup between these three factors. If we accept the first factor, as certain Catholic authors do, we cannot avoid respecting the other two factors also.

The natural order, for all its inner laws and conditions, ultimately rests upon a gratuitous happening (the Incarnation) and the history that flows from it. At its center and at every other point, this history is concreteness personified. To distance ourselves from it through abstraction is impossible and sinful. Within the natural order, to be sure, there is legitimate room for abstraction and universal concepts, but they always remain related to this concrete happening. It is this concrete happening that allows room for abstraction and contemplation, that gives full meaning to existence and nature, that allows us to use universal concepts (e.g., being) in a meaningful way.

Such use is legitimate, even in Barth's eyes, so long as we do not force Christ's Revelation and history into philosophical categories that drain it of substance and reality. Temporal truth is, in the last analysis, created truth. It is finite and mutable, and we cannot set it over against God's truth as an equal. Christian theology has done this all too often in the past, making *Platonic* concepts equal to God's concrete plans.[1] In an earlier age, when philosophy and theology were not neatly separated from one another, such Christian Platonism might be condoned. Today, when we have begun to demarcate the proper boundaries of created nature and reason, we must recognize the limitations of all human models and conceptual systems. Over against the concrete workings of God, they are relative and finite.

If we recognize this, there is little danger that the preambles of faith will tie Revelation down to a frozen philosophical system, as Barth once feared, and we in turn will appreciate Barth's concern to preserve and respect the chasm between divine Absolute and creaturely Relative.

II · THE CHURCH

There still remain many decisive differences between Protestants and Catholics, differences that justify schism in the eyes of Barth and other Protestants, e.g., the infallibility of the Pope, veneration of the saints, and Mariology, but the differences of opinion *in the topics considered here* (creation and Covenant) do not call for or justify a split on their own.

On the one hand, Barth's understanding of actualism in *Church Dogmatics* calls for an ecclesiology that stresses and justifies the happening character of history, but it does not call for an ecclesiology that *rules out all continuity for the sake of this happening.* The real happening for Barth is now the Incarnation, not the vertical descent of God's atemporal Word into the world. If ecclesiology is made a function of Christology (and it is by Barth in *Church Dogmatics*), and if Christology includes all the elements of the created ordier in it, then there is room for nature, continuity, and human conditions; in short, Barth's ecclesiology of an earlier period (1920–1930) is now superceded. No longer did he fear introducing temporal elements into theology and the Church, for now Christ stands at the center. The temporal concepts may be misused, but such misuse is not a foregone conclusion.

On the other side of the coin, the distinctive teachings of the Catholic Church are not tied up with the distorted notion of the analogy of being that Barth once entertained. Instead, they flow from Catholicism's attempt to respect the union of divine and created nature in Christ. In Christ, human nature is not ground under by the divine; it is given a chance to cooperate and serve. It is a service made possible and real by grace, but it is an authentic service. Whether we are talking about ecclesial structures (e.g., infallibility, sacramental grace) or man's cooperation with grace (e.g., merits, the saints, Mariology), we are really talking about God's free use of man and human realities in Christ. What the Protestant sees as a stress on human capabilities is, for the Catholic, the ultimate sign and high point of God's condescending grace.

We Catholics would do well to remember what we mean

when we say that grace elevates and perfects nature. At bottom, it means that grace descends into nature. It is grace that takes on hierarchial and institutional forms in the Church in order to lay hold of man better. It is grace that takes shape in the charismatic appeal of a person in order to reach men in their individual lives. Nature can never be the measure of grace, for every claim of nature fades away before the cross of Christ. It is in the cross of Christ that the seed of nature comes to fruition through grace. Of its own, nature has no fruit that could be relevant in the order of grace.

The biblical image of the grape vine and its branches may help to resolve the Protestant–Catholic differences in this area. Grace, like the vine, is the one source and principle of fruitfulness, but nature, like the branches, can bear much fruit if it is attached to the vine. The branches can bring forth much fruit (the Catholic stress), but only in conjunction with the vine (the Protestant stress). Like the vine, Christ gives the capability of bearing fruit to his branches. He is the head, the fullness of the godhead, who communicates to his body the capability of developing this fullness to the utmost, and, in doing this, his body will use all its natural organs.

To talk of a body, however, is to talk necessarily of interconnection, continuity, nature, and unconsciousness. A body cannot consist purely of sporadic moments of happening. The Church, as the body of Christ, originates from the vertical happening of the Incarnation; and its purpose is to continually bring its members into the grace happening and an encounter with the Head. But between these two happenings the Church perdures as a corporeal, substantial reality with natural and supernatural qualities. It will not last as such for all eternity, but it will last as such to the end of the world. Until that end comes, grace will make use of our frail and mortal corporeality.

Protestantism is reluctant to acknowledge that use. It prefers to view the Church on earth in the image of the heavenly kingdom to come. But we must allow grace to engage in the "folly" of using nature. In the alien realm of the natural world, its pure gratuitousness is most clearly revealed.

III · A FEW YEARS LATER

The first edition of this book came out in 1951. Framed in a particular historical setting, it sought to move discussion about Barth's theology out of strictly Protestant circles into the mainstream of interconfessional dialogue. It did achieve this goal, and the theology of Karl Barth became a lively topic.

In 1961, we began to think about publishing a second edition. But the general historical situation in theology had changed greatly, so it was not easy to decide upon the proper course of action. In Catholic circles, Barth's theology had been tackled with enthusiasm, as the works of Bouillard[1] and Küng[2] attested. In Protestant circles, the debate over the historical Jesus and demythologizing was taking up much time and energy. Finally, the stirrings of Vatican II had begun to excite hopes and speculations in all sectors of Christendom.

To match the historical impact of the original edition, a second edition would have had to undergo a thorough reworking. It would have to take into account the works of Bouillard and Küng, the new sections of *Church Dogmatics*, and the debate between Barthians and Bultmannians. It would also have to rectify the top-heavy emphasis of the first edition on fundamental theology and the modes of theological knowledge. The result would be an entirely new book.

This gave rise to several questions. Would such a revision contribute greatly to greater interconfessional dialogue? The answer seemed to be no. Wasn't it true that Barth's subsequent treatment of dogmatic issues (e.g., Christ as prophet, priest, and king) could be fully appreciated by Catholics in terms of the conclusions he had already reached in the earlier volumes? The answer seemed to be yes. So we decided to print the original edition unchanged, and to add a few remarks on what has happened since it came out.

To begin with, Barth himself had moved ahead but he had not changed his focal interest. Section after section embodied the same Christocentric emphasis that had lain buried in the *Epistle to the Romans* and broken to the surface in the earlier volumes of *Church Dogmatics*. It was still the story of God's salvific activity in the world through the human Jesus Christ, an activity that is only insofar as it is a happening. Barth described this happening as the "in-oneness" of two realities: the Lord's descent as a servant[3] and the servant's ascent to the Lord.[4]

Here there was no static Christology, such as that of earlier Catholic and Orthodox theology. Here we were not dealing with the essence of Christ, his intellect and will, or the relationship between his two natures. Here we were dealing with a dynamic and functional Christology similar to that proposed by Oscar Cullmann. It was only this happening that Christ could bear witness to as prophet and teacher, for he himself was the happening that bears witness to God, and theological Christology would be nothing, if it were not a witness to Christ's witness.[5]

Everything else in Barth's treatment of creation (cosmology, anthropology, divine providence and creaturely ethics[6]) converged towards this happening. Creation was the external ground for the Covenant, and the core of the covenant was Christ's work of reconciling the world to God. Any further treatment of redemption and eschatology could only represent the full unfolding of Christ's activity. Everything converged towards this central point.

Barth was now able to include more and more temporal issues and realities in his dogmatics, nor did he hesitate to introduce viewpoints from earlier dogmatic approaches (e.g., man's sanctification), even though he still rejected their methodology in principle. As long as everything was related to the central Christ-happening and judged by that norm, he could undertake an extensive analysis of marital, social, and political issues.[7]

One should not be deluded by this fact, however. Barth had definitely not abandoned his basic polemics against philosophical reflection. In his view, any and all philosophical reflection on human existence and its significance was still irrelevant. For this reason, I still have the same critical reservations about his later volumes that I had about his earlier ones (see pp. 198–200 in particular).

Put simply, my prime reservation is this. If one rejects the value or necessity of philosophical reflection because it is a purely temporal matter, then any and every truth about man must be deduced from a Christology (i.e., divine Revelation) that presupposes these truths. At the point where we are supposed to be talking about a *happening* between God and man, we must start from scratch to work up a doctrine about God, man, and the world. We introduce concrete, worldly elements, to be sure, but we cannot establish a real nexus between God's Word and *man's word*. God summons the creature, yes, but does the creature really respond with *his own word*?

Insofar as the debate over the analogy of being is concerned, Barth himself buried the issue once and for all. Let me quote one relevant passage:

Salvation is something more than being. Salvation is fulfillment—the total, definitive fulfillment of being. . . . Salvation is not proper to created being as such; it is something that lies in the future as fulfilled being. . . . It is something that created being does not possess of itself. It is being that *participates* in the being of God *himself*, from which it derives. . . .

Since salvation is not proper to created being as such, it can only *come to it*; and since it is a participation in God's existence, it must come *from God*. This coming of salvation is . . . the *grace of God*. . . . God grants it (the creature) something that is a *gift* and that only *he* can give. And he truly does grant it. . . .[8]

What more could a Scholastic theologian ask for? And any reflective Protestant will surely admit that the salvific happening that take place between God and the world is being, being in its fullest sense. So any attempt to set *act* over against *being* is absurd, inasmuch as Aristotelian and Thomistic thought picture real being as *energeia* or *actus*.

The attempt to set up a real opposition between the analogy of being and the analogy of faith is no longer meaningful either. One may choose to reserve the latter term for man's personal reaction to the self-revealing God, as opposed to the insight that man attains in the purely human process of reflection (i.e., that the world is not God, that it is pointed towards another outside itself). The terminology remains imperfect and misleading, however, because the grace-initiated response of faith is also *being*. To use the drastic terminology of Catholic theology, it is *infused* being poured down from above.

To be sure, the word *analogy* itself has a purely analogous sense in the two terms used here. This sense is justified, however, by the fact of creation; for in creation God determines the object of human reflection. It is rather arbitrary to restrict *analogy of being* to the relation established by creation and to set it in opposition to the highest relationship of being (the analogy of faith or grace).[9]

I would advise the present reader of this book not to confuse terminology differences with real theological opposition. The real source of controversy here was Barth's refusal to grant any trace of theological relevance to man's philosophical knowledge of God. In his presentation, does man truly have eyes to see the truth of God that is made manifest to them (Rom. 1:19)? Doesn't the analogy of faith (or grace) presuppose an analogous (by no means identical) analogy in the order of creation and even in the order of sin? Without the latter analogy as its external ground, can the analogy of faith become truly and effectively operative?

I must call attention once again to the purely *analogous* relationship between the analogy of being and the analogy of faith. Only when this point is clearly seen can one understand my treatment of nature and grace, of the dialectics in the concept of nature, and of man's natural desire for the beatific vision. Most critics of my first edition seem to have misconstrued my line of thought at one point or another.[10] In his recent book on Blondel,[11] however, Henri Bouillard provided a masterly exposition of this analogy and Gustav Siewerth evokes the same analogy in his recent survey of metaphysics.[12]

The first edition of this book received much careful attention and loving consideration from my fellow theologians in the Protestant Church. Besides the article of

W. Pannenberg cited earlier (footnote 9), I must mention the sensitive article of Walter Kreck,[13] and the clear article of Grover Foley[14] that goes right to the heart of the matter. Where Christian theology is concerned, they have followed me sympathetically and keenly even when the subject matter involved the most subtle relationships between theology and philosophy, but an iron curtain descends between us when it comes to the execution of a real philosophical act, and I should like to focus on this point for a moment.

These Protestant theologians speak as theologians, as outsiders to philosophy. They set limits on philosophical reflection from outside philosophy itself. They say: Philosophical reflection cannot be such and such, because it dare not be. But we can only prove the incompatibility of philosophical and theological reflection if we have tried to examine both from the inside. For all too long, Christian theology (both Catholic and Protestant) has treated philosophy as its lowly handmaid instead of seeing it as the queen of the sciences. The consequences of this tragic misunderstanding are all too evident today.

If there is no philosophy, then the whole hierarchy of values and scholarly disciplines collapses. If there is no philosophy, then there are no absolute truths and values any more. Man is left with the things that confront him in this temporal world, and no theology can save us from positivism. Christian theology in both churches must take its share of the blame for this situation.

I cannot conclude without saying a word about the works of Bouillard and Küng.[15] In his incisive article,[16] Grover Foley has brilliantly clarified the interrelationships between our three books. Bouillard has probed deeper into the nooks and corners of Barth's thought, and he has subjected Barth's theology to a thoroughgoing critique. In so doing, he has introduced elements from the theology of Rudolf Bultmann. In the last analysis, however, Bouillard and I are admittedly in agreement on the basic positions concerning fundamental theology.

Hans Küng speaks as a dogmatic theologian. His focal concern is Barth's doctrine of justification, which I only touched on briefly, and his basic thrust has been backed up by Karl Rahner.[17] It coincides with that of Barth, and it provides an even more determined profile of the Christocentric emphasis that I propounded as the proper plane for dialogue. Küng also seeks to break down the old, frozen lines of division on this issue that have existed since the Reformation and Trent.

We can only hope that the initiatives of Küng will be developed further, that bridges will be built to fundamental theology and philosophy, and that the whole history of theology will be revitalized by the new questions raised. We must not allow the dialogue in process to freeze over again.

NOTES

Citations of Barth's Works are keyed to the Bibliography that follows. Page numbers follow the original editions.

PART ONE. OVERTURE TO A DIALOGUE

I. THE TORN GARMENT

1. 1:101   **2.** 1:31   **3.** TK:286   **4.** G:163
5. TE 27:6–7   **6.** TE 27:9   **7.** G:167   **8.** TE 27:9–10
9. C:168   **10.** TE 27:12   **11.** TE 27:14
12. Cf. "Die Möglichkeit einer Bekenntnisunion," *Evang. Theol.* 1, 1935; "Die Kirche und die Kirchen," TE 27:14ff; "Wünschbarkeit und Möglichkeit eines allgemein reformierten Glaubensbekenntnisses," TK, 76ff; *Kirchliche Dogmatik* II/1, 693–740.
13. *Evang. Theol.*, 1935, 1:15   **14.** TE 27:18   **15.** TK:96ff.
16. TK:285ff; 329ff.   **17.** TK:286   **18.** TE 27:24
19. W:123   **20.** TE 27:24   **21.** TE 27:23
22. 1:30   **23.** C:128   **24.** TK:339
25. TK:349
26. A few decades ago, the possibilities of real dialogue between Barth and Catholics seemed quite dim. But much has changed in recent years. See the *Epilogue* in this volume.

II. PROTESTANT–CATHOLIC DIALOGUE

1. Yves M. J. Congar, *Chrétiens désunis*, 1937; Joseph Lortz, *The Reformation as A Problem for Today*, originally published in 1948.
2. Many recent Church pronouncements, from *Humani generis* through Vatican II, have stressed the need for studying and understanding different viewpoints and schools of thought.
3. Congar, *op. cit.*, pp. 34–36.
4. "Römischen Katholizismus als Frage an die protestantische Kirche," TK:329ff.
5. *Ibid.*, p. 331.   **6.** *Ibid.*, p. 333–334.   **7.** *Ibid.*, p. 336.
8. As *Humani generis* (Pius XII) puts it, the treasury of revealed truth is so immense "that it can never be exhausted."

9. Barth readily chided himself on the possibility of being too cocksure about one's own position. See 3:716.

10. 7:278–321   11. TE 14:41

12. TK:351   13. Congar, op. cit., pp. 355–357.

14. See Congar, "Sainteté et péché dans L'Eglise," *La Vie Intellectuelle*, Nov. 1947, pp. 6–40.

15. See, for example, Joseph Lortz, *Wie kam es zur Reformation?* Einsiedeln, 1950; Karl Rahner, *Kirche der Sünder* (Kleine Texte zur Theologie und Seelsorge, no. 7), Vienna, 1948; Damasus Winzen, "Büssende Kirche," *Catholica* 1, no. 2:108–112, 1932; Jean Daniélou, "Rahab: Figure de l'Eglise," *Irénikon*, 22:26–45, 1949.

16. *Cahiers* (ed. Grasset) I:470.   17. TK:363

III. A DIALOGUE WITH BARTH

1. 1:XI   2. *Ibid.*   3. W:100   4. 1:X

5. See Barth's lecture, "Die Neuorientierung der protestantischen Theologie in den tetzten dreissig Jahren," *Kirchenblatt für d. ref. Schweiz*, 96:98–101, 1940.

6. See 3:140–141; TS 1:4ff.; TE 47:18f.   7. 3:140   8. TS 5:7

9. See especially, Cornelius van Til, *The New Modernism*, 947.

10. 1:375–376   11. TE 27:6f.   12. C:6

13. 5:465; TS 6, 33–34; 7, 337–38

14. For example, on creation, 5:418–476; on God's perfection, 3:362–764; on faith, obedience, and prayer, 7:49.

IV. BARTH'S STANDPOINT

1. 1:33ff.   2. TK:339   3. ZdZ 8:62, 1924.   4. TK:20

5. W:201   6. W:182   7. ZdZ, 3:234, 1925.   8. See W:184–190

9. TK:338   10. TK:339   11. TK:343   12. TK:345–348

13. TK:336. See 1D:391–393.

14. This question is not one of our major concerns in the present volume. For some indications of Barth's position, see TK:300–312; TS 5, 32; 2:638, 654, 665.

15. ZdZ 8:49–64, 1924.   16. TK:240ff.

17. ZdZ 8:62, 1924.   18. TE 7:6

19. TE 1:23

20. The first section of *Analogia entis* appeared in 1932, and it was devoted to basic principles. One subheading was even entitled, "The anology of being as a principle" (pp. 149–154).

V. THE CATHOLIC STANDPOINT

1. *Catholica* 4:39, 1935.   2. *Catholica* 1:14, 1932.

3. 1:296   4. *Ibid.*   5. 1:293   6. 1:78

7. See the appraisal made by Ernst Wolf, "Der Mensch und die Kirche in katholischen Denken," ZdZ 11:34–57, 1933.

8. See Gottlieb Söhngen's reply to Emil Brunner on this point, *Catholica* 4:100–101, 1935.

VII. THE ROOTS OF CONTROVERSY

1. See TK:287	2. 1:VIII–IX	3. 2:690–720	4. TK:294–295
5. TK:295–296	6. 3:656–657	7. 3:661	8. 5:576
9. 1:70	10. 1:272	11. 2:639	12. 1:40–41

PART TWO. THE DEVELOPMENT OF BARTH'S THEOLOGY

I. INTERPRETING BARTH

1. 2:55–56; 3:715

2. This is one reason why we can go farther with Barth in Church Dogmatics than in his earlier Prolegomena. Moreover, certain issues are no longer crucial *denominational* doctrines in the later work.

3. C:159

4. *Evang. Theol.*, 1949, pp. 271–272. In the Foreword to the second edition (1928) of *Suchet Gott, so werdet ihr leben*, 1917, Barth cautions the reader: "A person can understand my earlier work only if he reads it in the light of my later work."

5. W:40

II. DIALECTICAL THEOLOGY

1. 1R:216	2. 1R:15, 73, *passim*.	3. 1R:106	4. 1R:202
5. 1R:60	6. 1R:420	7. 1R:55	8. 1R:207
9. 1R:61	10. 1R:237	11. 1R:194	12. 1R:60
13. 1R:413	14. 1R:131	15. 1R:34	16. 1R:221
17. 1R:220	18. 1R:190		

19. It should not be surprising that Barth was often viewed as a mystic in disguise. See E. Peterson, "Zur Theorie der Mystik," *Zeitschrift für syst. Theol.*, 1924, pp. 146–166; Heinzelmann, *Glaube und Mystik*, 1927; H. E. Weber, *Glaube und Mystik*, 1927; H. W. Schmidt, *Zeit und Ewigkeit*, 1927; Albrecht Oepke, *Karl Barth und die Mystik*, 1928; R. Otto, *Westöstliche Mystik*, 1926; J. L. Leuba, in *Verbum Caro*, 1947, p. 23; E. Przywara, *Ringen der Gegenwart*, I, 48f.

20. 1R:197	21. 1R:80	22. 1R:229
23. 1R:423	24. 1R:46	25. 1R:188
26. 2R:VII	27. 2R:237, 239	28. 2R:520

29. 2R:289   30. 2R:509   31. 2R:512
32. 2R:490   33. 2R:145   34. 2R:152
35. 2R:213   36. 2R:65   37. 2R:224
38. 2R:21, 188, 212, 224.   39. 2R:146   40. 2R:229
41. 2R:233
42. 2R:12f., 31, 112, 149, 150f., 169, 235.
43. 2R:73, 136, 186, 216, 264, 284.
44. 2R:155   45. 2R:154   46. 2R:143   47. 2R:229
48. 2R:279–280   49. 2R:149   50. 2R:51   51. 2R:246
52. 2R:228–229   53. R:136   54. 2R:186
55. Heinzelmann, "Das Prinzip der Dialektik in der Theologie Karl Barths," N. Kirchl. Zeitschrift, 1924; H. W. Schmidt, Zeit und Ewigkeit, 1927; Friedrich Traub, "Zum Begriff der dialektischen Theologie," Zeitschrift für Theologie und Kirche, 1929, pp. 388–389; W. Koepp, Die gegenwärtige Geisteslage und die dialektische Theologie, Tübingen: 1930, p. 70ff.; H. Volk, Die Kreaturauffassung bei Karl Barth, 1938, pp. 240–290.
56. ZdZ 8:378, 1930.   57. Ibid., pp. 378–385.
58. W:103   59. 1:454
60. TE 19:12   61. ZdZ 3:135, 1925.
62. A:76f.; 103f.; esp. 150f. 63. See 3:390f.
64. TK:319   65. 3:322
66. 1D:456–457   67. 1:459
68. 1:460   69. 3:416, 525, 554, and passim.
70. 1:462   71. W:135, 151; TK 357.
72. 2R:243   73. 2R:128
74. W:99   75. W:171
76. W:174   77. 2R:273
78. 2R:272–273

III. THE SHIFT TO ANALOGY

1. 1D:261   2. 1D:63   3. 1D:271   4. 1D:290
5. 1D:223   6. 1D:224, 229   7. 1D:295, 325f.   8. 1D:323
9. 1D:301f.   10. 1D:308–309   11. 1D:316   12. 1D:317
13. 1D:188   14. 1D:404–406
15. Evan. Theol., p. 272, 1948.
16. "Die Kirche und die Kultur," TK:364–391, 1926; "Schicksal und Idee in der Theologie," ZdZ: 309–348, 1929.
17. "Schleiermacher," TK:188; PT:386.
18. "Die Kirche und die Kultur," op. cit., p. 370.
19. Ibid., p. 387.   20. Ibid., pp. 374–376.
21. Ibid., p. 378.   22. Ibid., p. 380.
23. Ibid., p. 385.
24. "Schicksal und Idee in der Theologie," op. cit., p. 341.

25. *Ibid.*, p. 314.   26. *Ibid.*, p. 347.   27. *Ibid.*, p. 340.
28. "Das Problem der Ethik in der Gegenwart," W:125–155, 1922.
29. "Das Halten der Gebote," ZdZ 5:206–227, 1927.
30. "Rechtfertigung und Heiligung," ZdZ 5:281–309, 1927.
31. "Das erste Gebot als theologisches Axiom," ZdZ 11:297–314, 1933.
32. "Das Problem der Ethik in der Gegenwart," *op. cit.*, p. 125.
33. *Ibid.*, p. 135.   34. *Ibid.*, p. 145.
35. *Ibid.*, p. 147.   36. *Ibid.*, p. 153.
37. "Das Halten der Gebote," *op. cit.*, p. 217.   38. *Ibid.*, p. 221.
39. "Rechtfertigung und Heiligung," *op. cit.*, p. 293.
40. "Das erste Gebot als theologisches Axiom," *op. cit.*, p. 303.
41. Ph:123
42. "Kirche und Theologie," TK:302–338, 1926, a response to Peterson's *Was ist Theologie?* 1925; "Der Begriff der Kirche," TK:285–301, 1927; "Der römische Katholizismus als Frage an die protestantische Kirche," TK:329–363, 1928.
43. "Die Not der evangelischen Kirche," ZdZ 9:89–122, 1931.
44. Analyzed and criticized in an outstanding article by Georg Feuerer, "Der Kirchenbegriff der dialektischen Theologie," 1933.
45. 2R:324   46. "Der Begriff der Kirche," *op. cit.*, 1927.
47. *Ibid.*, p. 299.   48. *Ibid.*, p. 346.
49. ZdZ 9:96–97, 1931.   50. 2:236
51. 1:201   52. 1:252
53. 1:254   54. 1:257
55. 3:253–254   56. 3:258–259
57. 3:268   58. 3:271
59. 3:347–348   60. 3:461
61. Cf. 3:248, 251; C:33–34; G:52, 57, 63.   62. 7:98–99.
63. G:69   64. 3:671, 673, 575
65. G:178

IV. ANALOGY IN FULL BLOOM

1. 2:134–221   2. 2:141–143   3. 4:673–674
4. 6:175   5. 6:330–331   6. 6:339
7. 6:340   8. 6:340–343   9. 6:581
10. 5:53–54   11. 6:330   12. 6:266
13. 6:625   14. 6:82   15. 5:103–258
16. 5:258–377   17. 1:431   18. 3:80
19. 3:572   20. Cf. 3:573–574   21. 1:495
22. 3:579   23. W:62–63   24. 3:569–570
25. 3:331   26. 5:50   27. 5:64, 69
28. 5:262–263   29. 5:207   30. 5:83–84
31. 6:162   32. 6:170   33. 6:169, 174
34. 6:192   35. 6:414–439   36. 4:419

37. 1:469 38. 3:576 39. 3:651
40. 7:21 41. 7:52 42. 7:52
43. 7:53–57 44. 7:112 45. 7:113
46. 7:119 47. 7:153–157 48. 7:161
49. 7:325–326
50. J. L. Leuba, "Le Problème de l'Eglise chez Karl Barth," Verbum Caro 1:4–24, 1947.
51. 6:425
52. The first document indicating the transition is his book on the Anselmian proof for God's existence, Fides quaerens intellectum (1931). Barth himself called it the manifesto of his new approach. In Church Dogmatics I/1 he presents his doctrine on faith; II/1 discusses the possibility of knowing God; III/1 deals with knowledge of the creator as derived from creation; III/2 discusses the possibility of human knowledge; III/3 considers our knowledge of God insofar as it is derived from history and the course of world events.

In addition, there is his reply to Brunner, Nein! (1934), and his discussion of God's sovereignity (TS 5, 1939).
53. 5:399–400 54. 7:280 55. 7:280–281 56. 5:422–445
57. TS 5:16 58. 6:210 59. 5:400 60. 6:415
61. 6:157 62. A:149 63. A:179 64. A:188
65. A:190 66. 3:600–605 67. 6:86–157 68. 6:478
69. 6:485 70. 2R:143 71. 2R:142 72. A:41f.
73. 3:47 74. ZdZ 336–337, 1929.
75. See 1:40; 1:175; 1:180; 1:459–460; 2:88; 4:588f.; 5:19; 6:206f.; 6:219; 6:262; 6:390; 6:410; 7:115f.
76. See 1:252; 2:41; 2:48; 3:90; 6:413; 7:115
77. See 2:158; 2:262; 3:349; 6:168; 6:417
78. 2:91–92; 3:654f.; 4:717f.; 4:829–830
79. 5:206, 219 80. 6:262–264 81. 7:116
82. 3:89–90 83. 3:291–292
84. On man's capacity for faith (1:256); on love between God and man (2:435); on man's concepts of God (3:252); on created being (5:430–431; 6:390). In his book on Anselm, Barth described divine and created existence in terms that Scholasticism would easily recognize (A: 178–180).
85. 5:422–426
86. 5:171
87. 7:49
88. 3:463

PART THREE. A CLOSER LOOK AT THE FRAMEWORK

I. GOD'S ENTHUSIAST

1. 7:171f., 189f.   2. 5:444–445. See also 7:121–123.   3. 7:405

II. PRAEDESTINATIO GEMINA

1. 2R:310, 333f.
2. Cf. Max Strauch, *Die Theologie Karl Barths*, Munich: Kaiser, 1924, 2nd edition, p. 35.

3. 4:98–99	4. 4:100	5. 4:47f.
6. 4:157	7. 4:158–159	8. See 4:176–180
9. 4:182–184	10. 4:382. See also 4:387–391.	11. 4:461
12. 4:466–467	13. 4:373	14. 5:212–213

III. THE OVERALL CAST OF BARTH'S THOUGHT

1. 6:179   2. 3:90–91   3. 7:295   4. 7:311–312
5. 6:81   6. 6:418–419   7. 6:82
8. Zdz 5:37; W: 210; cf. Thurneysen, Zdz 6:10.

IV. THE INTELLECTUAL BACKGROUND

1. Brunner, *Die Mystik und das Wort*, 1924.   2. TK:165–66
3. See *Die protestantische Theologie im 19. Jahrhundert*, 1947.
4. TK:182
5. "Moderne Theologie und Reichgottesarbeit," *Zeitschrift für Theologie und Kirche* 19:317–321, 1909.
6. *Ibid.*, pp. 479–486.   7. *Ibid.*, p. 484.
8. A 1910 lecture, later published in expanded form as "Der christliche Glaube und die Geschichte," *Schweizerischen Theologischen Zeitschrift*, 1912, pp. 1–18, 49–72.
9. *Ibid.*, pp. 10–17   10. *Ibid.*, p. 58.
11. Reprinted as "Der Glaube an den persönlichen Gott," in *Zeitschrift für Theologie und Kirche* 24:21–32, 65–95, 1914.
12. *Ibid.*, p. 89.

V. IDEALISM AND REVELATION

1. 4:198; 5:258–259; 2:963–990; 5: 439   2. 4:204
3. 4:355–356   4. 7:332   5. 1:145

6. 4:600f.; 6:87   7. 6:294   8. 5:123–126
9. 4:820
10. 5:111f., 119, 136f., 141, 148f., 153f., 164f.; 7:84, 97, 406.
11. 4:179   12. 4:738–739
13. 4:193   14. 6:43, 328–329
15. 4:197   16. *See* 5:231; 6:234–236, 498, 501.

VI. RESERVATIONS AND UNANSWERED QUESTIONS

1. 7:158
2. 7:147
3. He himself admits this. *See* 4:161.
4. 6:176
5. 4:634

PART FOUR. CATHOLIC PERSPECTIVES

I. THE VARIETIES OF CATHOIC THOUGHT

1. *See* Hermann Schell, *Kleinere Schriften* (ed. by Hennemann), 1908, pp. 97–98.
2. 3:660   3. 3:658

II. BARTHIAN THEOLOGY AND THOMISM

1. Thomism is presented in this light by Gustav Siewerth, *Der Thomismus als Identitätssystem*, 1939.
2. Aquinas, *De an.*, q. un. a. 18 ad 16.
3. "Individual events (*singularia*) are treated in sacred scripture, but not because they are its main subject. They are introduced as examples for practical living . . . or to indicate the authority of the men through whom Revelation has come down to us. . . ." *S.Th.* I, q. 1, a 2, ad 2.

Here we must ask whether the individual events of the Christ mystery, from which all other *singularia* of Revelation history derive their reality, fall under this statement. The answer is a clear no; for Christ is truth itself, not the witness to an abstract doctrine. We would reject completely the view proposed by M. D. Chenu and others that the Incarnation is a contingent event. An absolutely gratuitous act of God's absolute freedom, this view maintains that the predestination of Christ is the chief event de facto in the economy but has no de jure place there. As Chenu puts it: "It is impossible to give it an a priori place in the series of divine decrees." See M. D. Chenu, Introduction à l'étude de S. Thomas d'Acquin, 1950, p. 270. For the other side, see H. Rondet, R.S.R. 38:144–160, 1951.

III. THE CONCEPT OF NATURE IN CATHOLIC THEOLOGY

1. See S.Th. III, q. 9, a 2, ad 3; Karl Eschweiler, Die zwei Wege der neueren Theologie, 1926, p. 272; Henri de Lubac, "Surnaturel," in Etudes Historiques, 1946, pp. 431–480.

The modern problem of nature and the supernatural arose later in the debate with Baius; it was developed by Bellarmine, Molina, Lessius, and Suarez. See Henri Rondet, R.S.R. 35:481–521, 1948.

2. The following remarks originated in a series of articles for Divus Thomas during 1944 and 1945. They were prompted, in no small part, by the work of Erich Przywara.

3. Emil Brunner, Natur und Gnade, 1935, p. 24.

4. See Scheeben, Dogmatik, II, 240; Aquinas, S.Th. I, q. 29, a 1, ad 4; ibid., I/II, q. 6, a 5, ad 2.

5. Cf. Aquinas, S.Th. I/II, q. 84, a 1, ad 3.

6. Söhngen rightly notes that the Platonic categories of "participation" (i.e., in God) are dangerous within philosophy, because they mix up God's grace relationship to creation with his natural causal relationship. See "Analogia fidei," Catholica 3:202–204, 1934. Just as the Platonic categories do not serve well to express the God–creature relationship, so the Aristotelian categories do not serve well to express the grace relationship.

7. Lercher, Institutiones Theologiae dogmaticae, 3rd edition, 1940, II, 344. More recent manuals repeat the same axiom.

8. See, for example, Pohle, "Natur und Übernatur," in Religion, Christentum, Kirche (ed. Esser-Mausbach) 1911, I, 318, 324.

9. Aquinas, S.Th. II/II, q. 111, a 1, ad 2; ibid., I, q. 21, a 1, ad 3.

10. Ripalda, De ente supernaturali, I, d. 1, S. 1 and 9.

11. This overlapping of these two roles—the philosopher as theologian versus the theologian as philosopher—is exemplified in Augustine and Thomas Aquinas. Augustine's genius was primarily theological. He took the philosophy of Neoplatonism (a disguised theology) and worked it up into a real theology of participation. Aquinas's genius, by contrast, was primarily philosophical. He took a philosophy with strong theological implications and worked it up into an explicit ontological philosophy of secondary causes.

For Augustine, the concrete concept of nature becomes more and more concrete as he unveils its theological content. For Aquinas, it becomes more and more abstract as one moves towards the limits of pure nature. He becomes more reserved about creaturely knowledge of God.

12. *S.Th.* II/II, q. 2, a 3, c.

13. Henri Rondet presents the alternatives this way: "Either nature was given such autonomy that it was completely independent of God (Nietzsche's superman, Pelagianism); or one arrived at Suarez's notion that a certain need for grace existed in every possible condition, and introduced the supernatural once again" (*R.S.R.*, 1948, p. 520). See also H. de Lubac, "Le Mystère du Surnaturel," *R.S.R.*, 1949, pp. 88–89.

14. Przywara, op. cit., p. 46.

15. See Söhngen, *Catholica* 4:110–111, 1935.

16. *Mélanges Joseph Maréchal* (Mus. Lessianum 1950) Vol. I: *Oeuvres*, p. 46. Maréchal influenced many philosophers in France and Germany. See, for example, Joh. B. Lotz, *Sein und Wert*, 1938; Max Müller, *Sein und Geist*, 1940; G. Siewerth, *Der Thomismus als Identitätssystem*, 1939; two early works of Karl Rahner, *Geist in Welt*, 1939, and *Hörer des Wortes*, 1941; B. Welte, *Der philosophische Glaube bei K. Jaspers*, 1949.

17. Maréchal, *A propos du sentiment de présence chez les mystiques*, 1908.

18. See Maréchal, *Etudes sur la psychologie des mystiques*, 1924, I, 179.

19. Maréchal, *Abstraction ou Intuition?* 1928, reprinted in *Mélanges*, op. cit., I, 102–180.

20. Maréchal, *Le point de départ de la métaphysique*, 1917 (*Mélanges*, 289); *Jugement "scolastique" concernant la racine de l'agnosticisme Kantien*, 1914 (*Mélanges*, op. cit., 278).

21. *Ibid.*, p. 286.

22. Maréchal, *De naturali perfectae beatitudinis desiderio*, 1930 (*Mélanges*, op. cit., 327–334).

23. Maréchal, *Le problème de Dieu d'après M. Ed. Le Roy* (*Mélanges*, op. cit., p. 258).

24. See A. Milet, in *Mélanges Joseph Maréchal*, op. cit., I, 32; Maréchal, *De naturali perfectae beatitudinis desiderio* (*Mélanges*, op. cit., p. 335).

25. See Henri du Lubac, *Surnaturel*, 1946; idem, "Le mystère du surnaturel," *R.S.R.*, 1949, pp. 80–121; P. Delaye, in *Orientierung* (Zurich, June 30, 1950), pp. 138–141.

26. Delaye, *ibid.*, pp. 138, 140.

27. See Michael Schmaus, *Dogmatik* (2nd edition, 1949) II, 194f.

28. K. Rahner, op. cit., 141–145.

29. E. Przywara, *Analogia entis*, p. 51.

30. The following works provide a variety of insights into the aims and teachings of Vatican I: H. Lennerz, *Natürliche Gotteserkenntnis*, Herder, 1926; J. M. A. Vacant, *Etudes théologiques sur les constitutions du Vatican*, 1895, 2 vols.; Michael Schmaus, *Dogmatik*, 2nd edition, 1948, I, 180–184 and 204; Gottlieb Söhngen, "Fünf Vorlesungen," reprinted in *Die Furche* (Vienna) Sept. 3, 1950; E. Przywara, *Ringen der Gegenwart*, 1929, I, 407.

The moral necessity of Revelation was again upheld by Pius XII in *Humani generis*.

31. Aquinas, *S.Th.* I/II, q. 89, a 6 c.
32. Heinrich, *Dogmatik*, V, 448.
33. Diekamp, *Dogmatik*, II, 51.

IV. CHRIST AT THE CENTER

1. *S.Th.* III, q. 1, a 3 c.
2. *Ibid.*, II/II, q. 2, a 7.
3. See C. V. Schätzler, *Das Dogma von der Menschwerdung Gottes*, 1870, pp. 316–324.
4. Suarez, *De Incarn.*, q. 1, disp. 5, sections 2–5.
5. E. Mersch, *Théologie du Corps Mystique*, 1946, I, 170.
6. Przywara, *Summula*, Glock und Lutz: 1946, p. 75.
7. See, for example, Przywara, *Analogia entis*, p. 80.
8. *Deus semper major*, esp. III, 91f.
9. See *Das Wesen des Christentums* (in book form), 1940, pp. 39, 52, 54–56.
10. Guardini, *Der Herr*, 6th ed., 1949, pp. 545–546.
11. *Katholische Dogmatik*, 3rd and 4th eds., 1949, II.
12. *Ibid.*, for example, pp. 185–186.
13. *Ibid.*, pp. 224–225; see also Eucharius Berbuir, *Zeugnis für Christus*, Herder: 1949, pp. 28–29.
14. *La Théologie du Corps Mystique*, 1946; see, for example, I, 47–48.
15. *Ibid.*, I, 99f.
16. "Natur und Geschichte," in *Catholica* 4/2, 49–60, 1935.
17. *Ibid.*, p. 57.
18. To mention but a few names: Josef Bernhart, *Sinn der Geschichte*, 1931; Peter Wust, *Dialektik des Geistes*, 1928; Theodor Haecker, *Der Christ und die Geschichte*, 1935; Karl Buchheim, *Wahrheit und Geschichte*, 1935; A. Schütz, *Gott in der Geschichte*, 1935; Philipp Dessauer, *Der Anfang und das Ende*, 1939; Oskar Bauhofer, *Das Geheimnis der Zeiten*, 1936; Karl Rahner, *Hörer des Wortes*, 1941; Alfred Delp, *Der Mensch und die Geschichte*, no date; Karl Thieme, *Gott und die Geschichte*, 1948; Michael Schmaus, *Von den letzten Dingen*, 1948; Josef Pieper, *Über das Ende der Zeit*, 1950; and almost all the works of Romano Guardini and Reinhold Schneider.

In France a major breakthrough was the book by H. de Lubac, *Catholicisme*, 1937. He was followed by others who tackled historico-theological material, e.g., Gaston Fessard, Y. de Montcheuil, Jean Daniélou, and Christopher Dawson.

The reality and meaning of history is the main concern of many Catholic philosophers and theologians. Among the philosophers are Theodor Haecker, A. Dempf, H. Meyer, A. Wenzl, H. E. Hengstenberg, M. Müller, E. Spiess, and B. Welte.

19. Schmaus, *Von den letzten Dingen*, 1948, p. 52; see also *ibid.*, p. 60; G. Söhngen, "Analogia Fidei," *Catholica* 3/4, 191f., 1934.

20. See, for example, *Wesen des Christentums*, pp. 68–69; *Die Offenbarung*, 1940, pp. 79–84, 88–93; *Jesus Christus*, pp. 129–151; *Welt und Person*, 1939, p. 71.

21. See also M. Schmaus, *Katholische Dogmatik*, II, 277–278; F. X. Arnold, *Untersuchungen zur Theologie der Seelsorge*, 2 vols, 1948–49.

22. Laberthonnière, *Le réalisme chrétien et l'idealisme grec*, 1904.

23. Maurice Blondel, *Action*, 1893.

24. Guardini, *Die Offenbarung*, pp. 76, 84.

25. Schell, *Das Problem des Geistes*, 1897; in *Kleinere Schriften*, ed. Hennemann, Paderborn: 1908, p. 189.

26. See Schmaus, *Dogmatik*, I, 445, 454; II, 477, 588, and *passim*.

27. See Przywara, "Corpus Christi mysticum: eine Belang," in *Zeitschrift für Aszese und Mystik* 15:212, 1940.

28. Guardini, *Welt und Person*, p. 23.

29. See Guardini, *Freiheit, Gnade, Schicksal*, Munich: 1948, pp. 163–166.

30. Daniel Feuling, *Katholische Glaubenslehre*, 1937, pp. 214–217.

31. See Oskar Bauhofer: *Das Geheimnis der Zeiten*, 1935; *Die Heimholung der Welt*, 1937; *Die rettende Gewalten*, 1950.

32. Bauhofer, *Das Geheimnis der Zeiten*, 1935, pp. 22–25.

33. Bauhofer, *Die rettende Gewalten*, Vienna: 1950, p. 128.

34. See Josef Pieper, *Über das Ende der Zeit*, Munich: 1950, pp. 18–27; idem, "Christliche Philosophie?" *Hochland* 40:503, 1948.

35. Berbuir, *Natura Humana*, Munich: 1950.

36. Schmaus, *Katholische Dogmatik*, II, *passim*.

37. Besides Josep Pieper, we can mention Dietrich von Hildebrand, Bernhard Rosenmüller, August Brunner, Peter Wust and Gabriel Marcel.

38. *Katholische Dogmatik*, I, 452 (my italics). The notion that all our knowledge is grounded in faith has been developed most completely by August Brunner, S.J. in *Glaube und Erkenntnis*, Munich 1951.

39. Bernhart, *Chaos und Dämonie* (Munich: Kösel, 1950).

40. See Von Balthasar, *Présence et Pensée* (Paris 1942) pp. 29–60. It is a study of the religious philosophy of Gregory of Nyssa.

41. See Bernhart, *Chaos und Dämonie*, pp. 92–94.

V. GRACE AND SIN

1. For example, the younger Blumhardt, H. Kutter, L. Ragaz, Joh. Müller, Joh. Weiss and Albert Schweitzer.

2. See 3:711–19

3. 2:181f.

4. 2:55

5. See 2:57–62

6. On what follows see Robert Grosche, "Simul peccator et justus," *Catholica* 4/3:132–139, 1935. For a general Catholic and Protestant explanation of the formula, see Alfons Kirchgässner, *Erlösung und Sünde im NT*, Herder: 1950. On the corresponding doctrine of Emil Brunner, see Hermann Volk, *Emil Brunners Lehre von dem Sünder*, Regensberg, Münster: 1950.

7. 3:707. See also 4:846; HK:30–41.

8. See 3:450

<hr>

Epilogue

<hr>

I. A LOOK BACK

1. See Gottlieb Söhngen, in *Catholica* 3/4:202, 1934.

III. A FEW YEARS LATER

1. Henri Bouillard, *Karl Barth*, 3 vols., Aubier: 1957.
2. Hans Küng, *Rechtfertigung: Die Lehre Karl Barths und eine katholische Besinnung*, Johannesverlag: 1957.
3. *Church Dogmatics*, IV/1.
4. *Ibid.*, IV/2.
5. *Ibid.*, IV/3.
6. *Ibid.*, III/1–4.
7. *Ibid.*, III/4.
8. *Ibid.*, IV/1, p. 7. Barth's italics.
9. This would be my basic complaint with the fine article of W. Pannenberg, "Zur Bedeutung des Analogiegedankens bei Karl Barth: Eine Auseinandersetzung mit Urs von Balthasar," *Theol. Lit. Zeitung*, 1953, no. 1; esp. p. 24.

On the analogy of faith see also Erich Przywara, "Analogia fidei," *Lexicon für Theologie und Kirche*, 1957, I, col. 474; Gottlieb Söhngen, "Analogie," *Wörterbuch theologische Begriffe* (Kösel); *idem*, "Analogia entis in analogia fidei," *Antwort*, 1956, pp. 266–271.

10. See for example, the article of P. Gutwenger, "Der Begriff der Natur in the Theologie," *Z f K Th* 461–464, 1953, and my reply in the same issue, pp. 452–461.

11. Bouillard, *Blondel et le Christianisme*, Seuil: 1961.

12. Siewerth, *Schicksal der Metaphysik von Thomas zu Heidegger*, Johannesverlag: 1959, pp. 361–517.

13. W. Kreck, "Analogia fidei oder analogia entis," *Antwort* (a Barth *Festschrift*) 1956, pp. 272–286.
14. Grover Foley, "The Catholic Critics of Karl Barth," *Scottish Journal of Theology* 14:136–155, 1961.
15. *Idem* 3
16. *Idem* 15
17. K. Rahner, *Schriften zur Theologie*, IV, 237–271.

BIBLIOGRAPHY

This bibliography lists works of Karl Barth that are cited or mentioned in the present volume. A key to the Notes section is provided at the left of each work that is cited in shorthand form. English translations are also indicated, but this listing is not meant to be exhaustive.

Barth's total corpus was enormous. For further reading, one may consult the *Bibliographia Barthiana* by Charlotte von Kirschbaum in the Barth Festschrift *Antwort*, Evang. Verlag, Zürich-Zollikon: 1956. It lists 406 titles up to 1955.

Die Kirchliche Dogmatik

1. I/1. Die Lehre vom Wort Gottes, 1932
        The doctrine of the Word of God
2. I/2. Die Lehre vom Wort Gottes, 1939
        The doctrine of the Word of God
3. II/1. Die Lehre von Gott, 1940
        The doctrine of God: Knowledge
        of God, the reality of God
4. II/2. Die Lehre von God, 1942
        God's predestination
        God's commandment
5. III/1. Die Lehre von der Schöpfung, 1945
        The doctrine of creation: the
        work of creation
6. III/2. Die Lehre von der Schöpfung, 1948
        The creature
7. III/3. Die Lehre von der Schöpfung, 1950
        The creator and his creature
    This major work is available in English. *Church Dogmatics*, ed. G. W. Bromiley and T. F. Torrance, Edinburgh, T. & T.

Clark. Subsequent volumes have appeared both in German and English. To gain a general understanding of the whole work, one may consult Otto Weber, *Introductory Report to the Dogmatics*, Lutterworth Press, 1953.

Other Major Works

Suchet Gott, so werdet ihr leben. Sermons, in collaboration with E. Thurneysen. Bern: 1917.

1R. *Der Römerbrief*. 1st ed. Bern: 1919.

2R. *Der Römerbrief*. 2nd ed. Munich: 1922.

The Epistle To The Romans. English translation from the sixth edition, with a new preface by Karl Barth. London: Oxford University Press, 1950. The reader may also wish to consult *Kurze Auslegung des Römerbriefs*, Munich: 1956; Eng. trans., *A Shorter Commentary on Romans*, SCM & John Knox Presses, 1959.

Komm, Schöpfer Geist! Sermons, in collaboration with E. Thurneysen. Munich: 1924. Eng. trans. *Come Holy Spirit*, Round Table Press & T. & T. Clark, 1933.

W. *Das Wort Gottes und die Theologie*. Munich: 1924. Collected articles, 1916–1924. Eng. trans. *The Word of God and the Word of Man*, Hodder and Stoughton, 1928.

AT. *Die Auferstehung der Toten*. Munich: 1924. Eng. trans., *The Resurrection of the Dead*, New York: F. H. Revell Company, 1933.

Ph. *Erklärung des Philipperbriefes*. Munich: 1927. Eng. trans., *The Epistle to the Philippians*, Richmond, Va.: John Knox Press, 1962.

1D. *Die Lehre vom Worte Gottes: Prolegomena to Christian Dogmatics*. Munich: 1928.

TK. *Die Theologie und die Kirche*. Munich: 1938. Collected articles, 1920–1928.

HG. *Zur Lehre vom Heiligen Geist*, with Heinrich Barth. Beiheft 1 to periodical *Zwischen der Zeit*, 1930.

A. *Fides quarens intellectum*. Anselm's proof for the existence of God. Munich: 1931. Eng. trans. *Anselm: Fides quarens intellectum*, Richmond, Va.: John Knox Press, 1960.

C. *Credo*. Munich: 1935. Eng. trans., *Credo*, New York: C. Scribners' Sons, 1936.

Die grosse Barmherzigkeit. Sermons, in collaboration with E. Thurneysen. Munich: 1935. Eng. trans., *God's Search For Man*, Round Table Press and T. & T. Clark, 1935.

G. *Gotteserkenntnis und Gottesdienst*. Zollikon: 1938. Eng. trans., *The Knowledge of God and the Service of God*, London: Hodder and Stoughton, 1938.

Eine Schweizer Stimme. Political talks and writings from 1938 to 1945. Zollikon: 1945.

PT. *Die protestantische Theologie im 19. Jahrhundert*. Zollikon: 1947. Eleven chapters of this book are translated in *Protestant Thought From Rousseau To Ritschl*, London: SCM Press and Harpers, 1959.

DG. *Dogmatik im Grundriss*. Zollikon: 1947. Eng. trans., *Dogmatics In Outline*, New York: Philosophical Library, 1949.

HK. *Die christliche Lehre nach dem Heidelberger Katechismus*. Zollikon: 1948. Eng. trans., *The Heidelberg Catechism For Today*, Richmond, Va.: John Knox Press, 1964.

Fürchte Dich Nicht! Sermons, 1934–1948. Munich: 1949.

BROCHURES AND PAMPHLETS

A. From the series, *Theologische Existenz heute* (Theological Existence Today). A selection from this series can be found in *God In Action*, New York: Round Table Press, 1936.

TE 1. *Theologische Existenz heute!* 1933.

TE 2. *Für die Freiheit des Evangeliums*, 1933.

TE   3. Reformation als Entscheidung, 1933.
TE   4. Lutherfeier, 1933.
TE   5. Die Kirche Jesu Christi, 1933.
TE   7. Gottes Wille und unsere Wünsche, 1934.
TE   9. Offenbarung, Kirche, Theologie, 1934.
TE 10. Der gute Hirte, Sermon, 1934.
TE 12. Der Christ als Zeuge, 1934.
TE 13. Der Dienst am Wort Gottes, 1934.
TE 14. Nein! Antwort an Emil Brunner, 1934.
TE 17. Drei Predigten, 1934.
TE 19. Vier Bibelstunden, 1934.
TE 22. Vier Predigten, 1935.
TE 25. Das Evangelium in der Gegenwart, 1935.
TE 27. Die Kirche und die Kirchen, 1935.
TE 28. Die theologische Voraussetzung kirchlicher Gestaltung, 1935.
TE 29. Das Bekenntnis der Reformation und unser Bekennen, 1935.
TE 32. Evangelium und Gesetz, 1935.
TE 37. Calvin, 1936.
TE 43. Calvinfeier, 1936.
TE 47. Gottes Gnadenwahl, 1936.

B. From the series, *Theologische Studien* (Theological Studies)

TS   1. Rechtfertigung und Recht, 1938.
TS   2. Evangelium und Bildung, 1948.
TS   5. Die Souveränität des Wortes und die Entscheidung des Glaubens, 1939.
TS   6. David Strauss als Theologe, 1939.
TS 14. Die kirchliche Lehre von der Taufe, 1943.
TS 20. Christengemeinde und Bürgergemeinde, 1946.
TS 22. Die Schrift und die Kirche, 1947.
TS 23. Die Botschaft von der freien Gnade Gottes, 1947.
TS 27. Die Wirklichkeit des neuen Menschen, 1950.
TS 28. Humanismus, 1950.

Five Important Articles from the Early Period

"Was sollen wir tun?" *Christl. Welt* 23:236–237, 1909.
"Moderne Theologie und Reichgottesarbeit," *Zeitschrift f. Th. K.* 19:317–321, 1909.
"Antwort an D. Achelis und D. Drews," *Z. f. Th. K.* 19:479–86, 1909.
"Der christliche Glaube und die Geschichte," *Schweiz. theol. Zeitschrift* issues 1 and 2, 1912.
"Der Glaube an den persönlichen Gott," *Z. f. Th. K.* 24:21–32, 65–95, 1914.

Selected Articles from the Periodical Zwischen den Zeiten (ZdZ)

(insofar as they are not compiled or cited in the anthologies W and TK)
"Brunners Schleiermacherbuch," 1924, pp. 49–64.
"Das Schriftprinzip der reformierten Kirche," 1935, pp. 215–45.
"Menschenwort und Gotteswort in der christlichen Predigt," 1925, pp. 114–119.
"Rechtfertigung und Heiligung," 1927, pp. 281–309.
"Das Halten der Gebote," 1927, pp. 206–227.
"Schicksal und Idee in der Theologie," 1927, pp. 309–348.
"Die Lehre von den Sakramenten," 1927, pp. 427–460.
"Die Theologie und der heutige Mensch," 1930, pp. 374–396.
"Die Not der evangelischen Kirche," 1931, pp. 89–122.
"Die Theologie und die Mission in der Gegenwart," 1932, pp. 189–215.
"Das erste Gebot als theologisches Axiom," 1933, pp. 297–314.

Autobiographical Writing

"Parergon: Karl Barth über sich selbst," *Evangel. Theol.*, 1948/49, pp. 268–282.

INDEX